Legacies of the Past

In memory of Andrea Noble

Legacies of the Past

Memory and Trauma in Mexican Visual and Screen Cultures

Edited by Miriam Haddu and Niamh Thornton

EDINBURGH
University Press

Edinburgh University Press is one of the leading university presses in the UK. We publish academic books and journals in our selected subject areas across the humanities and social sciences, combining cutting-edge scholarship with high editorial and production values to produce academic works of lasting importance. For more information visit our website: edinburghuniversitypress.com

Edinburgh University Press Ltd
The Tun – Holyrood Road
12 (2f) Jackson's Entry
Edinburgh EH8 8PJ

Typeset in 11/13 Monotype Ehrhardt by
Manila Typesetting Company, and
printed and bound in Great Britain

A CIP record for this book is available from the British Library

ISBN 978 1 4744 8053 6 (hardback)
ISBN 978 1 4744 8055 0 (webready PDF)
ISBN 978 1 4744 8056 7 (epub)

Contents

Figures

The Contributors

Julia Banwell is currently a Lecturer in Hispanic Studies at the University of Sheffield. Her research encompasses contemporary art, photography and film from Mexico, with a thematic focus on the cultural location of visualisations of death and corpses. Her monograph *Teresa Margolles and the Aesthetics of Death* was published in 2015. She has also published papers on the representation of death in the photography of the Mexican Revolution, and the reporting of death and injury in sports.

Miriam Haddu is Senior Lecturer in the School of Humanities, Royal Holloway, University of London. She specialises in Mexican film, photography and documentary filmmaking. She has curated Mexican photography exibitions in the United Kingdom, Mexico and the United States. She has published extensively on Mexican visual culture including articles on film, documentary and photography. She is the author of *Contemporary Mexican Cinema (1989–1999): History, Space and Identity* (2007) and *Violence, Conflict and Discourse in Mexican Cinema (2002–15)* (2020).

Chris Harris is Professor of Modern Languages and Cultures at Xi'an Jiaotong Liverpool University (XJTLU) where he is also the Vice-President, Academic Affairs. Concurrently, he is an Honorary Professor of Hispanic Studies at the University of Warwick. He is the editor, together with Amit Thakkar (Lancaster), of *Representations of Men and Masculinities in Latin American Cultures* (2010) and *Men, Power and Liberation: New Readings of Masculinities in Latin American Literatures* (2015). He has published on works by a range of post-Revolutionary Mexican writers including: Ángeles Mastretta, Rosario Castellanos, Mariano Azuela, Juan Rulfo and Agustín Yáñez.

Catherine Leen is Associate Professor of Spanish and Latin American Studies at Maynooth University, Ireland. Her teaching and research interests centre on Mexican and Chicana/o literature and cinema and Argentine and Paraguayan visual culture and literature. In 2008, she received a Fulbright Scholarship to conduct research at the Chicana/o Studies Centre, University of California, Santa Barbara. She is co-editor of the volume *International Perspectives on Chicana/o Culture: 'This World is My Place'* (2017) which explores the relevance of Chicana/o Studies outside the United States. Her most recent publications are 'Deconstructing the Divas: Music in Arturo Ripstein's *El lugar sin límites* and *La reina de la noche*', in *The Films of Arturo Ripstein: The Sinister Gaze of the World* (2019); and 'From Don Juan to Dolores Huerta: Foundational Chicana/o Films', in Francisco Lomelí et al. (eds), *Routledge Handbook of Chicana/o Studies* (2018).

Viviana MacManus is Assistant Professor in the Department of Spanish at Occidental College in Los Angeles, California. She received her PhD in Literature at the University of California, San Diego in 2011. She specialises in Latin American cultural studies and literature, Latin American/Latinx culture and history, Latin American feminist theory and literature, and film/visual culture. Her research focuses on cultural productions that document histories of gender and state violence during the so-called 'Dirty Wars' of Argentina and Mexico (1960s–80s). Her book, *Disruptive Archives: Feminist Memories of Resistance during Latin America's Dirty Wars*, is under contract with the University of Illinois Press's 'Dissident Feminisms' series and is forthcoming in late 2020.

Maximiliano Maza-Pérez is Associate Professor in Film and Cultural Studies and Director of the Master's Degree and PhD in Humanistic Studies at Tecnológico de Monterrey. Maza-Pérez' research focuses on the intersections between space, memory, cultural identity and gender identity in Mexican cinema and US–Mexican border films. He is author of *Miradas que se cruzan: El espacio geográfico de la frontera entre México y los Estados Unidos en el cine fronterizo contemporáneo* (2014). Maza-Pérez received his doctoral degree in Humanistic Studies from the Tecnológico de Monterrey. He is a member of the Mexican National System of Researchers, the Mexican Association of Researchers of Communication, the Technical Committee of Cinematography of the Council for Culture and Arts of the State of Nuevo León, and the Art-Kiné International Group of Cinematographic Research of the University of Buenos Aires, University of Vienna and University of Granada.

Niamh Thornton is Reader in Latin American Studies at the University of Liverpool. She is a specialist in Mexican film, literature and digital cultures with a particular focus on war stories, gendered narratives, star studies, cultures of taste, and distributed content. Her key research interest is in the multiple representations of conflict in literature and film. She has published extensively. Her books include *Women and the War Story in Mexico: La novela de la Revolución* (2006) and *Revolution and Rebellion in Mexican Cinema* (2013). Co-edited books include *Revolucionarias: Gender and Revolution in Latin America* (2007) and *International Perspectives on Chicana/o Studies: This World is My Place* (2013). She has recently completed a monograph on violence, curation and memorialisation in Mexican film: *Tastemakers and Tastemaking: Mexico and Curated Screen Violence* (2020).

Jessica Wax-Edwards is an independent researcher who received her PhD in Hispanic Studies from Royal Holloway, University of London in 2018. Her research interests include memory, violence, and politics in twentieth-century and contemporary Mexican visual culture. She has published articles on Latin American fiction and documentary cinema, graphic art and photography and is currently working on her monograph *Violence, Victims and the Ethics of Representation: The Visual Legacy of Felipe Calderón (2006–2012)*.

Acknowledgements

As is fitting for a work on memory, trauma and the spectral, this book evolved over time and against the backdrop of a dramatically changing world. The first airing of some of these ideas took place at a one-day symposium in September 2014 held at Senate House in London, and financially supported by the Institute of Latin American Studies (ILAS), the University of Liverpool and Royal Holloway, University of London. We are grateful for this support. We are also thankful for the administrative assistance provided by Olga Jiménez at ILAS in the lead-up to and during the symposium. Co-organised by the editors, the symposium brought together a range of scholars working in the field of Mexican film and visual culture in order to explore ideas about memory, representation, absence/presence of death and trauma in fiction/documentary filmmaking, installation, plastic/digital arts, photography, performance and necro-aesthetic arts, as a means of exploring and articulating traces of a collective condition. These included papers by Peter Watt, University of Sheffield, Nuala Finnegan, University College Cork, Anna Kingsley, Royal Holloway, University of London, Erica Segre, Trinity College, University of Cambridge, Dolores Tierney, University of Sussex, Debbie Martin, University College London, and Julia Tuñón, Centre de Recherches Interdisciplinaires sur les Mondes Ibériques Contemporains, Sorbonne University, Paris, as well as by many of the contributors to this volume. More detail can be found here: http://specularghosts.wordpress.com/. While not all are included in this present collection, because their contributions have led to publications elsewhere, the conversations that were conducted at the symposium, and the ensuing dialogues that took place informally and at conferences and symposia elsewhere, helped inform how the thinking developed. Our links to scholars in the UK, where we live and work, in Europe, and the Americas, resulted in this coming together and are intended to open out the conversation further. We are thankful for the opportunity to have held these conversations and to have this network of brilliant scholars with whom to share ideas.

We would both like to extend thanks to staff at Edinburgh University Press who shepherded this project to completion during a challenging global pandemic. In particular, we would like to extend our appreciation to Gillian Leslie and Richard Strachan for their care and attention as well as their patience in ever-shifting times. Additionally, we would like to thank our colleagues at our respective universities, the University of Liverpool and Royal Holloway, University of London, who have provided practical advice and support through the development and completion of this project.

Niamh Thornton would like to thank Charles Forsdick, University of Liverpool, for reading and commenting on a draft of Chapter 2, Abigail Loxham, University of Liverpool, for mentoring advice, the librarians at the University of Liverpool, and Elides Pérez Bistrain, Genoveva García Rojas and the rest of the staff at the Centro de documentación at the *Cineteca Nacional de México* in Mexico City for their support in sourcing material. Thanks to Maricruz Castro Ricalde and Guadalupe Pérez-Anzaldo for sharing work that would otherwise have been difficult to access outside of Mexico. Thanks to my virtual writing group made up of an ever-evolving network of enthusiastic and supportive academic tweeps whose presence and voices have helped keep up the momentum. As ever, to Liz, thanks for the support, listening ear, clear insight, and love. To Marmaduke and Rua for the entertaining distraction they prove to be.

Miriam Haddu would like to thank Tatiana Huezo for her generosity and for providing access to her films, and to the Santander Travel Award which allowed for a research trip to visit Mexico City and conduct fieldwork. Sincere thanks go to Niamh Thornton for her patience and understanding when life events got in the way. Thanks to all of the contributors in this book for their commitment, hard work and illuminating chapters. Finally, heartfelt thanks to Richard and to Miles for providing welcome distraction and helping to keep things in perspective.

Finally, this book, and the symposium from where it was born, came about thanks to a chance conversation over lunch in between panel sessions at the Latin American Studies Association (LASA) Annual Congress held in San Francisco in 2012. We are grateful to this organisation for bringing together scholars from all walks of life, from all corners of the globe, and with differing interests, allowing for the exchange of ideas and the birth of new projects.

An earlier version of Chapter 3 appeared in *The Journal of Latin American Cultural Studies* as '"Ghosts of another Era": Gender and Haunting in Cultural Narratives of Mexico's Dirty War', 24: pp. 435–52.

Revised sections from Chapter 7 have appeared previously in Haddu, M., *Violence, Conflict and Discourse in Mexican Cinema (2002–15)*, New York: Palgrave Macmillan, 2020.

Legacies of the Past:
Memory and Trauma in Mexican
Visual and Screen Culture

Niamh Thornton

Sanitised imaginings of death and violence constituted the formulation of the nation-state in Mexico in the early twentieth century. The foundational moment of the modern Mexican state is the Revolution (1910–20) whose dating is contested because it was deployed as a label for a political process reaching beyond the conclusion of the battles. The Revolution evolved into a 'master narrative' (Benjamin 2000: 14) in order to bring a divided and traumatised population on board a nation-building project by the party that dominated Mexican politics for most of the twentieth century, the Partido Revolucionario Institucional [Institutional Revolutionary Party] (PRI). This process of exhaustive monumentalisation and commemoration rendered the Revolution banal (see Billig 1995) through co-option, repetition and almost excessive deployment of key figures, tropes and visual iconography. This led to a flattening out of the experiences of war and the construction of myths of heroic battles without any real engagement with the memories or traumas of this past. An overt strategy of display and performance of the past has become a pattern that has continued as a national project of forgetting through saturation or co-option throughout the twentieth and twenty-first centuries. Therefore, the work of audio-visual creatives and filmmakers has been to find ways to resist this forgetting and remember and unearth the ghosts of the past in order to address the collective trauma of distinct violent events.

In the light of past and recent events, it is tempting to examine statistics of those who have died over the last one hundred years in Mexico as a result of traumatic violence in order to foreground the urgency and spread of the trauma. There are many events to choose from, starting with the Revolution, which relied on a smoothing out and forgetting of the up to two million who died as a result of battle, illness or hunger, to the approximated ten murders a day of women in 2019 whose deaths have largely gone unpunished (Villegas 2020). But to do so is both overwhelming and risks reducing individual experiences, memories and traumas to mere numbers.

What the works examined in this book do is to focus in on the individual or group experiences of loss and trauma in order to understand the legacy on the collective.

The authors in this edited collection were invited to analyse Mexican audio-visual and screen culture through three interrelated but separate concepts: trauma, memory, and the spectre. Approaching a selection of multi-layered historical presences and events, the chapters in this book examine legacies of the past by tracing how memory and trauma dominate Mexican audio-visual and screen cultures. This introduction cannot exhaustively pick its way through the wealth of scholarship related to each concept; instead, it aims to provide some signposts for the reader to understand key historical moments and the theoretical approaches that underpin the close textual analysis carried out by the authors.

Mexico is not alone in its hauntings. Ghosts of the recent past continue to maintain a presence that shifts, performs for and dominates the public imaginary in many countries across Latin America. The need to address their meanings has seen a rise in the region of the study of the recent past, propelling socio-political debates concerned with articulating the processing of loss, trauma, grief and mourning. These issues have become pertinent to nations such as Guatemala, Argentina, Uruguay, Chile and Brazil where public debate on the so-called 'Dirty Wars' of the 1960s and 1970s have begun to be reassessed in a contemporary light. Engaging with the work related to the legacy of the Holocaust, Southern Cone scholars such as Elizabeth Jelin (2003) and Cara Levey (2016) have provided models for translating such work to a distinct set of events and experiences. While during the past century the Mexican nation has experienced periods of significant political and social unrest where lives have been lost amid a context of conflict and violence, the state has a variable and unresolved engagement with this process. With the exception of 1968 and its aftermath, memory and trauma studies has yet to take hold in the study of Mexican audio-visual and screen culture.

Riven with multiple unresolved traumas, the past haunts the spaces in Mexican film and audio-visual culture because the political process has attempted to erase or appropriate their significance. These historical events act like ghosts or spectres haunting the present. In order to comprehend how they are manifest, this collection looks at a selection of traumas that haunt the present and considers how filmmakers and visual artists have found ways of understanding the haunted spaces. Their explorations, imaginings and counter-imaginings of the past bring the spectres to the foreground and create new narratives and, thus, propose new histories.

Therefore, a discernible presence in many of the chapters is the turn towards the spectre and spectrality as metaphor that has evolved since the 1990s to 'evoke an etymological link to visibility and vision, to that which is both *looked at* (as fascinating spectacle) and *looking* (in the sense of examining)' (Blanco and Pereen 2013: 2, italics in original). Taking the spectral to mean the injured, wounded and disappeared bodies who haunt Mexican politics, society and culture, the chapters reflect upon and closely examine how (audio)visual media can evoke loss and trauma. In addition to the idea of looking at and looking, there is the question of listening in film and other multi-media works. Taking the spectre and the ghostly as evocations of those whose presence lingers because their cases and conditions make them highly visible, intangibly oblique, silenced, or hidden in plain sight, the authors consider how the audio-visual can invite us to look (and listen) to absences.

Spectrality studies took root in largely anglophone literary studies in the early part of the twenty-first century and has gradually been adopted and deployed to understand Hispanic narratives with an emphasis on political violence and how memories of absent bodies irrupt coherent conceptualisations of temporality. Alberto Ribas-Casasayas and Amanda L. Petersen's (2016) edited collection traces these absent presences. In their introduction, drawing on the work of Jacques Derrida (1994) and Avery F. Gordon (2008), they assert that

> the theory of the ghost conveys the notion of a present disrupted by attempts to verbalize images or words that contradict the coherent, unproblematic, and historically decontextualized character of the representation of social reality in hegemonic discourse. (Ribas-Casasayas and Petersen 2016: 3)

This preoccupation with temporal disjuncture caused by hauntings is reiterated by Ribas-Casasayas (2019) in his introduction to a special issue of *iMex* where he asserts that such narratives have the power to stand outside of the 'condiciones o modos discursivos generados por la violencia militar, política o económica en el contexto de la modernidad' (2019: 13) [conditions or discursive modes operated by military, economic or political violence under modernity].[1] Spectral presences have a double function of making the forgotten visible and challenging the hegemonic mode of representing the past.

Of Time, Storytelling and Ethics

Time recurs persistently as a concern in writing about memory and trauma (see, for example, Gordon 2008; Kuhn and McAllister 2008; Hirsch 2014;

Bond 2018). Trauma and memory do not respect chronological time and, yet, temporal logic facilitates comprehension. When attempts are made to fit trauma into narrative form it can be incompatible with the ordering logic of storytelling and its conventional features. Idelbar Avelar addresses the risks involved in such attempts and finds conventional containment to be violent, asserting that converting 'the stark, brute facticity of experiences into a signifying chain in which such facticity perennially runs the risk of being turned into yet another trope' to be ripe for banal repetition (1999: 211). Linear sequencing of experiences that elide temporal fixity is at the heart of this problem for Avelar (1999). Trauma may be experienced in time but is not generally remembered sequentially. It is an 'unknowable truth' (Torchin 2012: 6). Avelar's analysis is concerned with survivor narratives of the Southern Cone dictatorships, but there are others who share his queasiness about the potentially reductive nature of some forms of culture to portray trauma.

Popular forms of visual and screen culture are often subject to criticism. Speeded up time, or accelerated action and excessive display, is the more usual concern for those writing about audio-visual culture. Nick Hodgin and Amit Thakkar (2017: 6–7) are critical of popular genre cinema's tendency towards the specularisation of trauma through the use of hyper-realist techniques favouring experimental and challenging portrayals of trauma. Generic conventions are too often associated with pleasure rather than mass communication, which is something Leshu Torchin (2012: 6–13) addresses as she argues in favour of the popular, asserting that that there is considerable potential for popular film to occupy the witness function. This lack of critical consensus gets to the heart of the ethical considerations and tensions in representing horrors experienced or shared by others. In the same way, there is no single approach by the authors in this collection. The chapters operate in an implicit and lively dialogue with one another. What the authors share is an ethical awareness of their positionality in relation to the work and the subjects haunting it.

If we consider genre and structure as framing devices that home in on the experiences of individuals or groups, it is useful to turn to scholars who examine subjectivity. How individuals or a collective are framed determines the value placed on their lives. In her analysis Judith Butler uses framing as a way of understanding how we 'apprehend' another and 'generate specific ontologies of the subject' (2009: 3). Framing is a form of focalisation that subtly places attention on certain subjects and excludes others, thus privileging their narrative. In her work, Butler is putting forward a philosophical argument about living beings in the world as they are read through public policy and political decisions. In this volume,

we are concerned with how these beings are represented and what privileging their stories means. While Butler's analysis is useful, Avery F.
Gordon's (2008) term 'complex personhood' helps to extend this and provides space for a highly nuanced apprehension of those who experience
trauma. Gordon explains that

> [c]omplex personhood means that the stories people tell about themselves, about
> their troubles, about their social worlds, and about society's problems are entangled
> and weave between what is immediately available as a story and what their imagina-
> tions are reaching towards. (Gordon 2008: 4)

She finds narrative storytelling to be a means of gaining insight into this
complex personhood and the traumatic events it is trying to capture. In
sync with Marianne Hirsch's call to develop 'a form of solidarity that is
suspicious of empathy, shuttling instead between proximity and distance,
affiliation and disaffiliation, complicity and accountability' (2014: 339),
woven into the chapters in this collection is the understanding that while
each attempt is contingent and partial, the artists and filmmakers portrayed are all trying to convey a sense of complex personhood on those
who lived through the traumatic events.

Temporal Disjunctures: 1968, 1994, 2006, 2012

The ordering of the chapters in this volume was made difficult by the
nature of how memory and trauma disrupt a linear understanding of
temporality, especially where most of the events lack resolution. Distant
events seep into subsequent periods and find their way into the present like
unbidden spectres quashing hopes for change or conjured as ghosts impel-
ling calls for justice. Gordon articulates the immanence of these traumas,
explaining, 'what's distinctive about haunting is that it is an animated state
in which a repressed or unresolved social violence is making itself known,
sometimes very directly, sometimes more obliquely' disrupting a smooth
linear resolution of the past (2008: xvi). While the chapters in this volume
conjure preceding events and moments, our chronology starts with 1968,
a watershed year in twentieth-century Mexican history. Although the
authors inevitably engage with traumas from previous decades, the focus
in this book is on subsequent years that echo one another and frame dramatic historical shifts: 1994, 2006 and 2012, with some continuing assessment of events and their legacies that have taken place right up to 2019.
We have limited ourselves to these years because they recur and haunt
the present and an exhaustive study would be impossibly encyclopaedic.

This collection is intended as a snapshot of current concerns and a further open invitation to extend this discussion. While acknowledging that a precise chronology is an impossibility when discussing trauma, it is still necessary to account for key events that haunt the chapters.

The spectatorial presence of 1968 recurs in visual and screen culture. In 1968 Mexico was the first Latin American country to host the Olympic Games with the aim of showcasing the country's dynamism, creativity and political stability. Mere days before the opening ceremony, this image was shattered when the army gunned down an as yet unaccounted for number of student and worker protesters in the historic city centre square, Tlatelolco/*Plaza de las tres culturas*. The absence of justice and the lack of accountability for those deaths and disappearances has had a significant legacy in Mexico. The official story is yet to be told, but there are monuments, testimonials, literature and a museum that assert a narrative in sometimes contestatory ways and place the dead and missing at the forefront (Allier Montaño 2018).

The question of 1968 is unresolved because the state has not yet acknowledged its role nor provided official figures for the dead or disappeared. Coinciding with the build-up to the Olympics in Mexico City and taking advantage of the international media presence, students and workers held a series of protests. Some of these concerned local issues around employment and educational freedom; others were more broadbased and inspired by the student and worker protests taking place elsewhere. The protests began in early summer and culminated in a large demonstration on 2 October, ten days before the opening ceremony of the Olympic Games. Concerned with its international reputation and eager to impose order, this protest was met with violence by state actors, some disguised as civilians, whose aim was to act as agent provocateurs. The exact numbers of the dead vary between tens up to hundreds and have yet to be officially verified (see Claire Brewster 2005; Keith Brewster 2010). Such estimates are an indicator of why numbers are unreliable measures of trauma.

A wealth of visual material from 1968 was generated by student protestors. Mostly unsigned and anonymously created, the banners, graffiti and posters created a store of visual motifs, largely drawn from an international array of revolutionary imagery indicating peaceful protest and resistance, such as doves, hammers and sickles, and raised fists, mixed with locally specific imagery depicting protests against those in power, such as sketches of government officials and a repressive police battalion. Soon after the massacre, these were re-made splashed with red ink to represent blood and marking a before and after, conjuring the dead and injured.

For Mónica Szurmuk and Maricruz Castro Ricalde (2014: 15–16) such ephemera conjure 'México 68' as a moment of rupture and are iterations of a highly contested memory site that challenge the foundational myths of modern Mexico. A more stable audio-visual record was created when the marches and protests were filmed by a multitude that was given access to university equipment. The footage was edited and distributed in the form of the documentary film *El grito* [The Cry] (Leobardo López Aretche, 1968). Although Chapters 1, 2, 3 and 6 in this book all directly address the legacies of 1968, it is because of its primacy that we find this event haunting all of the moments examined in this collection.

Unfortunately, as Guadalupe Pérez-Anzaldo (2014) has observed, the history of Mexico has been a series of cycles of violence committed against the populous from the colonial period to the present day, which makes its recurrence on screen inevitable. This observation evokes the poet and essayist Octavio Paz's (1959) infamous assertion of the Mexican affinity for death in *El laberinto de la soledad/The Labyrinth of Solitude* but goes beyond his quasi-romantic essentialism and, instead, looks at the multi-layered causes. In her work Pérez-Anzaldo (2014) maps out the multiple forms of violence that range from structural and racial inequality and which are a legacy of colonialism and the low-intensity state-controlled warfare ongoing in different forms since the 1970s in response to the tumult of 1968. Impelled by national and transnational tensions, these have continued up until the present day with a few periods of reprieve.

Continuing with the chronological trajectory, 1994 is the next significant focal point for the contributors to this volume. The year 1994 was one that held promises of positive political, social and economic change, and in itself carries very different hauntings. The inauguration of the North American Free Trade Agreement (NAFTA) in January of that year was supposed to deliver high employment and economic improvements, and the presidential nominee for the PRI, Luis Donaldo Colosio, promised political reform. Instead, Colosio was assassinated in March of that year, and the peso collapsed, plummeting the nation into the worst economic crisis of recent times. NAFTA has brought a lasting negative social and economic legacy, not least for the workers living along the border region. The year is also remembered as the beginning of the EZLN (Ejército Zapatista de Liberación Nacional/Zapatista Army of National Liberation) rebellion on 1 January, deliberately staged to disrupt the NAFTA celebrations and already much examined from multiple angles (see, for example, Womack Jr. 1999; Weinberg 2000; Holloway 2002; and Higgins 2004). The legacy and impact of 1994 is also felt through the violence of the border region that is a consequence of the neoliberal economic policies of this period. Chapters 4, 7 and 8 consider the legacies of 1994 from different historical viewpoints.

One of the lasting legacies of NAFTA is seen in the poor conditions of the factories, known as *maquiladoras*, situated on the US–Mexico border that draw internal migration from small towns. Women, who make up the majority of the workers in these *maquiladoras*, work long hours and live in precarious and unsafe neighbourhoods with poor services. Since the early 1990s these border regions have become associated with an increase in femicides or feminicides – both terms are used critically, subject to legal and activist debate (see Driver 2015). Therefore, even the language surrounding the deaths in this case has become a contested terrain. There is partial acknowledgement by the state of the disappearance and murder of women in the border regions of Mexico, but no conclusive investigation at the time of writing. Rumours and theories abound about who is/are responsible for the deaths, but there has been little police action (see, for example, Villamil 2011). A number of bodies have been recovered, and the murder sites remain scattered. Human remains belonging to the murdered women have been found in wasteland, rubbish tips, mass graves and abandoned warehouses. Memorials have been created by families of the women based on a common image, the pink cross, at times mounted where single or numerous bodies have been found, at others placed where the women were kidnapped. The pink cross becomes visual shorthand at 'synecdochic sites', although death can be found in multiple potential memorial sites and objects (Sion 2014: 20).

The gaps in the examination of memory and trauma in Mexico can be, in part, explained by the state's methods in tackling dissent, violence or illegal activities up to the early twenty-first century. This shift can be understood by looking at historical assessments of state violence. For example, writing in 1999, Alan Knight characterises the pervasive nature of political violence in Mexico as 'less extreme' than that of the Southern Cone 'because it is more discrete, anonymous, prolonged, and quotidian' (118), something that has clearly changed since 2006 with Felipe Calderón's *sexenio* [six-year presidential rule] and his decision to engage in open war against drug traffickers and related criminal operations. The intense battles that have emerged from tensions between the illegal narcotics trade and the failure of state and extra-territorial forces to control these, has ruptured normality for many civilians since 2006. Chapters 7 and 8 address the spectrality of 2006, reaching back and forth to preceding conditions and subsequent events and their aftermath. It is tempting to place much emphasis on 2006, as a singular moment or flashpoint. Instead, it should be seen as a date that marks an escalation of political, military and criminal tensions that at time of writing have yet to see resolution.

As a consequence of the bloodshed since 2006, 2012 became a year of reckoning and reflection. Another election year when the spirit of 1968 was evoked by a new generation through protest and political demands, 2012 emerges in importance in this collection as witnessing a flowering of production and responses to the violence more than as an indicator of any considerable political shift. Ongoing as we write, and reaching a recent peak in 2012, the graphic depictions of this violence are carried out to different ends. There is a range of such works ranging from the horrific to the activist. There are filmed videos of torture, dismemberment and death placed on video-sharing sites such as YouTube; families, activists and artists film and photograph the dead or their remains in order to seek justice; and journalists – serious or sensationalist – capture images of death and violence in order to report on the events, often risking their lives. The government then exploits some or all of these to legitimate their activities, further muddying the indexical and representational nature of the texts, and the intent of the images and films.

Despite the disruptive nature of trauma, memory and the spectral on temporality, dates persist to aid a mapping out of events and activities – and, yet, do not neatly coalesce. These temporal shifts between 2006, 2012 and the present day must be rooted in another key originating moment; this gendered violence is another legacy of the political corruption and social instability demarcated by the year 1994. Starting earlier but running concurrently, the brutal killing of women by unidentified assailants which began in the 1990s has, simultaneously, been exacerbated by and conflated with the violence related to the criminal activities of the drug cartels and the paramilitary and military responses to these.

Haunted by this recent violence and concerned with other moments, Chapters 3, 4, 5 and 6 all consider work from 2012, while Chapters 7 and 8 directly address 2006 and its aftermath. Haunting all of these is the spectre of 1968, which evokes other past traumas and is evoked through them. Moving back and forth through time, the works made in 2012 build on this legacy. By addressing the hauntings of these events, the chapters in this volume tackle the subject of loss through death, disappearances or displacement.

Tracing Memory, Trauma and the Spectre across Spaces and Times

Although not divided into distinct sections because of the chronological challenge supposed by memory, traumas and the spectre, this book opens with three chapters on the significance and legacy of the unresolved and repeating moment of 1968. Chapters 1, 2 and 3 examine how visual and screen arts can represent trauma using different modes of documentation – both fiction and non-fiction – that do not always serve fixed indexical functions, nor act as easy memory markers. The spectre of 1968 evokes other past traumas and is evoked through them. In Chapter 1 Chris Harris asserts that the comic, *Los agachados de Rius, número especial de los cocolazos de julio-agosto-septiembre y octubre quién sabe si tambor. . .* [the stooped: a special issue of the battles from July-August-September and October who knows if the drum beats. . .] by Rius about protests and published shortly after the massacre in 1968 can be used as a historical and testimonial source. Harris posits that the comic sits as both an integral part of the literary canon of Tlatelolco and as a form of Mexican visual culture that provides productive terrain for revisiting and re-thinking Jacques Derrida's (1994) concept of 'hauntology'. Using the interpretive framework of Derrida (1994) and Raymond Williams (1977), Harris argues that as one of the early works to emerge in the immediate aftermath of the events, *Los agachados* has the capacity to fill gaps in knowledge. For Harris these gaps produced a crisis that continues to haunt the present in the face of its attempts to, variously, co-opt and silence the memorialisation of 1968.

Successive Mexican governments have deployed different tactics whereby they establish ownership over national traumas. David Wood (2019) has written about the Mexican state's policy of forgetting by acknowledging what has taken place and performing an investigation that does not result in justice, all the while creating a smokescreen through media saturation. This pattern can be seen in many events including the state response to 1968 and its aftermath. A large state-supported museum exists in Tlatelolco square with an engraved monument at the spot where many were injured, killed and disappeared. Following on from the events in 1968 the government supported independent filmmakers to make films, none of which centred on the events, but some of which addressed them implicitly through their tone, style and approach (see, for example, Haddu 2007 and Thornton 2013). This performance of openness hides the truth in plain sight and evades accounting for what happened. It also allows space for other narratives to emerge, resulting in a polyphony of approaches and a range of alternative visions that operate within and beyond the 'often homogenizing properties of national memory regimes' evident elsewhere (Bond, Craps and Vermeulen 2016: 4). This simultaneous creation within and without can look totalising in its grandeur, scale and volume (if we look at the number of state-supported war narratives), but when examined closely has facilitated numerous and repeated examples of resistance, of speaking out and against, and of maintaining memories of the past for future generations. This all makes Mexico a contradictory, paradoxical and necessary case study.

Accordingly, 1968 haunts the case studies in Chapter 2, filtered through the perspective of its aftermath. Niamh Thornton considers how the archive has been deployed in films made in 1976 as a way of figuring through how screened violence is focalised. The legacy of 1968 can be found in films centred on three distinct events: *Los de abajo* [The Underdogs] (Servando González, 1976), a film set during the Mexican Revolution (1910–20), and two films by Felipe Cazals, *Los Poquianchis: (De los pormenores y otros sucedidos del dominio público que acontecieron a las hermanas de triste memoria a quienes la maledicencia así las bautizó)* [The Poquianchis: (On the particularities and other known occurrences that happened to the tragic sisters who were maliciously baptised as such)], on a notorious case of the exploitation and mass murder of female sex workers, and *Canoa*, a docudrama about an incident that took place in 1968 in rural Mexico.

As is explored in Chapter 2, Servando González was accused of complicity with the government in Tlatlelolco in 1968. By way of response to these accusations, in *Los de abajo* he deployed documentary footage to confront the audience with hyper-realist depictions of death and trauma from the archive of the Revolution, thus addressing an unresolved perpetrator perspective. From a different position, but with similar ambivalence towards screened violence, Cazals interrogates cinema's role in the creation of spectacle and explores its capacity to portray violence ethically in *Los Poquianchis* (1976) and *Canoa* (1976). Employing stylistic features of documentary film, Cazals questions the witness function (Torchin 2012) in film and the complicity of the filmmaker when capturing violence. Combining this with Marianne Hirsch's (2003 and 2014) work on re-appropriated material, Thornton examines how these films use the archive to reflect on the nature of looking at death.

Following on from this use of indexical traces as a means of playing with convention and challenging closure, in Chapter 3 Viviana McManus considers the documentary, *Flor en Otomí* [Flower in Otomí] (Luisa Riley 2012), as a mode of recovering the forgotten involvement of women guerrillas in the 'Dirty War'. Tracing their decision to shift from peaceful protest to armed struggle and examining the secret acts of the government to contain them, McManus uses interviews with subjects who were active in the movement and carries out close textual analysis of the documentary to propose it as a heuristic tool that can help understand gaps in the historical record. The fact that these first three chapters span the years from 1968 up to and beyond the new millennium (2012) indicates how present and recurrent the trauma of 1968 is for visual artists and filmmakers.

In a similar fashion, 1994 and 2012 are integral to and cast a shadow over the works examined in Chapter 4 by Maxmiliano Maza-Pérez. The year 1994 held promises of positive political, social and economic change, while 2012 saw a groundswell demanding justice for disappeared and missing people. Both carry very different hauntings. Colosio's assassination, although officially investigated, failed to provide a conclusive explanation for the many contradictory facets of the event; this resulted in a number of unexplained circumstances leading up to the murder, discarded witness statements from the scene of the crime and an unconvincing hypothesis framing the case. It is the inconclusive nature of this traumatic moment in the nation's history that is explored in the film *Colosio: El asesinato* [Colosio], released in 2012. Maza-Pérez compares *Colosio: El asesinato* to another film about the failed political assassination of President Porfirio Díaz, *El atentado/The Attempt Dossier* (Jorge Fons 2010). Focusing on the cinematic landscape in the film, Maza-Pérez explores a theme that recurs in the chapters: haunted spaces. Clearly, place is a central preoccupation in spectrality and trauma studies, collapsing boundaries between the past and present attached to specific locales. For Maza-Pérez, these films are an invitation to reflect on public spaces and consider the multiple horrors committed there, thus emphasising memories' localities and attachment to spaces.

A recurrent theme in the chapters is the subject of loss through death, disappearances or displacement primarily focused on the territorial. While the Mexican state as a boundaried entity is central to many of the analyses, there is a need to consider traumas beyond its borders. In memory studies there has been a shift towards 'mnemonic mobility' (Bond et al. 2016: 3), that emphasises how the nation state is a poor container for memory because of memory's 'transcultural, transgenerational, transmedial, and transdisciplinary drift' (Bond et al. 2016: 2). Memory and trauma can be carried and produced beyond borders and reoriented spatially and temporally with migrants as central figures in this process. As Emma Bond states, 'ghosts [can] oscillate between the poles of past and present, here and there' (2018: 201). Memory and its hauntings can migrate and move with people and across generations. In Chapter 5 Catherine Leen examines this need to open out our analysis beyond the state borders to consider those who live outside of Mexico and carry the legacies of the past intercut with the traumas of the present.

In the US, the migrant is the visible presence of Mexico bearing the burden of being the US's 'imago' (Alemán 2013: 509), a distorted mirror image. At best seen through the prism of 'romantic primitivism' (Alemán 2013: 509), at worst a malign racial profiling, the Mexican migrant in the US has to find a sense of self through potent spectres and the pull of the here and there. Leen examines the loss and trauma of immigration in the Mexican photographer Dulce Pinzón's 2012 series 'The Real Story of the Superheroes', re-configured and countered through playful photography and dress-up. Leen proposes Pinzón's photographs as subversive activist work that counter migrant imagery. The migrant experiences a doubling of their displacement through the traumatic loss of home and in the place they move to they are the other. Leen addresses the trans-, inter-, and supra-national legacies of trauma by considering Mexican artistic expression beyond national frontiers, assessing its impact across borders.

Reflecting the cyclical nature of trauma, in Chapter 6 there is a return to the ghosts of 1968. Linking 1968 and 2012, Jessica Wax-Edwards examines political protests that took place in the public squares of Mexico and were amplified via online platforms. It is significant that 2012 was an election year when the spirit of 1968 was evoked by a new generation through protest and political demands. Wax-Edwards considers the ways in which the #YoSoy132 [IAm132] movement and the attendant hashtag draws on its predecessors and signals the lasting legacy of 1968. Combining the affordances of social media to amplify #YoSoy132's message with the established mode of street protest, the digital becomes a means of mapping the movement as 'social interaction, shaped by political circumstances [. . .] and enabled by evolving media technologies' (Bond et al. 2016: 18). The hashtag is part of the 'impactful spectral moments' to be found in anti-violent protests (Petersen 2019: 29). As Wax-Edwards explores, what the #YoSoy132 movement is protesting in 2012 is another souring of the promises of the Mexican Revolution and a legacy of the political corruption and social instability demarcated by the year 1994 and the explosion of violence after 2006. Therefore, while 1968 dominates many of the chapters, the trauma, spectrality and legacies of other events also persist.

Chapters 7 and 8 address the ways in which 'psychological trauma and shock function in the blurred boundaries between the private and public spheres' (Clancy 2017: 218). In Chapter 7 Miriam Haddu examines loss and mourning in Tatiana Huezo's documentary *Ausencias* [Absences] (2015), focusing on those directly affected by Calderón's policies of 2006 and the consequential violence that has followed. In *Ausencias* Huezo tackles the problem of the thousands of enforced disappearances in Mexico, identified as 'casualties' of the drugs wars, and positions a grieving mother at the heart of her narrative. It is these internal spaces of mourning, as examples of affected experience after an enforced disappearance, that constitute the focus of this chapter's analysis. In the film we are guided by the subject's memory, which narrates the personal experience of longing and absence, predominantly felt by those left behind after an enforced disappearance. Haddu considers Huezo's work as an exemplar of a shift towards the poetic mode in documenting violence (see also Wood 2019). Framed within discourses of mourning, trauma, melancholia and loss, Haddu's explorations of Huezo's work illustrate how the filmmaker's visual language, which mediates between the observational and expository, articulates the often private experience of grief as indicative of a wider cultural trauma manifest in the collective. In this chapter the condition of perpetual mourning undergone by families of the victims of enforced disappearance is addressed as a legacy of grief that has been left behind by the perpetrators of such crimes. The condition of mourning, therefore, exemplified by the maternal figure at the centre of Huezo's documentary, becomes a visual motif conveying the state of national trauma experienced by thousands of civilians in Mexico who have lost loved ones to the drug wars.

In Chapter 8 Julia Banwell considers the work of the multi-media and transmedia artist Teresa Margolles who uses her art as a form of activism to draw attention to the trauma and aftermath of gendered violence in Mexico. This chapter takes a selection of works to examine the artist's use of space and emptiness to address issues around agency in the performance of bodies and ruins. The subjects of her work bring to the fore the challenge of imbuing individuals with complex personhood. Focusing on marginalised subjects, some of whom number among the thousands of women murdered since the early 1990s without legal consequences, space is central to Margolles' work. She is concerned with the collapse of the distance between public and private spaces as a result of violence. Drawing these strands together, Banwell considers how Margolles addresses the structural and physical violences enacted on marginalised people and the spaces they inhabit.

Like many of the audio-visual artists considered, Margolles is conscious of the commemorations and monuments that control the narrative, dominate the visual landscape and attempt to misdirect the victims' and families' responses. For example, there can be partial justice, such as the named centre for investigation set up in Juarez to investigate the disappearance and murders of women in the city as detailed in the special issue in 2011 of the Mexican news magazine *Proceso* (Villamil 2011). This establishes a bureaucracy and appearance of justice without actual justice. To navigate these acts of control over memory and its legacies, visual and screen representations are vital acts of recuperating and maintaining the past. Against this backdrop, Margolles demands that we look at the spaces inhabited by the absent presence of the 'haunted bodies' of those who have been wounded, disappeared or murdered (Cosentino 2019). Some of these spaces have been taken from the victims in the process of gentrification, a form of violence which attempts to erase the memory as well as the physical presence of those who formerly inhabited or occupied them. This results in further marginalisation. Using traces and remains of the dead and disappeared, Margolles' work is often confrontational and, in Chapter 8, Banwell considers the power of Margolles' work in the context of the wider cultural, economic and political sphere within which she is operating.

Official state-sanctioned justice and memorialisation of traumas has its own characteristics that can distort the past as well as be a means of regulating how the story is told, but its absence can cause greater damage. Brigitte Sion asserts that, '[o]bviously, a trauma neither precedes nor concludes with memorial construction' (2014: 20), be that a physical structure or through an audio-visual text. A memory text is an important intervention in the structuring of memory or of creating an opening for new debates that oftentimes can reach a new audience, viewer or readership and challenge the accepted state-sanctioned version (where these exist). The spectres of the past lie in, among, and beyond the official versions as well as haunt the sites and subjective experiences of victims and survivors.

This book will go some way towards offering its readers an insight into the interrelationship between sensory experience, artistic expression and self-definition, as we observe the trajectory of memories. These in turn are articulated through carefully constructed acts of memorialisation, which give rise to externalised reflections of lived and imagined traumas of the past, present and future. The past bumps up against the present because when it is unresolved it is often repeated. Picking up a series of case studies that explore the multiple facets of memory and trauma, this book proposes to be an opening out of a discussion within an urgent area of analysis in Mexican studies.

Mexican filmmakers, photographers, and cartoon and multi-media artists turn to address the traumatic events of the past and present, choosing to represent these moments and their legacies through a variety of visual and screen media. This book assesses a selection of cultural outputs emerging from the chaos and disorder of both past and present traumas as indicators of a process of mourning, re-appropriation and possible enlightenment. The aim is to signal the type of work that needs to be done in order to start to apprehend the legacy of the past on present-day Mexico.

Note

1. Unless otherwise stated, all translations are my own.

Bibliography

Alemán, Jesse (2013), 'The Other Country: Mexico, the United States, and the Gothic History of Conquest', in Maria del Pilar Blanco and Esther Pereen (eds), *The Spectralities Reader: Ghosts and Haunting in Contemporary Cultural Theory*, New York and London: Bloomsbury, pp. 507–26.

Allier Montaño, Eugenia (2018), 'Tlatelolco, lugar de memoria y sitio de turismo: Miradas desde el 68', *Revista Mexicana de Ciencias Políticas y Sociales*, 63:234, pp. 215–8. Available at <https://dx.doi.org/10.22201/fcpys.2448492xe.2018.234.65790> (last accessed 23 March 2020).

Avelar, Idelbar (1999), *The Untimely Present: Postdictatorial Latin American Fiction and the Task of Mourning*, Durham, NC and London: Duke University Press.

Benjamin, Thomas (2000), *La Revolución: Mexico's Great Revolution as Memory, Myth and History*, Austin: University of Texas Press.

Billig, Michael (1995), *Banal Nationalism*, London: Sage.

Blanco, Maria del Pilar, and Esther Pereen (2013), *The Spectralities Reader: Ghosts and Haunting in Contemporary Cultural Theory*, New York and London: Bloomsbury.

Bond, Emma (2018), *Writing Migration Through the Body*, London: Palgrave MacMillan

Bond, Lucy, Stef Craps, and Pieter Vermeulen (2016), 'Introduction: Memory on the Move', in Lucy Bond, Stef Craps, and Pieter Vermeulen (eds), *Memory Unbound: Tracing the Dynamics of Memory Studies*, New York and Oxford: Berghan Books, pp. 1–26.

Brewster, Claire (2005), *Responding to Crisis in Contemporary Mexico: The Political Writings of Paz, Fuentes, Monsiváis, and Poniatowska*, Tucson: University of Arizona Press.

Brewster, Keith (2010), *Reflections on Mexico '68*, Malden, MA and Oxford: Wiley and Blackwell.

Butler, Judith (2009), *Frames of War: When Life is Greivable*, Calcutta: Seagull Books.

Clancy, Fiona (2017), 'Flesh and Blood in the Globalised Age: Pablo Trapero's *Nacido y criado* (*Born and Bred*), and *Carancho* (*The Vulture*)', in Nick Hodgin and Amit Thakkar (eds), Scars *and Wounds*, London: Palgrave Macmillan, pp. 217–41.

Cosentino, Olivia (2019), 'Haunted Bodies: Spectrality, Gender Violence and the Central American Female Migrant in Recent Mexican Cinema', *iMex: México Interdisciplinario/Interdisciplinary Mexico*, 8:16, 2019/2, pp. 41–54. Available at <https://www.imex-revista.com/en/ediciones/xvi-spectral-mexico> (last accessed 23 March 2020).

Derrida, Jacques (1994), *Specters of Marx: The State of the Debt, the Work of Mourning and the New International*, translated by Peggy Kamuf, New York and London: Routledge.

Driver, Alice (2015), *More or Less Dead: Feminicide, Haunting, and the Ethics of Representation in Mexico*, Tuscon: University of Arizona Press.

Gordon, Avery F. (2008), *Ghostly Matters: Haunting and the Sociological Imagination*, Minneapolis and London: University of Minnesota Press.

Haddu, Miriam (2007), *Contemporary Mexican Cinema 1989–1999*, Lewiston, NY and Lampeter: The Edwin Mellen Press.

Higgins, Nicholas P. (2004), *Understanding the Chiapas Rebellion: Modernist Visions and the Invisible Indians*, Austin: University of Texas Press.

Hirsch, Marianne (2003), 'Nazi Photographs in Post-Holocaust Art: Gender as an Idiom of Memorialization', in Alex Hughes and Andrea Noble (eds), *Phototextualities: Intersections of Photography and Narrative*, Albuquerque: University of New Mexico Press, pp. 19–40.

Hirsch, Marrianne (2014), 'Connective Histories in Vulnerable Times: MLA Presidential Address', *PMLA*, 129:3, pp. 330–48.

Hodgin, Nick, and Amit Thakkar (2017), 'Introduction: Trauma Studies, Film, and the Scar Motif', in Nick Hodgin and Amit Thakkar (eds), *Scars and Wounds*, London: Palgrave Macmillan, pp. 1–29.

Holloway, John (2002), *Change the World without Taking Power: The Meaning of Revolutions Today*, London and Sterling, VA: Pluto Press.

Jelin, Elizabeth (2003), *State Repression and the Labors of Memory*, Minneapolis & London: University of Minnesota Press.

Knight, Alan (1999), 'Political Violence in Post-Revolutionary Mexico', in Kees Koonings and Dirk Krujit (eds), *Societies of Fear: The Legacy of Civil War, Violence and Terror in Latin America*, London and New York: Zed Books.

Kuhn, Annette, and Kirsten Emiko McAllister (2008), 'Locating Memory: Photographic Acts – An Introduction', in Annette Kuhn and Kirsten Emiko McAllister (eds), *Locating Memory: Photographic Acts*, New York and Oxford: Berghan Books, pp. 1–16.

Levey, Cara (2016), *Fragile Memory, Shifting Impunity: Commemoration and Contestation in Post-Dictatorship Argentina and Uruguay*, Oxford: Peter Lang.

Noble, Andrea (2010), *Photography and Memory in Mexico: Icons of Revolution*, Manchester and New York: Manchester University Press.

Paz, Octavio (1959), *El laberinto de la soledad* (Vida y pensamiento de México), Mexico: Fondo de Cultura Económica.

Pérez-Anzaldo, Guadalupe (2014), *El espectáculo de la violencia en el cine mexicano del siglo XXI*, Mexico City: Ediciones Eón and University of Missouri Press.

Petersen, Amanda L. (2019), 'Breaking Silences and Revealing Ghosts: Spectral Moments of Gender Violence in Mexico', *iMex: México Interdisciplinario/ Interdisciplinary Mexico*, 8:16, 2019/2, pp. 22–40. Available at <https://www.imex-revista.com/en/ediciones/xvi-spectral-mexico> (last accessed 23 March 2020).

Ribas-Casasayas, Alberto (2019), 'Editorial: el espectro, en teoría', *iMex: México Interdisciplinario/Interdisciplinary Mexico*, 8:16, 2019/2, pp. 8–20. Available at <https://www.imex-revista.com/en/ediciones/xvi-spectral-mexico> (last accessed 23 March 2020).

Ribas-Casasayas, Alberto, and Amanda L. Petersen (2016), 'Introduction: Theories of the Ghost in the Transhispanic Context', in Alberto Ribas-Casasayas and Amanda L. Petersen (eds), *Espectros: Ghostly Hauntings in Contemporary Transhispanic Narratives*, Lewisburg, PA: Bucknell University Press.

Sion, Brigitte (2014), 'Introduction', in Brigitte Sion (ed.), *Death Tourism: Disaster Sites as Recreational Landscape*, London and New York: Seagull Books, pp. 1–8.

Szurmuk, Mónica, and Maricruz Castro Ricalde (2014), 'La memoria y sus sitios en el México contemporáneo', in Mónica Szurmuk and Maricruz Castro Ricalde (eds), *Sitios de la memoria: México post 68*, Santiago, Chile: Editorial Cuarto Propio, pp. 7–29.

Thornton, Niamh (2013), *Revolution and Rebellion in Mexican Cinema*, New York: Bloomsbury.

Torchin, Leshu (2012), *Creating the Witness: Documenting Genocide on Film, Video, and the Internet*, Minneapolis and London: University of Minnesota Press.

Villamil, Jenaro (2011), 'Fábrica de muertas . . .', *Proceso, Special Issue, La tragedia de Juárez*, 34: August, pp. 8–13.

Villegas, Paulina (2020), 'In Mexico, Women Go on Strike Nationwide to Protest Violence', *The New York Times*, 9 March. Available at <https://www.nytimes.com/2020/03/09/world/americas/mexico-women-strike-protest.html> (last accessed 11 March 2020).

Weinberg, Bill. (2000), *Homage to Chiapas: The New Indigenous Struggles in Mexico*, London and New York: Verso.

Williams, Raymond (1977), *Marxism and Literature*, Oxford: Oxford University Press.

Womack, Jr, John. (1999), *Rebellion in Chiapas: An Historical Reader*, New York: The New Press.

Wood, David (2019), 'Nombrar lo ausente: cine documental y la 'verdad histórica' después de Ayotzinapa', in Adriana Estrada Álvarez, Nicolas Défossé, and Diego Zavala Scherer (eds), *Cine político en México (1968–2017)*, New York and Bern: Peter Lang, pp. 125–41.

CHAPTER 1

On the Commemoration of Mexico '68:
Los agachados de Rius, número especial de los cocolazos de julio-agosto-septiembre y octubre quién sabe si tambor. . .

Chris Harris

A la fecha nadie sabe el número exacto de muertos y desaparecidos que nos deparó la Trinca Infernale GDO-LEA-MGB. Es decir, traducido al cristiano: Gustavo Díaz Ordaz, Luis Echeverría Álvarez y Marcelino García Barragán, el de la Defensa. Es cuando da coraje que no exista el infierno de todos tan temido . . . ¡Ay, si hubiera Dios! (Rius 2014: kindle loc 1776)

[To this day nobody knows the exact number of deaths and disappearances that the Infernal Trio GDO-LEA-MGB delivered to us. That means, in other words: Gustavo Díaz Ordaz, Luis Echeverría Álvarez and Marcelino García Barragán, the one from Defence. That's when it becomes infuriating that the hell we all fear doesn't exist . . . If only there was a God!].[1]

El movimiento estudiantil de 1968, localizado en la ciudad de México, pretendió desestabilizar al gobierno del presidente Díaz Ordaz; su verdadero objetivo, que nunca conocieron los estudiantes, era establecer un gobierno socialista en México. (Corona del Rosal, 1995: 276)

[The student movement in 1968, localised in Mexico City, tried to destabilise the government of President Díaz Ordaz; its real objective, which the students never understood, was to establish a socialist government in Mexico].

In October 2018, and for several months prior to that, there were numerous academic and cultural symposia as well as new publications dedicated to remembering and re-analysing the story of the 1968 Mexican student movement (see Carpenter 2018). The focus of such activity was on the students' conflict with the state, the Partido Revolucionario Institucional (PRI), President Gustavo Díaz Ordaz (1964–70), and especially on the Tlatelolco massacre of 2 October 1968. The slogan '2 de octubre no se olvida' [October 2nd is not forgotten] reappeared, most frequently as a Twitter hashtag shortened to #2deoctubre. There were ceremonies and commemorative acts in Mexico City, which included flying the national flag at half-mast in the capital city's main square. Those ceremonies recalled the events of 1968 while simultaneously calling for social justice in relation to specific contemporary issues of the twenty-first century. The president-elect, Andrés Manuel López Obrador, promised he would never enlist military force to thwart student protests (see Malkin 2018). This annual political fervour, fuelled by historical events and legacies, can be positively influential for a new youthful Mexican generation. Yet that will only be the case when public understanding focuses both upon remembering for the purposes of present-day political protest and on a more complex consideration of the affective and shifting practices of commemoration in relation to the Tlatelolco massacre and the myriad conjunctural factors that produced it. In other words, if the ends of remembering Mexico '68 are effectively limited to voicing new forms of protest and to celebrating the very freedom to protest in contemporary Mexican society, this will tend to efface the student movement's longer-term goals of radical social transformation and of protesting with a view to eroding the structural and physical violence, or better, 'slow violence' (see Nixon 2013), still associated today with the neoliberal Mexican state.

One of the most problematic aspects of engaging with the history of Mexico '68 is that there continue to exist significant gaps in our knowledge; a number of important unknowns like the precise death toll and, of course, radical narrative variations depending on the starting points and authorial convictions and perspectives. It is always, therefore, a highly risky endeavour to try to produce a summarised account of events. I do so at the beginning of this chapter for one reason only: to make what follows on Rius and *Los agachados* more intelligible to readers who are coming to these narratives and the issues they raise for the first time. In the same vein, the title of this chapter and the epigraph also merit brief comment. *Los agachados de Rius, número especial de los cocolazos de julio-agosto-septiembre y octubre quién sabe si tambor. . .* [The Downtrodden: special issue on the July–August–September beatings and possibly drumbeats in October . . .] is the full title of the special issue.[2] It is shortened hereafter in this chapter to '*número especial de los cocolazos*'. The use of 'tambor' is ambiguous but menacing. It could refer to 'tambores de guerra' [drums of war], or the cylinder of a pistol. Either way, an event of the nature and magnitude of the Tlatelolco massacre is portentously and metonymically suggested. The lines in the epigraph appear in Chapter 31, 'Mi 68 particular' (Rius 1968). Rius reveals that he was invited to attend the Tlatelolco rally and stand on the balcony of the Chihuahua Building with the student leaders. The only reason he was not there was because Guillermo Mendizábal, the founder of the publishing house Editorial Posada, forgot to tell Rius he was invited. Curiously, Rius makes no significant mention of his work on the special issue of *Los agachados*. He simply alludes to the students using his drawings and to student leader Roberto Escudero collecting them.

On 26 July 1968 a protest march concerning the incursion of armed police officers, *granaderos* [grenadiers, 'military riot police'], into Mexico City's Vocational School Number 5 of the Instituto Politécnico Nacional [National Polytechnic Institute/IPN] coincided with a communist march to mark the anniversary of the Cuban Revolution (see Hodges and Gandy 2002: 93–106). A violent confrontation between *granaderos* and protesters in the heart of the capital left buses upturned, shop windows smashed, numerous injuries and two deaths. Further protest marches involving other institutions then followed. On 1 August the *rector* [vice chancellor] of the Universidad Nacional Autónoma de México (UNAM) 'led a demonstration of at least 50,000 people as a sign of mourning for the fallen students and the violation of university autonomy' (Hodges and Gandy 2002: 95). Subsequently, the Consejo Nacional de Huelga [National Strike Council] was formed and it made six demands:

1. Freedom for political prisoners.
2. Dismissal of the police chiefs.
3. Abolition of the Grenadiers.
4. Abrogation of the crime of 'social dissolution'.
5. Compensation for the families of the dead and wounded.
6. Determination of responsibility for the repression.

The support for the students and for their demands was growing, reaching its highest numerical point in August. Two large marches to the *Zócalo* [main square] gathered some 200,000 people on the 13th and 400,000 on the 27th (Hodges and Gandy 2002: 96–8). September brought a change in policing. In his state-of-the-nation speech on 1 September, President Gustavo Díaz Ordaz announced that if force were necessary, his regime would take that route. A third and silent march to the *Zócalo* on 13 September saw the number of protesters drop to somewhere in the region of 250,000 as hard-line policing, injuries and deaths increased. On 18 September the UNAM campus was occupied by 5,000 soldiers before, tragically, at Tlatelolco square on October 2, the protests were brought to an end through military intervention and massacre. Rius, in his autobiography, records that: 'La intención del gobierno fue descabezar el Movimiento con el terror de la Noche de Tlatelolco, para poder inaugurar alegremente los Juegos Olímpicos de México 68' (Rius 2014: kindle loc 1776). [The intention of the government was to guillotine the Movement with the terror of the Night of Tlatelolco, so they could cheerfully open the Mexico '68 Olympic Games].

In the contemporary and shifting processes of commemorating Mexico '68, accelerated and reinvigorated by the 2018 anniversary, one Mexican cultural icon and one popular publication that have somehow, and so far, escaped popular assimilation into the ongoing discussions and debates are the leftist artist Rius and his satirical comic book *Los agachados* [The Downtrodden] (see Roberts 2014). This oversight is most notable in the case of *Los agachados* with the *número especial de los cocolazos* [literally meaning special issue about blows to the head] (1968): the principal textual focus of this essay. Rius is the pen name of Eduardo del Río (1934–2017), a prolific Mexican intellectual, comic book writer and political cartoonist whose death from complications of prostate cancer on 8 August 2017 at his home in Tepoztlán brought him momentarily back into the global public eye (see Galindo 2017; Roberts 2017). A few years earlier, when he celebrated his 80th birthday in 2014, Rius had also fleetingly been an object of media attention because he opened a retrospective exhibition called *Rius para principiantes* [Rius for Beginners]. The exhibition was located in Mexico City's Museo del Estanquillo. It ran until January 2015 and contained 220 exhibits. While few reviews remain online, a taster of this exhibition can be found through the Museo del Estanquillo's site (2020). In spite of his numerous readers, Rius was not always in the Mexican public eye. After leaving formal education at fifteen he worked in a number of jobs, including earning his living variously as a barman, a civil servant and an undertaker. He had to wait until the 1960s for his first taste of artistic success and, even then, his controversial left-leaning political views brought him his first experiences of censorship and pressure from the state. On Rius's artistic success in that decade, Hinds and Tatum record that Rius 'wrote and illustrated 291 issues of [. . .] *Los agachados* between 1968 and 1977, [and that] initial circulation figures were around 50,000 rising to 150,000' (Hinds and Tatum 1992: 72–3). With regard to political pressure from the Mexican state, Hinds and Tatum also inform us that two years after Rius had walked away from his first comic book *Los supermachos* [The Supermen] in 1967 because of censorship, his life was threatened when, following arrest and a day in a military prison in Toluca, he was 'taken out to the nearby mountains, where the police told him he would be executed for crimes against the government' (Hinds and Tatum 1992: 71). Fortunately, this attempt to scare Rius into ceasing production of his political satire failed. He told Tatum in a personal interview: 'I continued with the only thing I knew how to do. And I wasn't about to turn my back on my work that I considered useful to everybody' (Hinds and Tatum 1992: 71–2).

An appreciation of Rius's biography, his career as a self-taught cari-caturist and his multiple satirical publications is essential for our under-standing of twentieth-century Mexico and contemporary cultural history. Moreover, his contributions to Mexican culture and his attempts to shape Mexican popular political discourse require urgent recognition and reval-orisation, especially in the case of his comic book representation of Mexico '68. *Los agachados*, drawn and designed by Rius, was on sale weekly in Mexico from 1968 to 1977 (Figure 1.1). Circulation of the fifth in the series was delayed by a week in order to allow for the publication of the 1968 special issue – a fact that the special issue records on the inside back cover. The special issue was completed in late September 1968, just days before the Tlatelolco massacre of 2 October. Curiously, the back cover is dated '2 de noviembre de 1968'. Further historical research is needed on the exact publication date, distribution and circulation of this issue, as this may shed light on the question of why this text has not previously figured prominently in intellectual discussions of the history of 1968. There is no listing, for example, in the bibliography of Jorge Volpi's *La imaginación y el poder: una historia intelectual de 1968* (1998). Similarly, in Claire Brewster's (2005) analysis of the responses to 1968 in the works of key journalists and authors, there is no reference to this comic. While it is obvious that Rius and *Los agachados* fall outside of the project parameters of Volpi and Brewster, the absence of even a pointer to another domain of necessary research is indicative of the fact that Rius's views on the state–student conflict have remained marginal.

Although the exact publication date for the special issue is not given, the final part of the comic's narrative refers to the military occupation on 24 September of the campus at the Instituto Politécnico Nacional. The Mexican state–student conflict was then at a very advanced stage with the Tlatelolco massacre just eight days away (though the massacre is not cov-ered in the comic's narrative and it appears that the comic circulated prior to the acts of state terror). On the opening page Rius positions himself and his collaborator AB (Emilio Abdalá) as citizens of integrity in a situa-tion of national crisis characterised by misunderstandings and the delib-erate and widespread deception of the public by the state. Rius claims that despite the constant criticism from students of a state-controlled 'prensa vendida' [state co-opted press], he still sees himself as a journalist and caricaturist who is attempting to produce an account of unfolding political events that is 'objetivo, aclarador de paradas y fácil de entender' (Rius 1968: 1) [objective, insightful about contradictory points of view and easy to understand]. The comic's images and dialogue locate the reader in the imaginary village of Chayotitlán where a public meeting is being held about

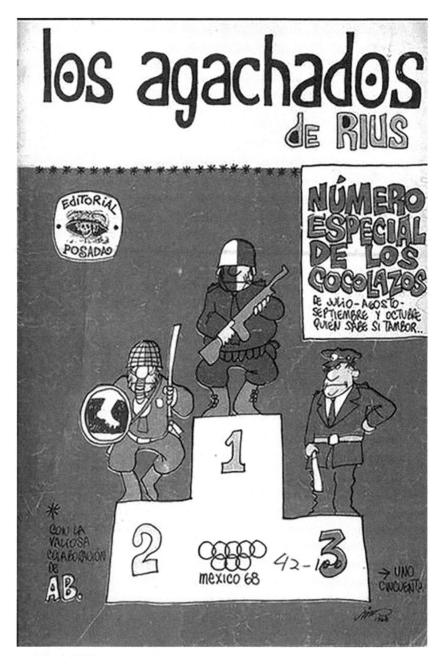

Figure 1.1   Cover of *Los agachados* (1968, número especial).

the alarming events in the capital. The meeting is chaired by Licenciado Güacache, the local *cacique* [political boss] and friend of the local RIP delegate. Rius consistently uses this fictional acronym RIP instead of the historical and real acronym PRI. In addition to the significance of the acronym RIP in English, this looks to be a typical move by a political satirist with a view to preventing legal action for libel from the offices of the ruling Partido Revolucionario Institucional (PRI). The main speaker is 'Profesor' Gumaro, a trainee teacher who has just returned from Mexico City. Objectivity, though, is a concept used here by Rius with considerable irony. The cover image immediately links preparations for the Olympics with the state–student conflict, portentously depicting the medals podium and suggesting a victory for Mexico's state authorities and thus a defeat for students and sympathisers. The cover also immediately references the increasing levels of violence that were being experienced with its titular reference to blows to the head. This provocative reference to police brutality is quickly transformed into an enduring image of Mexico City's police officers using truncheons to beat student protesters. When the principal character and narrator, Gumaro, is asked '¿Y cómo se salvó de los rojos, profe?' [So how did you save yourself from the reds, teach?] he replies: '¡Dirás de los azules! Por poco y me dejan lisiado de la choya' [You mean the blues! They came close to giving me a head wound] (Rius 1968: 7). Rius also ends a brief prologue by asserting that if his account is biased, that's because he and AB are part of civil society.

One main reason for turning our attention to Rius's special issue of *Los agachados* is an urgent need to explore the implications of the marginalised status of this special issue within the broad canvas of 1968 literature. Indeed, with some obvious exceptions such as the photographic essay included in Poniatowska's *La noche de Tlatelolco* (1968) and Jorge Fons's film *Rojo amanecer / Red Dawn* (1989), as well as more recent studies such as Steinberg (2016), the visual more generally has until now remained marginalised as a source of evidence within research on Mexico 1968. While there is no doubt that this special issue of *Los agachados* should play an important part in research on Mexico '68, and that it can come to play such a role following the renewed academic interest leading up to and during 2018, the issue does not yet figure prominently in any academic discussions. There is a critical literature available on Rius and on *Los agachados* but the special issue is not brought into focalised, in-depth discussion (see Alicino 2015; Agnew 2004). Another reason for selecting this textual, visual and spectral trace is that it affords us a new point of departure for approaching the commemorative narrativisation of 1968 as a contribution to the field of Mexican cultural studies. In this regard *Los agachados* is best viewed as a cultural practice, as one instance among many of story-telling about Mexico '68, and it must be related to those other narratives for us to begin to understand Mexican culture in the days of the Díaz Ordaz presidency (1964–70). As we think this through, William Rowe's 'The Place of Literature in Cultural Studies' is an insightful position paper. This is because Rowe emphasises the crucial importance of 'focus' or 'selection', and so calls upon practitioners of cultural studies to assume responsibility 'for the type of "cut" made through the unbounded events called culture' (2003: 38). At the same time he urges multiple contex-tualisation, and a thoroughgoing search to identify and explain 'all the ways in which meaning is produced in a given instance' (Rowe 2003: 39). Beyond this, but also in connection with Rowe's claim that 'cultural studies is a regional practice in that the relationships between its mate-rials are regional' (2003: 39), I want to suggest that Raymond Williams's thinking around structures of feeling continues to be highly illuminating for research around issues of cultural representations of Mexico's state–student conflict. Williams writes in *Marxism and Literature* that: 'The idea of a structure of feeling can be specifically related to the evidence of forms and conventions – semantic figures – which, in art and literature, are often among the very first indications that such a new structure is forming' (1977: 133). He continues by claiming that these forms and conventions themselves may 'in turn be seen as the articulation (often the only fully available articulation) of structures of feeling which as living processes are much more widely experienced' (1977: 133). Thereafter, Williams adds that structures of feeling can be defined as 'social experiences in solution', and that 'it is primarily to emergent formations [. . .] that the structure of feeling, *as* solution relates' (1977: 133–4). This special issue of *Los agacha-dos* is an instance of focused, issue-driven popular storytelling, a cultural practice (or convention, with the comic as form) which in its relations with other instances of specifically Mexican storytelling (and therein lies what Rowe identifies as 'regional') constitutes and illuminates our under-standing of Mexico '68 at the same time as it enacts the commemorative (re)narrativisation of those events and articulates emergent and principally subaltern structures of feeling.

July 1968: The Role of Alfonso Corona del Rosal

In his account to the people of Chayotitlán of the origins of the Mexican state–student conflict in July 1968, Gumaro places a very definite empha-sis on the role played by Alfonso Corona del Rosal, then Mayor of Mexico City (or more precisely, Jefe del Departamento del Distrito Federal), in provoking and escalating tensions. Firstly, Gumaro overtly connects Corona del Rosal with the initial skirmishes between Mexican students and the security forces as a possible agent provocateur. It is true that Gumaro refers to the initial fight on 22 July between students from the Polytechnic's Vocational Schools 2 and 5 and the Isaac Ochoterena Preparatory School and reports nothing political about the events: 'El pleito no tiene nada de político: son agarrones que siempre hay entre estudiantes de dos distintas escuelas por causas y cosas de muchachos' (Rius 1968: 9). [The argument is not in any way political: these are the sorts of fights that always happen between pupils from two different schools because boys have their issues and their reasons]. Yet it is also true that other commentators on 1968, especially Raúl Álvarez Garín, have suggested that this fight was not simply a post-football match brawl between young boys but an event provoked by *porristas* in the employ of Corona del Rosal. Álvarez Garín defines *porristas* as 'grupos de choque financiados por las autoridades para mantener el control en las escuelas' (1998: 30) [shock troops financed by the authorities to maintain control in schools]. He refers again to the involvement of *porristas* on the 23rd of July: 'todos apadrinados por el grupo político de Alfonso Corona del Rosal' (Álvarez Garín 1998: 35) [all in the pay of Alfonso Corona del Rosal's political group]. In line with this, Gumaro also asks his audience to see political motivations and the possible involvement of Corona del Rosal in the unnecessarily brutal intervention of the *granaderos* on the 23rd of July after the boys who had come off worse physically had attempted to take their revenge. He does so by highlighting the strangeness of an intervention by the *granaderos* after the fighting had already stopped: 'Y a pesar de que el desorden ya había terminado [*los granaderos*] entran a los salones de clase y a puro gas y trancazos sacan a estudiantes y profesores sin importarles nada' (Rius 1968: 9). [And even though the disturbance had already ended (the military riot police) enter classrooms and, willy-nilly, drag out pupils and teachers using tear gas and truncheons].

Secondly, Gumaro's account distinctly suggests that Corona del Rosal had it within his power on 24 July to resolve the emergent conflict involving the two Vocational Schools and the *granaderos*, but that he opted to escalate rather than de-escalate tensions. He is shown in the comic saying: 'Archiven la queja . . . si nos ponemos a cesar granaderos salvajes, nos quedamos solos..!' (Rius 1968: 10). [Archive the complaint . . . if we start dismissing savage *granaderos*, we're on our own. . .!]. In the next panel there is a hand tossing a ball of paper into a waste basket and the dialogue balloon says 'Archivado jefe' (Rius 1968: 10) [Archived boss]. The implication from Corona del Rosal's statement is that he sees the *granaderos* as allies in whatever goal he is pursuing by way of the violent tensions they provoke. Further to this apparent desire not to take preventative measures, Corona del Rosal is then linked to additional acts of provocation. As Gumaro continues, Corona del Rosal's decision to approve a march on behalf of the Vocational Schools on 26 July – in the full knowledge that a communist march to commemorate the attack on the Moncada barracks in Cuba already had approval – is presented as 'muy raro' (Rius 1968: 10) [very odd]. Other subsequent events are presented as equally mystifying: why did some of the participants in the IPN march hijack buses and head for Mexico City's main square, the *Zócalo*, via the known rallying point for those who had participated in the communist march?; why did the leader of the Federación Nacional de Estudiantes Técnicos (FNET) [the National Federation of Technical Students/FNET], the organising force in the polytechnic-based march and a body known to be linked to the PRI telephone the *granaderos* and request help to restore public order?; and why did the beatings in the streets adjacent to the *Zócalo* fall upon students from the San Ildefonso Preparatory School who were completely unconnected to either of these two marches? In this latter instance, Gumaro highlights Corona del Rosal's part in the early militarisation of the conflict by co-authorising, with Luis Echeverría as Secretario de Gobernación [Home Office minister], army action at the San Ildefonso Preparatory School. Gumaro draws attention to indiscriminate beatings and detentions as well as the infamous destruction with a bazooka of the ornate hand-carved colonial door of San Ildefonso.

Corona del Rosal's motivation for provoking public disturbance and for escalating tensions deliberately is communicated clearly. Gumaro conveys the view that as Mayor of Mexico City, and together with General Luis Cueto Ramírez, Mexico City's Chief of Police, Corona del Rosal was determined to ensure the effective disempowerment of Mexican communists ahead of the Olympic Games that were scheduled to open on 12 October. Moreover, it is intimated that Corona del Rosal knew that he could use the threat of communist subversion in Mexico as a perfect justification for heavy-handed policing and, if necessary, militarisation. Even fatalities could be explained convincingly with students used as 'chivos expiatorios' (Rius 1968: 12) [scapegoats]. By the end of July, Gumaro reports, there were already four dead in the conflict: 'Fuentes, Quiroz, Colín y De la O' (Rius 1968: 12). In this context, Cueto is shown saying 'Los agitadores crean zozobra para dañar la Olimpiada' (Rius 1968: 12) [The agitators are creating unrest to disturb the Olympics], and Corona del Rosal alongside is shown saying 'Fueron agitadores comunistas' [They were communist agitators]. In his narration of the events of July Gumaro catalogues the pressures placed by the state security forces on communists. He reports that on 26 July the police invaded and sacked the offices of the Communist Party and arrested those they found there; on 27 and 28 July they detained those considered agitators. Most were Communist Party members. And on 30 July five leaders were interned at Lecumberri prison for being communists. Moreover, even before we follow Gumaro's narrative as readers of this comic, we see that Rius uses humour to establish a specifically Mexican cold-war context for this special issue of *Los agachados* while simultaneously dismissing a certain degree of paranoia and exaggeration surrounding communist subversion. In the opening sequence in Chayotitlán the agrarian delegate Pitacio claims that communists want to destroy the institutions of Mexico and that '200 mil guerrilleros quieren tumbar al supremo gobierno', 'ya tomaron la catedral de la capital . . . y han asesinado a miles de gentes..!!' (Rius 1968: 3). [200,000 guerrillas want to overthrow the Mexican government, they already took control of the cathedral in the capital . . . and they have assassinated thousands of people!!]. A peasant called Chimuelo doubts this is true. His name, Chimuelo, means toothless and is therefore chosen by Rius to be descriptive, metaphorical, and a metonym for the Mexican peasantry. When another peasant, Pitacio, names the RIP delegate as his source of information, Chimuelo retorts that the RIP delegate is 'rete mentiroso' (Rius 1968: 4) [a real liar]. Pitacio then insists that they should show their loyalty to the government by organising a meeting and having their photos published in the capital: 'Nosotros no estamos para discutir sino para obedecer, aunque no sepamos la causa'. [We are not here to question, only to obey even if we don't know the reason why]. Their mission, he claims, is to oppose 'los enemigos de la patria' (Rius 1968: 4) [the enemies of the homeland].

　　Looking at the ideas communicated in *Los agachados* from the perspective of the present, and projecting them into the renewal of research on the histories of Mexico '68, we are compelled to consider the possibility that in late July Corona del Rosal was feeling confident that he could disturb the public realm of law and order and then re-establish it once the communists were detained and his pre-Olympics goal of a guaranteed social peace had been achieved. If that is accurate, then Corona del Rosal was misguided. He was misguided because, given the emergent and even pre-emergent nature of any oppositional structures of feeling, he could never have predicted the groundswell of public and principled opposition to the state's disingenuous statements concerning a communist threat to national security, nor the persistence of public outrage at unjustifiable police brutality. Less still could he have predicted the rapid rise of a protest movement supported by influential leaders in Mexican higher education. In *Los agachados* Gumaro tells the people of Chayotitlán that on 31 July three requests were made with support from the highest educational levels emblematised by the *rector* and vice chancellor of the UNAM, Javier Barros Sierra. These were: '1. Destitución del jefe y sub-jefe de la policía por salvajes; 2. Libertad para los injustamente detenidos; 3. Indemnización para los muertos' (Rius 1968: 13). [1. Dismissal of the savage head and deputy head of the police; 2. Freedom for the unjustly detained; 3. Compensation for the dead]. Looked at from the perspective of subsequent events, with influential responses like this, Corona del Rosal as the man supposedly in charge of the capital had suddenly lost control of his terrain.

August 1968: The Role of Gustavo Díaz Ordaz (Part One)

If July is portrayed in *Los agachados* as a month characterised largely by Corona del Rosal's uncompromising attitude towards those he perceived as communist agitators, the portrayal of the events and developments of August 1968 sees a continuation of this assertive standpoint from the state authorities but now with an emphasis on Gustavo Díaz Ordaz's public and private responses to the specific demands made by the Mexican student movement (Figure 1.2). The dual image created is of a president who is both eager to present his democratic credentials in public by insisting on a negotiated settlement and simultaneously annoyed in private that his authority is being questioned. For example, Gumaro tells the people of Chayotitlán that on 1 August Díaz Ordaz confidently asserted that he would restore law and order in the capital. Speaking from a visit to Guadalajara, Díaz Ordaz said: 'es una algarada sin importancia; ¡orden y nos amanece-mos!' (Rius 1968: 13) [it's an insignificant disturbance; restore order and start afresh!]. This is a reference to a presidential address often referred to as the 'mano tendida' [extended hand] speech because Díaz Ordaz also called upon students to return to study rather than enter into conflict and, as Ramírez reports, the president said:

> Una mano está tendida: es la mano de un hombre que a través de la pequeña histo-ria de su vida ha demostrado que sabe ser leal. Los mexicanos dirán si esa mano se queda tendida en el aire o bien esa mano, de acuerdo con la tradición del mexicano, con la veradadera tradición del verdadero, del auténtico mexicano, se vea acom-pañada por millones de manos de mexicanos que, entre todos, quieren restablecer la paz y la tranquilidad de las conciencias. (Díaz Ordaz 1968)

> [One hand is outstretched ... it's the hand of a man who throughout the minor history of his life has demonstrated that he knows how to be loyal. The Mexican

Figure 1.2 Image of President Gustavo Díaz Ordaz from *Mis confusiones: memorias desmemoriadas* de Rius.

people will decide whether that hand remains outstretched or whether that hand, in accordance with the Mexican tradition, with the real tradition of the real, authentic Mexicans, will be joined with millions of Mexican hands of those who, all together, want to re-establish peace and easy consciences].

This public call by the Mexican president for a peaceful, negotiated end to the state–student conflict is contradicted by the comic's emphasis on the president's unwillingness to be pressured into a course of action by anybody. Gumaro explains that in the first week of August it was already time to solve the most burning of problems and that the student demands amounted to nothing more than further requests that could be met without any impact on the stability of the regime. However, there were no state–student conversations. An image of Díaz Ordaz sees him saying: '¿Quiénes son los estudiantes para exigirnos a nosotros?' (Rius 1968: 15) [Who are the students to make demands of us?], and also pondering on what has happened to the ideal of authority – '¿y el sagrado principio de autoridad?' (Rius 1968: 13) [and what of the sacred principle of authority?]. Similarly, the image of a dialogue between peasants from Chayotitlán sees the claim made that the government will not engage in meaningful dialogue with the student leaders because everything in Mexico is decided by the president. Where Corona del Rosal had failed to restore public order in July, in August Díaz Ordaz was determined to succeed, and he expected the students to do as they were ordered, to shake his hand, metaphorically speaking, and then return to the classrooms. His vision was patriarchal, patronising and infantilising all at once. This particular attitude, this hardline fatherliness from a monolithic and supposedly revolutionary state, has been described by Krauze (1997) as 'presidentialism' and by Hodges and Gandy (2002) as 'presidential despotism'.

So, with Díaz Ordaz, despite his 'mano tendida' speech, resolute in his unwillingness to negotiate a settlement at the start of August, the Mexican student movement continued to grow and to focus on the six demands listed above and reiterated in Rius's special issue. At this point in the comic book narrative, Gumaro charts the rapid rise of the Student Movement for the people of Chayotitlán: on 1 August, the very day of Gustavo Díaz Ordaz's speech, Javier Barros Sierra as *rector* of the UNAM led a demonstration protesting against the violation of university autonomy and the unjust detention of students and teachers; on 5 August the IPN organised another march (this time without the FNET and without Massieu, the organisation's head) calling for the savage repression to end, and for dialogue with 'papá gobierno' (Rius 1968: 14) [father government]. In view of a non-response from the state, Gumaro continues, on

8 August the students called a strike involving the UNAM, the IPN, the *Escuelas Normales*, the agricultural college at Chapingo, the Iberoamerican University and the provincial universities. Two very large marches to the *Zócalo* followed. On 13 August there was a march of some 200,000 protesters from Santo Tomás to the *Zócalo*. There was no violence, no police intervention and significant popular support for the students. On 27 August even more marched, as 300,000 walked from Chapultepec to the *Zócalo*. With permissions granted, the cathedral bells were tolled. Without respect for authority though, graffiti was painted on the walls of the Palacio de Gobierno [National Palace; seat of the Mexican government] and a red and black flag signalling a workers' alliance and strike activity by socialists and anarchists was raised in the *Zócalo*. Gumaro's account of developments in August 1968 stops at this point, just after the march that inspired the highest turnout but which also marked both the peak and the turning point in the state–student conflict.

With the Mexican student movement at the height of its popularity towards the end of August, and with the opening of the Olympic Games on 12 October drawing ever closer, there was what we might call a second wave of state violence, worse than that which occurred at the end of July but also a continuation of that violence. It appeared that Díaz Ordaz's patience was wearing thin, and his private annoyance with the protesters was winning out over his desire for a semblance of a negotiated peace. In his account of these tense moments, Gumaro explains that the students were making use of 'mitines relámpago' [lightening meetings] throughout the city but that 'la policía golpea cuando puede' (Rius 1968: 16) [the police are using beatings whenever they can]. Gumaro records that on 27 August, after the march to the *Zócalo*, the red and black flag was removed and the national flag was returned to its place, though a group of some 3,000 students remained there waiting for a dialogue with Díaz Ordaz. At 1am they were attacked, and by dawn a different red and black flag of considerable proportions was flying over the *Zócalo*. On that day, 28 August, Corona del Rosal called for a 'desagravio a la bandera' [an act of respect for the national flag], a public ceremony of taking down the red and black flag and replacing it with the Mexican one. When the ceremony was over, Gumaro reports, there were calls from the state for the crowd to disperse. After the third such call there was a 'balacera en pleno zócalo' (Rius 1968: 18) [shoot-out right in the main square]. Furthermore, that night there was an assassination attempt on Professor Heberto Castillo, one of the National Strike Committee leaders. So, with President Díaz Ordaz at the helm of the ship of state, Corona del Rosal's July campaign against communist subversives and especially foreign agitators was renewed with another show of force. There was no effective dialogue in August as Rius's image of a man with a chain on his mouth announces; public opinion is not heard in Mexico, only the opinion of the government.

September 1968 and the Present Moment: The Role of Gustavo Díaz Ordaz (Part Two)

In its representation of July 1968 one key question implicitly raised by this special issue of *Los agachados* is: did Corona del Rosal systematically provoke social unrest in the prelude to the opening of the Olympic Games as a pretext to arrest communists? In the narrativisation of August the principal tacit question changes: did Gustavo Díaz Ordaz systematically allow promised negotiations with student leaders to fail in order to preserve his own authority as president of Mexico? In this respect, Hodges and Gandy (2002: 101–2) point out that once 1968 was over, and over the course of the following three years, Díaz Ordaz did repeal the law on social dissolution and the railway workers Demetrio Vallejo and Valentín Campa were released from prison. Luis Echeverría subsequently removed the chiefs of police from office. In other words, student demands could have been met but were not because the power of the state, perceived and real, was paramount.

Now, as Gumaro tells the people of Chayotitlán about the events and developments of September, a still darker implicit question emerges: did Gustavo Díaz Ordaz systematically implement a campaign of state terror in order to bring the student protests to an end? In this context, Gumaro begins his account with reference to the annual presidential state-of-the-nation speech on 1 September. He draws attention to the frustrated public expectation that Díaz Ordaz would announce a negotiated solution to the conflict, a solution first promised by the 'mano tendida' speech made in Guadalajara in July. Díaz Ordaz, the Chayotitlán listeners are told, instead referred the problem to the 'autoridades competentes' (Rius 1968: 18) [relevant authorities]. Here, we must read this to mean 'security forces'. The presidential speech contained an unambiguous statement concerning the use of force to end the conflict. As Ramírez records, and citing the Mexican Constitution's reference at Article 89 to the nation's legitimate capacity for military response to attacks on national security, the president concluded: 'No quisiéramos vernos en el caso de tomar medidas que no deseamos, pero que tomaremos si es necesario; lo que sea nuestro deber hacer, lo haremos; hasta donde estemos obligados a llegar, llegaremos' (Ramírez 1969: 284). [We do not wish to find ourselves in a situation where we adopt measures we do no wish to adopt, but we will adopt them if necessary; whatever our duty may be, we will fulfil it; whatever lengths we must go to, we will].

Beyond the state-of-the-nation speech, Gumaro's account of September places a considerable emphasis on the rise of state violence against protesters and sympathisers. His listeners learn that although 200,000 participated in the silent march on 13 September, the Mexican student movement was losing momentum because of the state's threat and use of force. They also hear that on 18 September, in a major show of state power, sixteen tanks and thousands of soldiers occupied the UNAM campus because it was functioning as a site of subversion. Gumaro explains that although there were continuing public protests over the violation of the university's autonomy and the ongoing processes of repression and imprisonment, from 19 September to 24 September the heavy-handed repression continued. On 23 September there was an armed attack on Vocational School 5 of the IPN involving machine-gun fire from a car but the police denied this. In addition, as the repression increased, Barros Sierra found himself being scapegoated. Gumaro's overall account of September's key events is undoubtedly one of state terror. In his last chronological reference for 24 September he reports that: 'El ejército toma el Poli con sangre y fuego por ambos bandos. Hay muertos, heridos y un chorro de detenidos' (Rius 1968: 30). [The army occupies the Poli with gunshots and blood on both sides. There are fatalities, injuries and a huge number of arrests]. Subsequently, the people of Chayotitlán hear Gumaro say: '¿Qué clase de gobierno temenos, que todo lo "resuelve" con tanques y policías?' (Rius 1968: 23) [What sort of government do we have that everything is "resolved" with tanks and police officers?].

When Gumaro finishes his account of Mexico's state–student conflict, he then enters into a present-moment debate with Licenciado Güacache and the RIP delegate which centres on a number of key issues. The present moment is 25 September, as it is the day after Gumaro leaves Mexico City. One key issue is social dissolution and political prisoners. Gumaro explains that nobody questions the importance of Articles 145 and 145a that Díaz Ordaz quoted in his 1 September speech on national sovereignty and the territorial integrity of the nation, but he also explains that Díaz Ordaz omitted another part of the legal text referring to anyone who engages in acts of sabotage or subversion. Gumaro points out, on that basis, that lawyer Trueba Urbina is right when he claims that anyone can be accused of social dissolution; the law is a catch-all open to use by the state as required. Moreover, to the suggestion that Mexico's prisons hold only criminals and there are no political prisoners, Gumaro pointedly asks what about Vallejo, Campa, Unzueta and Rico Galán? All four of these men were political prisoners. Demetrio Vallejo and Valentín Campa were leaders of Mexico's railway workers imprisoned for strike activity during the presidency of López Mateos (1958–64). Gerardo Unzueta and Víctor Rico Galán were both leftist journalists who supported the Mexican student movement. Another key issue at the heart of this debate is the idea of communist subversion in Mexico and its impact upon the country's standing in global arenas. Güacache and the delegate from the RIP both agree that the UNAM needed to be occupied by the military because it had become a 'foco de anarquía, de agitación y de ataques a nuestras instituciones para subvertir el orden público' (Rius 1968: 23) [focal point for anarchy, for subversion and for attacks on our institutions to undermine public order]. They also agree that the students are part of a campaign to blacken Mexico's global reputation and they ask: '¿Qué van a decir de nosotros en el extranjero?' (Rius 1968: 26) [What will foreigners say about us?]. Gumaro will not accept these claims and argues that the idea of a foreign-led conspiracy to overthrow the Díaz Ordaz regime is not true. Those who believe this 'están mafufos' (Rius 1968: 27) [are off their heads]. He adds that there is institutional corruption everywhere. He argues that this explains why people have lost respect for those who govern and, at times, have lowered the tone to personal insult. He insists that foreigners will not believe Mexico's 'prensa vendida' [state-co-opted press] either. Gumaro asks what they will think of a government that hosts peaceful Olympics with prisons full of innocent people; of a government that assassinates students and converts its university campus into a barracks and prison. He also asks how Mexico can speak of democracy with a fascist body like the *granaderos*; and how the government can call students to respect the constitution if civil servants fail to do so: '¿Con qué cara les pide el gobierno a los estudiantes que respeten la constitución si los funcionarios son los primeros en violarla, robando, golpeando, violando domicilios, deteniendo inocentes y pasándose por el arco de triunfo las leyes..?' (Rius 1968: 27). [How can the government hypocritically ask students to respect the constitution if civil servants are the first to violate it, stealing, hitting, violating homes, detaining the innocent and gloriously overlooking laws..?]. Visually, at this point, a biting and dark sense of humour reinforces the political statement and the constitution is represented as a toilet roll. Ominously Gumaro sees the national situation as anxiety-producing because the students face 'un gobierno que todo lo quiere resolver a trancazos' (Rius 1968: 31) [a government that wants to resolve everything with truncheons]. The imagined threat of a military solution, a Tlatelolco massacre, is left hanging in the air.

Conclusions

My initial conclusions arising from this close reading of one special issue of *Los agachados* on Mexico '68 are as follows. The issue itself as a material trace of traumatic histories needs to be duly valorised in the broad category of Tlatelolco literature, where there is also a need to examine more fully the wide range of visual representations of Mexico '68 including the now extensive materials available online (see Nelsson 2015). This special issue of *Los agachados* poses questions of the contemporary moment in 1968 that have not yet been fully answered and that need to return to a position of centrality in today's debates, or possibly even be given such centrality for the first time. The emphasis on the importance of the role played by Corona del Rosal is particularly revealing because only Álvarez Garín makes similar claims and he, too, like Rius, was engaged with the movement. I hypothesise that further archival investigation will shed new light and offer explanations and connections that can for now only be surmised concerning Corona del Rosal and cold-war contexts. Finally, on a theoretical plane, Raymond Williams's discussion of structures of feeling is strikingly relevant and useful in the analysis of a comic which, I argue, not only captures and articulates some emergent structures but, in doing so, already recognises the fact that positive change in the Mexican political system – the end of PRI dominance in 2000 – had become inevitable by 1968. The structures of feeling that Rius articulates are not exclusively middle class, despite Louise E. Walker's convincing and undoubtedly urgent broadening of our understanding:

> The desires and fears of the middle classes, as well as their actions, shaped the economic and political history of late twentieth-century Mexico. Most scholars have pointed to the 1968 student movement as the beginning of the end of the PRI's hegemony, but this was only one symptom of a larger upheaval. The emphasis on the student movement has eclipsed a more important historical point: that the most consequential struggles over the future of the PRI's system took place among the middle classes. The leftist student who took to the streets to protest the authoritarianism of the PRI can and should be analysed alongside conservative housewives enraged at the rising cost of living, alienated engineers suffering ennui, consumers falling into debt to support their lifestyle, yuppies who believed the world was their oyster, and angry homeowners struggling to defend their privileged access to housing. These reactions to crisis, which span the political spectrum, represent different threads by which the one-party system was coming undone. (2013: 2)

If the structures of feeling that this comic captures and expresses belong, then they belong to students and workers alike in such complex ways that they cannot strictly speaking be class bound. The contents include various beliefs: that the PRI is in crisis, that the state is in crisis, but also, more specifically, that the origins of Mexico '68 are not somehow accidental, but rather are intimately bound up with Corona del Rosal's aspirations to prevent communist disruption of the Olympic Games so effectively that he would be a credible candidate for the 1970 presidential elections. Ultimately, it is popular culture, working-class memories and traumas – the subaltern dimensions of Mexico '68 – that must be reconsidered in the years that follow 2018. Rius's (1968) *Los agachados*, número especial de los cocolazos offers an exemplary point of departure.

Notes

1. Unless otherwise stated, all translations are my own.
2. I would like to thank Quetzalli de la Concha, especially, as well as Dora Hernando and Yolanda Cortés of Penguin Random House for their assistance with permissions to reproduce the images drawn by Rius. For their kind and enthusiastic support, I would also like to thank Manuel Barrero and Félix López at Tebeosfera, Seville, as well as Eduardo Soto Díaz from the Museo de la Caricatura y la Historieta 'Joaquín Cervantes Bassoco' (MUCAHI) in Anenecuilco, Morelos, Mexico.

Bibliography

Agnew, Bob (2004), '¡Viva la Revolución! *Los agachados* and the Worldview of Eduardo del Río (Rius)', *Studies in Latin American Popular Culture*, 23: pp. 1–20.

Alicino, Laura (2015), 'Historia e historietas en la obra de Rius: el cómic como forma de arte', *Confluenze*, 7:1, pp. 303–30.

Álvarez Garín, Raúl (1998), *La estela de Tlatelolco: una reconstrucción histórica del movimiento estudiantil del 68*, Mexico City: Grijalbo.

Brewster, Claire (2005), *Responding to Crisis in Contemporary Mexico: The Political Writings of Paz, Fuentes, Monsiváis, and Poniatowska*, Tuscon: University of Arizona Press.

Carpenter, Victoria (2018), *The Tlatelolco Massacre, Mexico 1968 and the Emotional Triangle of Anger, Grief and Shame: Discourses of Truth(s)*, Cardiff: University of Wales Press.

Corona del Rosal, Alfonso (1995), *Mis memorias políticas*, Mexico City: Grijalbo.

Díaz Ordaz, Gustavo (1968), '1968 Discurso en el día del ejército', *Memoria Política de México*, 19 February. Available at <http://www.memoriapolitica-demexico.org/Textos/6Revolucion/1968DAE.html> (last accessed 18 September 2017).

Galindo, Felipe (2017), 'Remembering Rius'. Available at <https://nacla.org/news/2017/08/14/remembering-rius> (last accessed 14 September 2017).

Hinds, Harold E. Jr, and Charles Tatum (1992), *Not Just for Children: The Mexican Comic Book in the Late 1960s and 1970s*, Westport, CT: Greenwood Press.

Hodges, Donald, and Ross Gandy (2002), *Mexico under Siege: Popular Resistance to Presidential Despotism*, London and New York: Zed Books.

Krauze, Enrique (1997), *La presidencia imperial: ascenso y caída del sistema político mexicano 1940–1996*, Mexico City: Pablo Tusquets.

Malkin, Elizabeth (2018), '50 Years after a Student Massacre, Mexico Reflects on Democracy'. Available at <https://www.nytimes.com/2018/10/01/world/americas/mexico-tlatelolco-massacre.html> (last accessed 10 October 2018).

Museo del Estanquillo (2020), 'Rius para principiantes'. Available at <https://www.museodelestanquillo.cdmx.gob.mx/storage/app/media/RIUS%20PARA%20PRINCIPIANTES.pdf> (last accessed 27 May 2020).

Nelsson, Richard (2015), 'How the Guardian reported Mexico City's Tlatelolco massacre of 1968'. Available at <https://www.theguardian.com/cities/from-the-archive-blog/2015/nov/12/guardian-mexico-tlatelolco-massacre-1968-john-rodda> (last accessed 18 September 2017).

Nixon, Rob (2013), *Slow Violence and the Environmentalism of the Poor*, Cambridge, MA: Harvard University Press.

Ramírez, Ramón (1969), *El movimiento estudiantil de México (julio/diciembre de 1968)*, Tomo I. Mexico City: Ediciones Era.

Rius (1968), *Los agachados: número especial de los cocolazos*, Mexico City: Editorial Posada S.A.

Rius (2014), *Mis confusiones: memorias desmemoriadas*, Mexico City: Grijalbo.

Roberts, Sam (2017), 'Eduardo del Río, Cartoonist who Mocked Politics and Religion, Dies at 83'. Available at <https://www.nytimes.com/2017/08/11/business/media/eduardo-del-rio-political-cartoonist-known-as-ri-us-dies-at-83.html> (last accessed 14 September 2017).

Rowe, William (2003), 'The Place of Literature in Cultural Studies', in Stephen Hart and Richard Young (eds), *Contemporary Latin American Cultural Studies*, London: Arnold, pp. 37–47.

Steinberg, Samuel (2016), *Photopoetics at Tlatelolco: Afterimages of Mexico, 1968*, Austin: University of Texas Press.

Volpi, Jorge (1998), *La imaginación y el poder: una historia intelectual de 1968*, Mexico City: Ediciones Era.

Walker, Louise E. (2013), *Waking from the Dream: Mexico's Middle Classes after 1968*, Stanford: Stanford University Press.

Williams, Raymond (1977), *Marxism and Literature*, Oxford: Oxford University Press.

CHAPTER 2

Felipe Cazals and Servando González Grapple with the Aftermath and the Archive: 1976 and 1968

Niamh Thornton

From the late 1950s and through to the 1960s there were frequent worker and student protests in Mexico. Some of these were over specific grievances and at other times were ideologically motivated, spurred by the apparent success of the Cuban Revolution (1959). In advance of the Olympic Games in October 1968 there were a series of worker and student protests, which culminated in the massacre of a still unidentified number of students on the 2nd of October of that year, ten days before the opening ceremony (Brewster 2010). The protests and violent army reactions were well documented by student filmmakers from the film school, the *Centro Universitario de Estudios Cinematográficos* [University Centre for Cinema Studies] (CUEC), founded in 1963, and resulted in a documentary, *El grito* [The Cry][1] (Leobardo López Arretche, 1968), which was widely disseminated among student and worker organisations, but which had limited release because of government controls on funding and distribution of material relating to the events. The first feature film to get local distribution, *Rojo amanecer / Red Dawn* (Jorge Fons), wasn't made until 1989. In a country preoccupied with making films about the 1910 Revolution as its foundational conflict, 1968 marked a shift in how the war story was told on film, in part because of the numbers of cameras following the protests (Thornton 2013). The protestors and filmmakers drew on the iconography of the Revolution that functioned as both inspiration and haunting. As a consequence of the controls, filmmakers encoded representations of the violent repression either through the use of footage that implicitly evoked 1968 or through the careful placement of such footage in the edit. The year 1968 is highly significant for two such filmmakers, Servando González and Felipe Cazals, for distinct reasons. An analysis of their work exemplifies different approaches to the use of the found footage. In this way, 1968 becomes a form of haunting in their use of the archive.

The 1960s and 1970s saw a flourishing of auteurist filmmakers in Mexico. Some came out of university film schools, others got training in a studio system in decline, and a small number were eager cinephiles who learned their craft through trial and error. They represent a generation deeply and personally affected by 1968. Among these is Cazals. His docudrama about a lynching linked to the tense atmosphere of 1968 in a village in central Mexico, *Canoa* (1976), was the first film to deal with the political turmoil and killings. As well as *Canoa*, Cazals released another film in 1976, *Los Poquianchis: (De los pormenores y otros sucedidos del dominio público que acontecieron a las hermanas de triste memoria a quienes la maledicencia así las bautizó)* [The Poquianchis: (On the particularities and other known occurrences that happened to the tragic sisters who were maliciously baptised as such)], that mixes documentary and fiction filmmaking techniques. *Los Poquianchis* (I will use the shorter title) is based on the exploitation, abuse and mass murder of sex workers in Mexico, an event that received considerable coverage in the popular press. Cazals shifted through the coverage that 'was often exaggerated and supplemented with imaginary and colourful details to satisfy even the most morbid readers' to reveal the horrors experienced by the women and the complicity of the state in the crimes (Lange 2009: 454). Less explicitly about either conflict and more focused on the broken promises of the Revolution, *Los Poquianchis* evidences Cazals' ongoing awareness of how he has had to navigate his implication as a filmmaker in the multi-layered, systemic and specific perpetrator violence as well as the mediatised violence of the tabloid press.

Among the filmmakers recording the protests of the students was the director Servando González. The difference between him and many of his fellow filmmakers was that where they spoke out or filmed the activities in solidarity with the students, González was tasked by the government with filming the protesting students and capturing the moment of their deaths. The film he made was never screened publicly and it has been suggested by a documentary released in 2012 that most of the footage was lost in a fire at the national film archive (Estrada 2012: np). Where Cazals' work has been hailed, González carried the stigma of this act of complicity for the rest of his career; his work has been haunted by his association with the perpetrators of the violence and his name barely graces the literature in the field of Mexican film studies.

The shadow of 1968 can be found in González's 1976 adaptation of the novel *Los de abajo* [The Underdogs] by Mariano Azuela (1915) based on the novelist's experiences as a medic with Pancho Villa's forces. It is generally agreed to be the first 'novela de la Revolución' [novel of the Revolution], but one with a complicated publishing and reception history (Sánchez Prado 2016: 50–1). Although it largely follows conventional storytelling techniques, there is a brief interlude in *Los de abajo* when González employs archival footage from the Revolution that acts as a commentary on the narrative and provides a space to reflect on the nature of filming the war story, whose aesthetic conventions have been determined by who can tell the story and to what end.

Los Poquianchis, *Canoa* and *Los de abajo* all employ archival footage and documentary elements which ground the films in reality. Cazals and González deploy iconography familiar to a Mexican audience in ways that subvert their original meaning and function as reflexive, meta-texual commentaries. With the ghosts of 1968 haunting the films as well as the spectres of the distinct events they portray, Cazals' and González's specific uses of the archive become an exploration of the audio-visual techniques utilised by perpetrators. This chapter will explore how the films navigate this controversial terrain in ways that uphold and disrupt the perpetrators' position.

Dark Travel and Perpetrator Material

A generative means of understanding Cazals and González's foregrounding and engagement with the audio-visual discursive strategies of the perpetrator is to draw on scholarly work around death tourism and re-inscribe it as dark travel. The three films I consider challenge the parameters of perpetrator filmmaking, because each one deploys techniques that evoke the perpetrator's position or are burdened by an unresolved tension between the winners and losers in Mexican conflicts. By doing this, they are uncomfortable objects of study and, furthermore, provide an opportunity to question the researcher's role in the investigation and recuperation of films that circulate among a select grouping of interested scholars, but which rarely get seen beyond the academy. Any gaze is not just one made by a simple series of audio-visual interventions and conveniently occupied by the viewer, rather it is one that is contingent on the individual's experiences. Therefore, intersecting with this core question is the need to acknowledge my own position as a researcher of realist violence and to propose that I, too, am a dark traveller finding my way through difficult terrain.

Dark travel is distinct to death (also known as dark) tourism. Travel suggests a bespoke, carefully curated route that deliberately takes the less traversed trail. It may step into the tourist routes, but it more usually eschews these in favour of the locally inflected and 'authentic' experience. Death tourism is a label used to describe visits to sites of violent death and, for Brigitte Sion, '[t]his form of negative sightseeing is incorporated into an industry that is otherwise dedicated to pleasure' (2014: 1). Memory and memorialisation are integral to these sites, whether through re-enactments, display or commemoration. The function of audio-visual representations of trauma in cinema has some commonality with death tourism insofar as they are interventions with aesthetic and often narrative concerns that have their concurrent pleasures; there is escape and there are durational facets grounded in a dedication to building consciousness of the original event(s); and there is an attentiveness to drawing in the viewers, ensuring they take away greater knowledge and awareness of the trauma, and share common feeling with the victims and/or survivors. As consumers of these texts, we become visitors to an uncomfortable audio-visual world where we are witnessing and watching others bear witness to terrible events.

Death tourism, a growing area of study in academia, is an experience for large numbers who care to venture into terrible moments in history and is marked by a particular mode of didacticism and ethics of presentation. Dark travel is an individual attempt to navigate history's horrors and find a way into explaining its violent past. It often involves esoteric and unique experiences that are to be replicated only by following an expert guide with certain exclusionary or exclusive access points. The ways in which González and Cazals employ archival material in carefully curated and disruptive fashion can be described as a form of dark travel.

In her chapter 'Ethical Spaces: Ethics and Propriety in Trauma Tourism', Laurie Beth Clark explores the different ways in which behaviour and responses to sites of trauma and killing are regulated by authorities, curators and fellow visitors, through layout, norms, architecture, 'social consensus' (2014: 18) and other forms of 'implicit or explicit guidance' (2014: 15). The tools available to filmmakers are different, and they are marked by film's capacity to create (usually fictional) vicarious pleasure in watching cruel and inhumane actions performed upon others. It is when the story is based on fact and, particularly, on the recent past, that there is an expectation of self-regulation and propriety in the representation comparable to that described by Sion (2014) and Clark (2012). The three films under consideration here employ documentary archival footage to different ends and do so with due regard for the events and individuals represented. This chapter considers the integration of archival footage in *Los Poquianchis*, *Canoa* and *Los de abajo*, three distinct films that challenge the audience to examine its imbrication into this culture of dark travel. All were released in the same year, yet were set at different moments in the past, respectively, the 1910–15 period of the Revolution, the 1950s-60s, and 1968. Aside from having the release year in common, 1968 is a date that haunts all three films as evident from the use of found footage.

The first film I want to consider is *Los Poquianchis*, where the move between fact and fiction is part of a more extended sequence and is not always as clear or as boundaried as the other examples. It serves as a generative exploration of the ways in which Cazals navigates the challenging terrain of the dark traveller to allow spaces to consider the filmmakers' complicity in the creation of films that deal with terrible crimes burdened with salacious and excessive representation.

Los Poquianchis (Felipe Cazals, 1976)

I have chosen an exemplary sequence from the last ten minutes of the hybrid experimental docudrama film *Los Poquianchis*, where Cazals uses a mix of audio-visual sources from the archive, documentary footage, and fiction storytelling modes. Set in Guanajuato in the mid-1950s to mid-1960s, *Los Poquianchis* tells the true story of a prostitution ring led by two women nicknamed Los Poquianchis. Protected by corrupt police and politicians, the women bought young women and girls from their impoverished families, kept them prisoner, abused them, fed them drugs and forced them into prostitution. When the women and girls were no longer able to work, Los Poquianchis and their accomplices murdered them and disposed of their bodies in mass graves. Around ninety young women were murdered until the case was uncovered and subject to investigation. For over a year after the revelations were made public in 1964, the tabloid press covered it in salacious detail. In the same year as Cazals' film was released, the story was the subject of a novel, *Las muertas*, by the crime novelist and satirist Jorge Ibargüengoitia.

Like Cazals' other film from 1976, *Canoa*, *Los Poquianchis* does not have a linear structure. Moving back and forth in ways that refuse an easy resolution, *Los Poquianchis* shifts between following the action; recreating key moments; talking head-style interviews; origin stories; set pieces that serve to critique the sensationalist mediatisation of the discovery of the bodies, arrests and trial; and the inclusion of documentary audio-visual elements. In addition, there is a secondary narrative thread involving land rights that serves as a significant context and commentary on structural violence against workers in Mexico and signals the struggles that led up to the organisation of students in 1968.

The segment I want to discuss begins with a talking head-style interview. These are interspersed throughout the film. Here, one of the victims who has been implicated in the crimes, Adelina (Diana Bracho), speaks direct to camera. She describes how the two sisters, Chuy (Malena Doria) and Delfina (Leonora Llausás), abused her and pleads innocence, having been accused by the authorities of being complicit in the murders of her fellow captives. It is a poignant scene rendered powerful by the subtle and realist style of Bracho's performance as well as the documentary techniques employed by Cazals. The scene ends with Adelina/Bracho looking straight at the camera for a few beats (Figure 2.1). The talking head style mimics that of a documentary and the close shot encourages the viewer to empathise with the speaker. It is a performance by a professional actor and, therefore, characterised by her ability to embody the character and respond to the needs of the narrative. The documentary talking head-style interview means that Bracho's look to the camera both breaks the fourth wall of fiction film and returns the gaze in ways that challenge the viewer to believe what she says. It is indicative of the techniques Cazals employs that blur the boundaries between fiction and factual narrative, thereby eliciting empathy while creating ambiguity and leaving it the performance open to multiple interpretations.

Adelina's statement has the hallmarks of court testimony designed to plead her case and, as such, bears the traces of evidentiary value and attempts to convey the traumatic weight of the experience (Torchin 2012: 13).

Figure 2.1   Adelina's (Diana Bracho) look direct to camera, *Los Poquianchis* (Felipe Cazals, 1976).

Justice systems are performative insofar as they have procedures and rules
and are determined by human expectations of what innocence and guilt
appear to be. Furthermore, Bracho is performing a woman's performance
of her innocence. Therefore, there are multiple performances taking place
or implicit in this sequence. Although based on actual testimony that has
its own performativity, what we are watching is a performance by a highly
acclaimed actor of an accused's performance. This is one of the many ways
in which Cazals reminds us of the difficulties inherent in uncovering and
portraying the truth behind the victims' and perpetrators' stories. In the
next sequence he continues this shift between the archive and fiction using
distinct sources. This signals to the viewer that realism in fiction and documentary film may have its techniques to convey reality, but that reality as
captured by technology has limitations.

     After Adelina's interview, the next shot is of Tadeo (Manuel Ojeda), one
of the women's fathers, leaving jail. He is a farmer who has been arrested
for protesting against land grabs by wealthy investors. As the camera follows him walking away, on the soundtrack there is an interview between
unidentified men. This interview is uncredited and is from the archive.
The male interviewer, whose accent is markedly educated and urban,
is asking about land rights, worker exploitation and abuses of power by
caciques. The respondents' accents are rural. They describe the terrible
conditions they have experienced as subsistence farmers and labourers.
All the while we follow repeated sequences of Tadeo going to sell goods
at the government cooperative in the local town. This is repeated three
times, suggesting temporal changes. Suturing this sequence to the next,
the interview continues. In what appears to be documentary footage, in
the next shot the camera pans and tilts over the faces and upper bodies
of eight men waiting to be paid for their goods at the cooperative. The
interview comes to an end just as the camera pauses on a photo of the then
president Adolfo López Mateos (1958–64) and tilts downwards to a man
reading what looks like a photomontage news report of the Poquianchis'
case. In this way, Cazals indicates that the government is responsible for
both the impoverished conditions of the farmworkers and the women's
plight. There is a temporal distance between the men we see on screen
and the voices on the interviews – even if it is their voices –because they
are not shown to be speaking. This asynchronicity and deliberate layering
of voices and images is not jarring; instead it has an authority because the
quality of the recording bears traces of being the field notes of a researcher.
These work together to create a sense of indexicality that is marked by
time and its passing. The men haunt this film even as we see and hear
them because of the deliberate marking of time through this technique.

These sequences at the cooperative are bookended by Adelina's challenging look and a return to the trial, thereby inviting the viewer to make further connections between the conditions for labourers and the women's enslavement and murders.

The blurring of fact and fiction storytelling techniques continues in the next sequence. We see and hear a rally by the *Confederación Nacional Campesina* [National Farm Labourer Union] (CNC), an agrarian union affiliated to the ruling party that has dominated government, the Partido Revolucionario Institucional (PRI). Again, Tadeo is the focus of the action in this sequence. He walks into the shot as the speaker is coming to the final flourish of a rousing speech about how the union supports the workers. At the end of the speech the gathered crowd applauds, but Tadeo/Ojeda just stands and looks around at them. The speech is a real event, Tadeo is a character. The awkwardness of the crowd's behaviour in front of the camera and their looks to camera underline this and function to suggest at the indexicality of the image. That he does not clap is scripted and, therefore, is artifice and performative. At the same time, his inaction is not only out of sync with those around him, but is also a commentary on their scripted behaviour. Through this gesture of absence, Cazals highlights the everyday performance of complicity. He is suggesting that blame lies with the politicians and at the feet of those who support them.

The connection between the women's plight and that of the conditions of the labourers resonates with the narrative and thematic approaches taken by Ibargüengoitia in *Las muertas*. In her analysis of the novel Carolyn Wolfenzon finds a metaphorical exploration of state responsibility for the crimes, signalling that this is the 'hilo conductor' [guiding theme] (2016: 872) of *Las muertas*. In the novel truth is impossible to ascertain and the policeman-narrator, Captain Bedoya, couches his discoveries and conclusions as uncertain through his use of the conditional tense or phrases that qualify their veracity (Wolfenzon 2016: 873–4). It gradually becomes clear that Bedoya is 'cómplice y autor intelectual de los sucesos' [accomplice and mastermind of the events]. He is an unreliable narrator because not only is he employed by the state and therefore implicated in the crimes but also directly responsible for facilitating and covering up the murders (Wolfenzon 2016: 873). The novel tells the story from a perpetrator's point of view, implicating the reader in his world in a way that is deeply uncomfortable. As texts released in the same year, both novel and film convey a distrust of witness reports and individual points of view.

In *Los Poquianchis* Cazals adopts a similar approach by inviting us to observe the banality of state violence (*pace* Hannah Arendt). A tragic example of this is a figure who becomes a perpetrator because he works for the state as a lawyer who imposes violence through bureaucratic means. He appears for the last time after the aforementioned speech by the union leader. In this scene there is a return to the clearly fictional in a cut to the unnamed lawyer (played by Marcelo Villamil) sitting at his desk studying a file, who then gets a call from the attorney general. We hear only his side of the conversation. His only responses are 'sí señor' [yes sir]. After hanging up, he stops for a beat and looks at the file in his hands. The voice off camera of an assistant asks him whether he wants anything else. He replies that he does not and sits back in contemplation. He moves his hand to his mouth in a gesture that is suggestive of turmoil or possible powerlessness in the face of the decision that has been made over his head in which he is now complicit (Figure 2.2). He opens a drawer, pulls out a lighter and cigarette, and contemplates it for a beat. This civil servant acts as an intermediary between the women and the justice system. It is his responsibility to enforce the judge's decision irrespective of his own assessment. His resigned responses and subsequent actions can be read as the uncomfortable acknowledgement of his lack of power and his complicity with the system.

Figure 2.2 The Lawyer (Marcelo Villamil) sits in despair, *Los Poquianchis* (Felipe Cazals, 1976).

The next cut is to the title 'epílogo' [epilogue]. Informing us of the consequences of the lawyer's actions, a voiceover explains what happened next in the case as the camera pans over an abandoned space in a state of disrepair. It is a ruin with only walls and floors partially intact and few traces of the horrors of the past haunting the space. Ruins recur in the other films. In this instance, this brief sequence looks like actual footage of the place the women were captured, although there is nothing that makes this explicit. As the camera pans over the space, Cazals uses voice to imply the link to the past. An authoritative male voiceover, typical of documentaries of this time, states that five months later 'en uno de los procesos más rápidos de la justicia mexicana' [in one of the fastest processes of the Mexican justice system], the three ringleaders were sentenced to forty years in prison. Seventeen others (eight women and nine men) were jailed as accomplices, many of whom had already spent most of their lives 'prisioneras en las casas de las Poquianchis' [prisoners in the houses of the Poquianchis], and would serve a further twenty-six years in jail. This includes Adelina. The shift between fact and fiction and even the blurring of these through having actors move through real events (such as the rally) allude to the impossibility of knowing the full story or of discerning reality from fiction.

Los Poquianchis goes some way to explain the reasons why so many parents sold their children into prostitution and the terrible lives and deaths that they endured. The structural violence experienced by the farmers results in the awful tragedy that we have just watched unfold. Cazals (and Ibargüengoitia) ask us to consider the banality of evil in the perpetrator actions, and our own implication in the violence that takes place in the narratives. In addition, he foregrounds the complicity of the filmmaker in the horrors that befell these women and the injustices experienced by the farm labourers. There is a sense of an impossible bind for Cazals that he foregrounds through these techniques. These stories must be told, but too often the tools of the perpetrator must be used to tell them. Unlike with Canoa and Los de abajo, dead bodies are not the focus of the documentary footage used, but their absence has its own effect in the form of a haunting because the case was so familiar to Mexican audiences from tabloid reports.

Canoa (Felipe Cazals, 1976)

Canoa (Felipe Cazals, 1976) was the first of what is still a small number of feature films to have addressed the 1968 massacre, but it does so at a distance, in a village removed from the centre of activities in Mexico City.

It tells the story of four young University of Puebla employees who go out to a small village called San Miguel de Canoa on a hiking trip. They are caught out in bad weather and have to find somewhere to stay in the village. Due to their age and urban clothing, they are mistaken for students and are thereby accused of being seditious by the parish priest, who incites the fearful locals to banish the hikers in order to protect the village from communism. The hikers are given refuge by one of the locals only for his house to be attacked, and he, and the four men, are badly beaten. The army enters to wrest control and are implicated in the violence. Using a similar blend of fact and fiction techniques to *Los Poquianchis*, *Canoa* is told in a documentary style using re-enactments and talking-head interviews.

The film opens with shots of soldiers marching to a military band inter-cut with a funeral procession. Family members carry signs saying, 'exigi-mos justicia' [we demand justice]. The soldiers and the funeral procession meet at an unidentified (but recognisably Mexico City) intersection and move in opposite directions down different roads.

The pre-credit sequence is fictional, that, in turn, is preceded by an intertitle with a quotation from Act III of the seventeenth-century play, *Fuenteovejuna* (1619) by the Spanish dramatist Lope de Vega, 'El rey sólo es señor, después del cielo/y no bárbaros hombres inhumanos/si Dios ayuda nuestro justo celo/¿qué nos ha de costar?' (Vega 2010: 69). [The king's our only lord by heaven's laws,/Not that barbaric and inhuman horde. If God assists us in our righteous cause,/What have we all to lose?]. The choice of a quotation from *Fuenteovejuna*, a drama that 'raises ques-tions about truth itself', functions to signal a key concern of the film (Blue 1991: 295). Taken from the last act of the play, when the villagers are dis-cussing whether to take up arms against their masters, this quotation res-onates with similar debates that took place in the aftermath of the student massacre. In *Canoa* this allusion to a well-known Renaissance play studied at secondary schools throughout Mexico establishes the difficulties inher-ent in arriving at the truth of an event and sets the tone for the docudrama. In addition, the location of the play compares to that of the film. Up to this point in Mexican film, the rural was idealised whereas 'Cazals' film changed archetypal perception of the provinces as the paradise lost of the Mexican cinematic landscape inhabited by a simple, virtuous folk' (Haddu 2007: 213). By referencing *Fuenteovejuna* Cazals is signaling the parallels between the villages in both the play and *Canoa* as microcosms of larger society.

This is immediately followed by two further intertitles, 'Esto sí sucedió' [This really happened] and '15 de septiembre de 1968./Madrugada' [15th of September 1968./Early morning]. The event in *Canoa* took place in the weeks preceding the massacre in Mexico City on 2 October 1968, thus allowing for an exploration of the generalised tensions stirred up by political rhetoric as well as their subtle displacement in time and place. In this opening sequence, the sound heard is a phone conversation between a night editor and a reporter filing news of the dead 'students', as they erroneously call them. In these ways, from its opening sequence *Canoa* mixes fact and fiction by blending audio-visual realities.

This cuts to archival footage of the dead workers with no sound recorded live. It is accompanied only by the droning clicking sound of the sprockets of a camera, which works to underscore its authenticity as do the shaky movements of the handheld camera, which also draw attention to the means of production. A hand comes in from an oblique angle to stop the filming. Initially, it is unclear whether this is to censor the cameraperson or out of respect for the dead. Then the shot cuts to a soldier looking directly into the camera with his hand held up in a halt motion. It is then clear that it is an attempt to control what is being filmed. The camera pulls back and pans left to show a wide shot of two bodies on the ground covered with blankets. Part of their bodies and faces are visible. Evidently, they are dead. The camera pans right and the soldier motions to the ground (Figure 2.3). He does not want to be on camera but wants the bodies filmed. The camera zooms in on one of the bodies. This shot shows a man's body lying on his side. His hair is visible as is an outstretched arm. A blanket covers the rest of his upper body. His trousers are pulled down

Figure 2.3   The soldier motions to the ground, *Canoa* (Felipe Cazals, 1976).

around his knees and his underwear and upper thigh are covered in mud. This display of the body denies him dignity. The camera tilts down his body and reveals that he has no shoes. A man holding a light comes into shot. He is evidently assisting the cameraperson in capturing the scene as it is nighttime. He shines the light at each man so that they are visible to the camera. They are squatting down looking impassively at the bodies in a semi-circle and are dressed in apparel that suggests that they are farmers. There is a hard cut – but with the same lighting and sonically sutured by the sound of the camera – to shots of soldiers roughly pushing the same men against a wall with their rifles.

   This sequence lasts just under two minutes (5:53 to 7:07) and forms the credit sequence. As a credit sequence it exists outside of the text and within it simultaneously. It is a form of paratext that is sandwiched between the pre-credit sequence and the film itself. The only sound is that of the camera. After the diegetic percussive music of the army band and the footsteps of the army and funeral procession in the opening sequence, the quieter drone sound of the camera in the credit sequence feels like empty air. The sound of the camera draws attention to the means of recording but lacks the voices and other sounds of the people and the space. The 'ground noise', as the sound of the technology in filmmaking is called, is usually cleaned up in post-production because it 'is understood to threaten the representational by interference, disruption and distraction' (Birtwistle 2010: 85). But here it acts to evoke the spectres of 1968 and invites us to read this as authentic archival material because such 'audible material-ity announces pastness' (Birtwistle 2010: 92). The type of pastness is the sound of analogue technology no longer used to document such events, but for the audience in 1976 it is familiar from budget documentary film. Consequently, it operates on multiple temporal levels: the variable present of the viewing moment and the deliberate pastness foregrounded by the ground noise. For Andy Birtwistle, because of the drone-like quality of the sound of a film with ground noise, it 'is haunted by the shadowy, nebu-lous presence of this region of the unactualised' (2010: 121). Ground noise both evokes a specific type of technology and creates its own subconscious meanings of pastness, displacement, and unease.

   The interaction between the soldiers, the local people and the cinema-tographers suggests unease and uneven power relations. By foregrounding the cameraperson's attempts to film the soldiers while they are, simulta-neously, being controlled by one of them is significant. For the soldier who directs him or her, the cameraperson's role is to film the bodies, but it is unclear for whom, or to what end. If it is for the army as actors on behalf of the government, as the controlling hand and soldier's signalling suggest, this a record of a successful maneuvre to control unrest. Yet, this is complicated by the reporter's account of the event, which suggests that the villagers murdered these men thinking they were seditious anarchists. The villagers' actions elide with those of the state, but by taking power into their own hands, they too must be quelled, which is indicated by the jostling of the villagers by the soldiers, also recorded on film. From the opening sequence of the documentary the very nature of fiction and fact-based historical storytelling techniques are being called into question. It is a concise critique of the indexical capacity of documentary footage and of the gaps in reportage and journalism. We have partial views obscured by the dark and by the censorious actions of the soldiers. The means of production is foregrounded visually, through the assistant with the light who moves through the crowd showing individuals and groups. Thereby, this also alludes to that which we cannot see. The sound effect heightens the analogue mechanics of the camera, and the droning whirring effect is partially meditative – simultaneously noise, silence and self-conscious sound design.

The soldier's control of this footage carries the burden of complicity with the perpetrator. He acts as a proxy for the director, a nuanced position for Cazals to take in its acknowledgement of his compromised position and implicit acknowledgement that '[b]earing witness is a process, an encounter that implicates speaker and listener' as well as those capturing it on film (Torchin 2012: 5). Even if the cameraperson is there to record the events as a neutral observer, they have had their movements curtailed and controlled. This is an example of perpetrator control over the film-making process which, through its exposition in the soldier's onscreen presence as a director, draws attention to itself. To understand this as perpetrator footage we are to read it as such through the audio-visual cues presented to us and to allow space for it to be witness to the process of control itself.

The credit sequence of *Canoa* is a form of commentary on government control over cinematic practice and the filmmakers' role in it, which suggests that Cazals was aware of his own complicity because it is inherent in such filmmaking. He is a filmmaker who has received considerable acclaim from his contemporaries and national cultural organisations. In contrast, González's films are largely ignored, because of his implication in activities that were seen to go beyond what was deemed acceptable by his contemporaries. That is, he was specifically employed by the government to film the students. However, his version of the foundational novel of the Mexican Revolution, *Los de abajo*, serves to complicate this commonplace reading of his output, particularly in his use of original archival footage of the Revolution, which serves as a guide to the dark traveller attempting to understand his work.

Los de abajo (Servando González, 1976)

There are two film adaptations of Mariano Azuela's novel *Los de abajo*: a 1940 version by the popular filmmaker of the Golden Age, Chano Urueta, and a 1976 adaptation by González. Neither film was critically nor commercially successful. The plot of *Los de abajo* follows Demetrio Macías, a peasant farmer, who gathers a band of unlikely soldiers, first from among his neighbours inspired by his leadership. The force eventually builds to a considerable size as they move through the countryside and go on to join a larger troop on its way to the infamous and bloody Battle of Zacatecas (1914) to fight alongside Pancho Villa and Venustiano Carranza's army. After their success at Zacatecas, Macías and his army continue to fight on with Villa's army until, battle fatigued and disillusioned, they decide to turn for home. On this homeward journey they are ambushed by the federal army and killed. The 1976 adaptation covers these key plot points and conveys the horrors of war in the narrative. In a brief sequence that occurs at the apex of Macías' success in battle, we cut to archival footage from the Mexican Revolution. In this use of the found footage González provides clues to understand his ethical position in relation to the war story.

Like the films of the Revolution by his contemporaries (Paul Leduc, Marcela Fernández Violante, José Bolaños), González shot *Los de abajo* in realist mode. Unlike these others, his inclusion of the archive in this way is unique and, consequently, highly meaningful. The transition from fiction to archival footage in *Los de abajo* takes place using an iconic trope of films of the Revolution: the army boarding the train. This typically takes place after a success in battle and on a high note, usually accompanied by a *corrido*, a Mexican ballad form that frequently focuses on the Revolution. González employs some of the techniques familiar from *¡Vámonos con Pancho Villa!/Let's Go with Pancho Villa* (Fernando de Fuentes, 1936), for example, but with a dark and sombre musical score that proves to be a commentary on this trope. Rather than using a hard cut between the fictional narrative and the archival footage, the fiction film was treated to make it look like the early documentary films of the Revolution. This gives the impression of a gradual fade. The fiction film is first sepia tinted then fades to black and white. Additionally, it is speeded up to give the juddery effect of early film. Non-diegetic music starts to play. A slowed-down version of the normally lively *corrido*, 'Si Adelita se fuera con otro' [If Adelita were to go with another], is performed on the pianola, which has a tinkling effect that evokes silent film. After this transition, the fiction film gives way to quick cuts of a seemingly random series of archival film footage from the Revolution.

The footage is not taken from a single source. There were camerapeople who accompanied all sides in the Revolution. Some of these original news reels have been edited to form part of compilation films, the most famous of which is *Memorias de un mexicano* [Memories of a Mexican] (Carmen Toscano, 1950) (Pick 2010). But there is a considerable volume of footage from this conflict that is seldom, if ever, screened. None of the footage used by González is from the oft-repeated repertoire, which gives it a sense of 'foundness' that produces what Jaimie Baron calls the 'archive effect' and gives it 'an aura of being directly excavated from the past' (2014: 6). Integral to this archive effect is a 'temporal disparity' whereby the distance between the time the film was shot and the present is defined by a sense of the changes that have taken place in the intervening years (Baron 2014: 20–1). In *Los de abajo* temporal disparity is smoothed out, and even collapsed, when read through the haunting presence and congruence between the deaths in the Revolution and those in 1968.

In the archival footage used in *Los de abajo* there are few clear markers of the army or political affiliation of the bodies and no accompanying text or voiceover by way of explanation. Further, the montage effect serves to suggest the chaos of war. There are wide shots of action from multiple angles without identification of any of the individuals. This is reinforced by repetition of specific types of sequences, in particular: the setting up of machine guns and artillery; a series of explosions; and the movement of people by foot and on horseback from left to right and right to left, without evident coherence. The noise, dust and movement are confusing and look confused. Again, this reinforces the sense of the madness of war. Then, the music stops, the soundtrack is silent, and the footage shows dead horses lying on their sides, with their stomachs swollen and bloated. There is a certain foreshadowing to these images, but they also have other thematic and meta-narrative functions in the film.

The choice of *corrido* is unusual for a filmmaker at this time and one that González unexpectedly shares with Cazals in the soundtrack to *Canoa*. *Corridos* are associated with the films of the studio era from which many filmmakers of the 1970s were trying to distance themselves aesthetically and ideologically. There are several studio films named after *corridos*, and the 'Adelita' song in particular; *Si Adelita se fuera con otro* was a popular 1948 film by Chano Urueta. The eponymous song re-occurs in many other films, usually sung by a chorus accompanying the army riding into battle. In Catherine Leen's analysis, 'Cazals uses the corrido in an

attempt to redefine the nature of mexicanidad during the turbulent era of
1968' at key points in *Canoa* 'as a vehicle for dissent and a call for justice'
(2014: np). Evoking its association with the popular, the *corrido* is a way
for both directors to reference the past and situate their films within the
revolutionary fervour of 1968. For González to use the *corrido* at a slow
tempo goes against the usual jaunty pace at which it is performed in studio
films, thereby serving as a commentary on the footage being shown, and
as an intertextual referent that should be highly resonant for his audience.
He counters the presumed jingoistic nature of *corridos* whose usual function is to normalise war through displacing the motivation for war onto a
romantic heroic narrative. The Adelita figure is a *soldadera* [female soldier
and companion] for whom the male soldier is fighting and who follows
her partner into battle to support his heroic cause. There are no words
in the version González uses and no evidence of any woman on screen.
Therefore, this absent Adelita and the pace at which the tune is played
render the musical accompaniment poignant. When considered alongside
the visuals accompanying the *corrido*, it suggests that Adelita may have
gone with another because the soldier-hero is buried in a mass grave. Or,
she may also lie in there alongside him, thus puncturing the heroic quest.
Through music and editing, González is challenging the idea of glory in
battle or violent insurrection.

When the music is replaced by silence the imagery of death continues
and is followed by footage of dead people alongside their horses. The men
are only partially clothed and the horses lack riding equipment. Someone
has obviously removed these and abandoned the horses' bodies. The eco-
nomics of the Revolution, with scant resources for the ordinary combat-
ant, determined that those who took their clothing and equipment may
have been friends or foes. This cuts to mass graves of people disposed of
and thrown into trenches haphazardly, followed by workers covering up
these cadavers with soil. It is difficult material to watch because of the way
in which these people are being disposed of, that is, without dignity and,
apparently, anonymously with no ceremony. The sequences are to be read
as indexical traces, lacking in the markings of affiliation. The filmmaker
seems to be suggesting that there is a neutrality to the image captured and
that death is horrific irrespective of the affiliation of the cinematographers.

Trying to situate the original intention of filmmakers in such re-
appropriated material is something that is far from neutral, as Marianne
Hirsch (2003) has explored. She examines a series of photographic images
that have been cropped, altered and re-circulated in their edited versions
to become unrecognisable as perpetrator images. For her, this intensifies
the distance between the viewer and the subject, in particular when these

images are haunted by death (2003: 25). Where González appears to be contending that we are all equal in death and that the chaos of war flattens out the distinction between right and wrong, Hirsch disavows this when she states that there is 'an uncomfortably tainted position we always occupy when we view perpetrator images' (2003: 34). This is further complicated when discussing a civil war, such as the Mexican Revolution, where reconciliation is integral to the formation of a stable government, which means that there is no clear-cut perpetrator, unlike the apportioning of responsibility that is integral to memory work that Hirsch discusses in relation to the Holocaust. But when seen in the light of González's perpetrator footage taken at the scene of the 1968 protests and subsequent massacre, this sequence can be read as a coded message about the indexicality of documenting violence that the viewer needs to be attuned to in order to read against.

This sequence then cuts to Pancho Villa delivering a short speech, whereupon another jolly *corrido* begins to play. This gradually segues to footage that reveals itself to be a return to sepia, then colour and a resumption of the fiction film. At nearly two minutes forty seconds (54.03–56.40), this is an extended sequence which acts as a commentary on the fiction narrative being told, critiques the generic tropes of the films of the Revolution, and both questions the nature of archival footage to connote authenticity and implicitly alludes to its use as a tool for propaganda. It acts as a powerful and uncomfortable exploration of the ways in which González's work has been haunted by 1968 even when not addressing it explicitly.

Conclusion

In Mexico 1976 was election year and the last year of Luis Echevarría's presidency. Echevarría had supported filmmaking with a historical focus as a means of glossing over the events of 1968 and of creating a distance between his presidency and that of Gustavo Díaz Ordaz, who had ordered the repression of the students. In 1976 José López Portillo took over the presidency from Echevarría and his sister, Margarita López Portillo, became head of the film and cultural institutions. She is blamed for the fire in the Cineteca in 1982 with the resultant loss of archival footage and old film reels, because she starved it of funding. López Portillo did not prove supportive of filmmaking. These three films are part of the legacy of Díaz Ordaz and Echevarría's presidencies and Cazals and González had access to resources and found footage that the López Portillo era rendered impossible. In their use of archival footage, the films draw attention to the

multiple ways in which such footage can be remediated to open out discussion around the meaning of a text and are haunted by the loss of a large
quantity of this same archive.

The presence of 1968 looms large over all of these films. Not only
because it was relatively recent but also because it was integral to the
formation of these filmmakers. The archival footage used has an indexical function but also acts as its opposite. That is, a recognition of the
impossibility of footage to record an event. In *Canoa* the short sequence
shows events that took place in 1968 at a short distance from the primary
trauma site in Mexico City. In the case of *Los de abajo* the footage used
is doubly evocative. It is meant to conjure up the horror of war (specifically the Revolution), and act as a substitute for the trauma of the massacre of the dead students. It is about gaps. The missing footage from 1968
shot by González is replaced with terrible images from another foundational moment, the 1910 Revolution. Meanwhile, the final sequence of
Los Poquianchis is a continuation of the exploration of the impossibility of
truth-telling in either fiction or documentary form.

The films stand as examples of filmmakers grappling with what
Marianne Hirsch describes as 'an aesthetics of the aftermath' (2014: 334),
which prompts her to ask, '[h]ow can we allow the knowledge of past atroc-
ity to touch us without paralyzing us?' Her response is to conclude that
solidarity can be forged through being 'suspicious of empathy, shuttling
instead between proximity and distance, affiliation and disaffiliation, complicity and accountability' (2014: 339). This move from affect to analysis and action is significant in the study of trauma and post-memory and
proves a useful way to navigate perpetrator imagery because it does not
discount emotion. Instead, it asks us to respond with a view to taking
account of our own place in the regimes of power that govern scholarly
dark travel and the navigation of cultural knowledge.

When a filmmaker draws on the audio-visual language of the perpetrator to represent violence realistically it increases the discomfort and
ambivalences that are inherent for an academic studying such dark matters. Realist violence on screen invites the audience to consider horrors
that are visceral and affecting. It may not always be spectacular and large
in scale, but it is deployed to provoke a response. To describe such material
as realist violence is to try to synthesise in two words a range of objects
from fiction to archival artefacts that signal the intention of the author of
these materials to capture something real in a way that documents lived
experience but also acknowledges the impossibility of capturing a version
of reality that is unaffected by the medium employed.

All of the sequences discussed are deliberately disruptive and also act as commentaries upon the films themselves and the genres being employed. They ask the viewer to consider the nature of telling true stories or of relating history, all the while making truth claims. Such an approach must be understood in the light of the historical processes Mexico was going through in this period and also in the light of how such events impact the careers of the filmmakers themselves. The three films use archival footage to self-consciously create moments of meta-fictional reflection on the ethics of screening death thereby creating opportunities for us to pause on our own dark desires to seek pleasure from past traumas.

Note

1. Unless otherwise stated, all translations are my own.

Bibliography

Azuela, Mariano (1997), *Los de abajo*, edited and with introduction by Marta Portal, Madrid: Catedra.

Baron, Jaimie (2014), *The Archive Effect: Found Footage and the Audiovisual Experience of History*, Oxford and New York: Routledge.

Birtwistle, Andy (2010), *Cinesonica: Sounding Film and Video*, Manchester: Manchester University Press.

Blue, William R. (1991), 'The Politics of Lope's *Fuenteovejuna*', *Hispanic Review*, 59:3, pp. 295–315.

Brewster, Keith (ed.) (2010), *Reflections on Mexico '68*, Malden, MA and Oxford: Blackwell Publishing.

Canoa, film, directed by Felipe Cazals. Mexico: Concite Uno/S.T.P.C., 1976.

Clark, Laurie Beth (2012), 'Ethical Spaces: Ethics and Propriety in Trauma Tourism', in Brigitte Sion (ed.), *Death Tourism: Disaster Sites as Recreational Landscape*, London and New York: Seagull Books, pp. 9–35.

El grito, film, directed by Leobardo López Arretche. Mexico: Centro Universitario de Estudios Cinematográficos, 1968.

Estrada, Luis Armando (2012), '¿Quién quemó la Cineteca Nacional?', *Quo*, 10 October. Available at <http://quo.mx/noticias/2012/10/10/quien-quemo-la-cineteca-nacional> (last accessed 6 September 2017).

Haddu, Miriam (2007), *Contemporary Mexican Cinema 1989–1999: History, Space, and Identity*, Lewiston, NY and Lampeter: The Edwin Mellen Press.

Hirsch, Marianne (2003), 'Nazi Photographs in Post-Holocaust Art: Gender as an Idiom of Memorialization', in Alex Hughes and Andrea Noble (eds), *Phototextualities: Intersections of Photography and Narrative*, Albuquerque: University of New Mexico Press, pp. 19–40.

Hirsch, Marianne (2014), 'Connective Histories in Vulnerable Times: MLA Presidential Address', *PMLA*, 129:3, pp. 330–48.

Ibargüengoitia, Jorge (1976), *Las muertas*, México: Joaquín Mortiz.

Lange, Charlotte (2009), 'The "Truth" Behind a Scandal: Jorge Ibargüengoitia's *Las muertas*', *Neophilologus*, 93:3, pp. 453–64.

Leen, Catherine (2014), 'The corrido as Counterculture in Felipe Cazals' Canoa', *Modern Languages Open*. Available at <https://www.modernlanguagesopen. org/articles/10.3828/mlo.v0i0.22> (last accessed 22 August 2017).

Los de abajo, film, directed by Serrvando González. Mexico: CONACINE, 1976.

Los Poquianchis (De los pormenores y otros sucedidos del dominio público que acontecieron a las hermanas de triste memoria a quienes la maledicencia así las bautizó), film, directed by Felipe Cazals. Mexico: Alpha Centauri/CONACINE, 1976.

Memorias de un mexicano, film, directed by Carmen Toscano. Mexico: Archivo Salvador Toscano, 1950.

Pick, Zuzana M. (2010), *Constructing the Image of the Mexican Revolution: Cinema and the Archive*, Austin: University of Texas Press.

Rojo amanecer, film, directed by Jorge Fons. Mexico: Cinematográfica Sol S.A., 1989.

Sánchez Prado, Ignacio M. (2016), 'Novel, War, and the Aporia of Totality: Lukács's *Theory of the Novel* and Azuela's *Los de abajo*', *Mediations*, 29:2, pp. 47–64. Available at <www.mediationsjournal.org/articles/novel-war-and-the-aporia-of-totality> (last accessed 23 March 2020).

Si Adelita se fuera con otro, film, directed by Chano Urueta. Mexico: Diana Films, 1948.

Sion, Brigitte (2014), 'Introduction', in Brigitte Sion (ed.), *Death Tourism: Disaster Sites as Recreational Landscape*, London and New York: Seagull Books, pp. 1–8.

Thornton, Niamh (2013), *Revolution and Rebellion in Mexican Cinema*, New York: Bloomsbury.

Torchin, Leshu (2012), *Creating the Witness: Documenting Genocide on Film, Video, and the Internet*, Minneapolis & London: University of Minnesota Press.

Vega, Lope de [1619] (2010), *Fuenteovejuna*, translated by G. J. Racz and with introduction by Roberto González Echevarría, New Haven and London: Yale University Press.

Wolfenzon, Carolyn (2016), 'Las muertas y los relámpagos de agosto: la violencia como esencia de lo mexicano en la obra de Jorge Ibargüengoitia', *Bulletin of Spanish Studies*, 93:5: pp. 859–75.

CHAPTER 3

Spectres of Mexico's 'Dirty Wars': Gendered Haunting and the Legacy of Women's Armed Resistance in Mexican Documentary Film

Viviana MacManus

La historia oficial no nos contempla, nos ve como fantasmas de otro reino. Y estamos aquí para contar nuestras versiones, para mostrar que un discurso que nos excluye no puede aspirar a la universalidad. Y en realidad esta, la historia que estamos recuperando, reconstruyendo en este espacio, es ya otra historia. (Alejandra Cárdenas, *Partido de los pobres*, Guerrero, Mexico, quoted in Aguilar Terrés 2007: 30)

[Official history does not see us, it regards us as ghosts from another realm. We are here to tell our stories, to show that a narrative that excludes us cannot be considered universal. In fact this history that we are recovering, re-drafting in this space, is another type of history.]

To exorcise not in order to chase away the ghosts, but this time to grant them the right [. . .to a] hospitable memory [. . .] out of a concern for justice. (Derrida 1994: 220)

After my interview in July 2012 with Bertha Lilia Gutiérrez Campos, former member of Guadalajara's Frente Estudiantil Revolucionario and La Liga Comunista 23 de Septiembre guerrillas, she shared with me documents from her personal archive. Rifling through the papers, she pulled out a pamphlet made for a 2006 photographic exhibit in Guadalajara. The exhibit, 'To forget is to forget ourselves', featured photographs housed in Mexico's General National Archive and captured the visual history of the so-called Dirty War that the nation had systematically kept from public record. 'Dirty War' refers to the largely unacknowledged history of political repression that the Mexican government waged against armed and unarmed socialist movements, beginning in the late 1950s and lasting until the early 1980s. Gutiérrez Campos handed me the pamphlet and recited the stanzas by Mexican poet Enrique Macías Loza included in the flyer: 'No son las calles / lo que duele / son los muertos / nuestros muertos / los que no me dejan / dormir / ni vivir / y a veces ni morir.' [It is not the streets / that cause pain / it is the dead/ our dead / who do not let me / sleep / or live / and sometimes won't let me die.] Afterwards she added,

'Dice más, dice, no son las calles lo que nos duele sino lo que dejamos en ellas.' [He says more, he says, it isn't the streets that hurt us but what we leave in them.] She then took me to the area of Guadalajara where the prison, Penal de Oblatos, where she and other *guerrilleras* were detained for several years, used to be located.

As we approached the site, she told me that the prison was demolished in 1982 and an elementary school erected in that location. As we circled the block, she pointed to the playground and told me that this was where the *guerrilleras* were detained. Classes were out for the summer and the empty playground created a sense of haunting and loss. As we drove away from the site of the former prison, Gutiérrez Campos said, 'Los espacios conservan cierta energía del pasado, ¿no?' [Isn't it the case that spaces hold a kind of energy from the past?]. As we drove away from this former site of trauma and political persecution, I sat in silence with Gutiérrez Campos, just one of the many women protagonists of Mexico's little-known history of the armed struggle.

I begin with this anecdote as it captures the theory of haunting and spectrality that has emerged in my research on the legacy of women's participation in Mexico's armed struggle during the 'Dirty War'. Read alongside Cárdenas' epigraph, these former guerrillas' accounts of the past reveal a significant element that is absent from contemporary Mexican historiography: women's participation in the armed socialist movements of the 1960s and 1970s. The history of the armed movements in Mexico holds a marginal place in contemporary Mexican history, yet there is even less information on the history of women's participation in these movements. Gutiérrez Campos and Cárdenas allude to the haunting of Mexico's revolutionary past and the unsettling of two dominant narratives of the armed struggle: the state's criminalisation of armed organisations in contemporary cultural discourses, *and* the masculinisation and romanticisation of the armed struggle, narrated primarily by male protagonists. I argue that these dominant narratives on the armed insurgencies evince a *gendered haunting* of Mexico's revolutionary past on the present, where the spectres of the armed struggle unsettle and re-script the discourses that have failed to acknowledge the legacy of women's resistance.

While the history of the *guerrilleras* is rendered invisible in contemporary Mexico, visual culture has played a critical role in documenting women's histories of revolutionary struggle and capturing the gendered haunting of this past. This is evident in Luisa Riley's 2012 documentary film, *Flor en Otomí* [Flower in Otomí], which centres on the life and death of Dení Prieto Stock, a nineteen-year-old member of the Mexican urban guerrilla group, the Frente de Liberación Nacional (FLN) [National

Liberation Forces]. By centring my analysis on *Flor en Otomí*, I investigate how visual culture makes central these silenced narratives and how the history of the *guerrilleras* is rendered illegible and irrelevant in contemporary neoliberal Mexico. The film documents how Mexico's unresolved history of violence, and the *guerrilleras*' erasure from state and masculinist discourses, has resulted in a generation of spectres whose histories of revolutionary struggle continue to haunt contemporary Mexico. The film disrupts the neoliberal present as it documents Mexico's violent history and evokes the gendered memories of these ghosts who resisted the free market economic policies of the 1970s.

Although *Flor en Otomí* importantly documents the unrecognised legacies of this era and contests the Mexican government's role in committing human rights abuses, we are confronted with a critical limitation of the film: documentary film and other audio-visual texts face the vexing task of representing reality, especially when focusing on trauma and violence. *Flor en Otomí* is haunted by its own subject matter and by this difficulty of representing the un-representable: the violent loss of the gendered spectres of Mexico's 'Dirty War'.

Yet despite this limitation, the film is an important cultural text that portrays the gender politics of haunting, albeit in a contradictory, complex way. *Flor en Otomí* investigates how the presence of these ghosts contests the legacy of state violence and also destabilises dominant, masculinist histories of Latin American socialist movements. Rather than reading *Flor en Otomí* as a counter-narrative to dominant narratives on the armed struggle, it is critical to examine how the ghostly presences evoke the legacy of this *gendered haunting* of Mexico's 'Dirty Wars'. *Flor en Otomí* evinces the gendered nature of haunting in precisely what *cannot* be audio-visually or textually captured in relation to the violence of Latin America's revolutionary past. It is important, however, that these narratives of gendered haunting are not read as 'authentic' or true historic accounts of women's elided experiences in the armed struggle. In *Haunting Violations*, Hesford and Kozol caution against reading women's narratives of resistance to trauma and violence as 'authentic or "real" experiences to prove abusiveness of power' (Hesford and Kozol 2001: 2). Thus it is critical to interrogate what impact the legacy of these women's histories of repression has had on cultural productions, rather than reading them as authentic accounts of women's marginalisation. And while *Flor en Otomí* relies on testimonies of 'Dirty War' survivors and former *guerrilleros* to provide an important counter-narrative to the state's official account of this history, *Flor en Otomí* does not idealise these testimonies as the locus of truth. Instead, the film alludes to the haunting created by the eradication of political dissidents from Mexico's national consciousness and illuminates the important role that visual culture plays in tracking down the gendered ghosts of this history of political violence.

In my analysis of *Flor en Otomí*, I argue that haunting serves as a heuristic tool that can assist us in examining the erasure of women's political subjectivity from the history of Mexico's armed struggles of the 1960s and 1970s. As Avery Gordon notes in *Ghostly Matters*, haunting is 'an animated state in which a repressed or unresolved social violence is making itself known, sometimes very directly, sometimes more obliquely' (Gordon 2008: xvi). For Gordon, this 'animated state' represents that which cannot be documented empirically beyond that which is not seen, but felt; in other words, haunting reflects a 'structure of feeling that is something akin to what it feels like to be the object of a social totality vexed by the phantoms of modernity's violence' (Gordon 2008: 19). I am concerned with these 'phantoms of modernity's violence', or rather, the gendered ghosts of the Dirty Wars whose presences are felt in *Flor en Otomí*. The 'seething presence' of the gendered 'fantasmas de otro reino' [spirits from another realm] is evoked throughout the film, making themselves known to us. This kind of haunting that emerges vis-à-vis the 'structure of feeling' is to offer ghosts, as Derrida asserts, 'a hospitable memory out of a concern for justice', and I argue that *Flor en Otomí* creates such a 'hospitable memory' for these gendered ghosts of Mexico's 'Dirty War' (Gordon 2008: 64).

Ultimately, I argue that *Flor en Otomí* is a critical visual text that conjures the ghosts of the *guerrilleras* 'out of a concern for justice'. It is within the film's spaces of un-representability, gaps, and silences that the ghosts are conjured and given a chance for a 'hospitable memory' – a chance the state has effectively denied them for decades. While the film does not purport to offer the *real* history of the armed struggle in Mexico and although *Flor en Otomí* provides us with a contradictory portrayal of *guerrilleras*' experiences, the film's limits of representation create a political space that allows these 'fantasmas de otro reino' to teach us about histories of resistance and to help us envision alternative forms of justice for human rights crimes.

Searching for the Ghosts of Mexico's Armed Struggles

Flor en Otomí is one of the few cultural texts that focuses on women's involvement in Mexico's armed socialist movements of the 1970s. The 78–minute film traces the life of Dení Prieto Stock and the events that led to her death in 1974. Riley, Prieto Stock's childhood friend, decided to create a documentary film about Dení's life in an attempt to unearth the hidden history of guerrilla activism in 1970s Mexico and to document the egregious forms of human rights violations sanctioned by the state. Using first-hand testimonials, photographs and personal letters, the film recounts the life of Prieto Stock, who was born in Mexico City in 1955 to a Jewish-American mother, Evelyn Stock, and Mexican playwright father, Carlos Prieto Argüelles. The film relies on family and friends' testimonies to describe Prieto Stock's life before and after she joined the FLN and briefly lived clandestinely outside of Mexico City. Raised in a bilingual, middle-class and politically left family, Prieto Stock's personal world was immersed in politics, and the film reveals how this shaped her decision to become active in socialist organisations. However, increasing state repression in late-1960s Mexico impelled her to pursue the more radical decision and join the FLN. On 14 February 1974, Prieto Stock and four other FLN members were killed when the Mexican army ambushed their safe house in Nepantla de Sor Juana Inés de la Cruz, southeast of Mexico City.

Released decades after the death of Prieto Stock, *Flor en Otomí* emerges during a time when human rights organisations and activists were recuperating the historical memory of Mexico's armed struggle. In 2007, journalist Laura Castellanos published *Mexico armado*, focusing on the genealogy of Mexico's armed movements in the twentieth century. Contemporary Mexican literature has also reflected this interest in the 'Dirty War'; Carlos Montemayor's publications *Guerra en el paraíso* (1991) and *Las mujeres del alba* (2003) represent the history of the *Partido de los pobres* and *La liga comunista 23 de septiembre*, respectively. Recent feature films have also alluded to the legacy of Mexico's 'Dirty War', evident in the character of former *guerrillero* El Chivo (Emilio Echevarría) in Alejandro González Iñárritu's *Amores perros* (2000). However, very few cultural works centre on the role the *guerrilleras* played in this history; *Flor en Otomí* – along with *Las mujeres del alba* and the theatrical performance 'El rumor del incendio' (2010) – is one of the few texts that brings visibility to Mexico's *guerrilleras*. *Flor en Otomí* addresses this gendered, historical absence and the haunting that is created with the lack of justice achieved for these state crimes.

The haunting subject matter of *Flor en Otomí* is revealed in the discordances presented in the film's narrative arc and the limitations in portraying the 'real' history of the FLN and Prieto Stock's life. In Latin America, many documentary films produced in the 1960s and 1970s were in response to political strife and provided counter socio-political narratives. This tradition has continued in contemporary Mexican documentary filmmaking in productions that address present-day human rights crises, such as Marc Silver's *Who is Dayani Cristal?* (2013) and Lourdes Portillo's *Señorita extraviada* (2003). Similar to these films, *Flor en Otomí* documents a history of political repression and contributes to the small body of work that explores the unknown history of Mexico's 'Dirty War'. In the summer of 2012, I met with Riley and when I asked her what compelled her to make the film, she responded, 'es un granito de arena, sin duda contribuye a la recuperación de la memoria histórica [de la guerra sucia]. Se trata de la vida de Dení, pero para mí Dení representa el espíritu de los jóvenes de esa época'. [It's a grain of sand, without a doubt it contributes to the recuperation of historical memory (of the dirty war). It centres on Dení's life, but for me Dení represents the spirit of the youth of that era].

Flor en Otomí evokes the history of state-sponsored violence that took place thirty years before the film was initiated, and this temporal remove not only indicates a haunting that is evident in contemporary Mexico's inability to reckon with its traumatic past but also reflects a deviation from the emphasis on representing truth that many social documentary films purport to do. Rather than offer us a chronological account of Prieto Stock's life, the film explores the cultural legacy of these ghosts and what they can teach us about the audio-visual archiving of historical narratives.

In the attempt to track down Prieto Stock's ghost, *Flor en Otomí* draws on different archival materials, such as photographs, testimonials, personal letters and news sources. Riley's presence in *Flor en Otomí* illustrates her role as documentarian and family friend, yet also refers to the impossibility of documenting 'the way things truly [were]' when tracking down the spectres of the 'Dirty War' (Nichols 1983: 18). Despite being absent for the majority of the film, Riley's positionality is clearly noted throughout the documentary as she re-traces Prieto Stock's political subjectivity and life events. Riley has intimate access to material sources in the creation of her film, which include video reels from the Prieto Stock family, photographs and, most critical in the film's reconstruction of Prieto Stock's subjectivity, personal letters sent to her cousin Laura Stock in New York.

Riley's personal involvement with the subject matter is depicted in the first minutes of *Flor en Otomí*. The opening scene reveals headlines from the *Excelsior* and *El Universal* newspapers dated Thursday 15 February 1974, praising the Mexican government for dismantling 'una conjura roja contra México, cuyo objetivo era implanter por medios violentos un gobierno de tipo socialista' [a red conspiracy against Mexico whose aim was to establish a socialist government by violent means]. The camera then focuses on the text of the article, which claims that five 'extremistas' were killed in a 'balacera' [shoot-out] against the army and federal police. These images are accompanied by discordant, unnerving, minimalist minor keys of a piano, which eventually give way to the brash sound of trumpets as the text of the article lists Prieto Stock as one of the deceased. The abrupt, 'forte' notes of the piano played in the first few minutes of the film are unsettling and evoke the traumatic effect of the extra-legal violence sanctioned by the Mexican state. The original score, composed and performed by musicians Onésimo García and Steven Brown, provides the aural backdrop to this scene sequence. As the camera pans over the text of the newspaper documenting the ambush at the Nepantla safe house, we see green ink underlining portions of the text (Figure 3.1).

Riley's inclusion of these headlines from Mexican newspapers challenges the government's official discourse of the armed insurgency – and the media's corroboration of this discourse – and relays the immediacy of the filmmaker's relationship to Prieto Stock. These markings on the newspaper reveal the shock that Riley described to me when she read the 1974 *Excelsior* article at the Archivo General de la Nación [General Archive of the Nation] in 2007. She relates that she was left 'paralizada' the first time she read the newspaper in 1974, and that 'cuando lo volví a ver [en los archivos en 2007], grité. Te da la sensación de que es cierto. Realmente sí ocurrió.' [when I saw it again (in the archives in 2007), I cried out. You have the feeling that it is true. That it really happened]. Riley's absent-presence emerges at the commencement of the film and the loud, green ink underlining the name – Dení Prieto Stock – evokes this shock of re-encountering the reality of her friend's death in 2007.

This haunting in *Flor en Otomí*'s portrayal of past traumas is evident in its narrative structure and use of archival materials. Riley does not offer a historically chronological narrative, but rather her film compresses

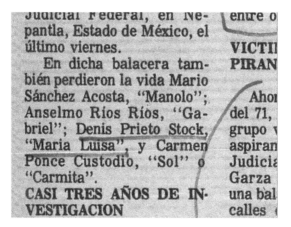

Figure 3.1   Image of the *Excelsior* newspaper that reveals director Luisa Riley's underlinings in ink.

temporal distance by moving between three narrative arcs while incorporating distinct sources. The first narrative line offers a biographical sketch of Prieto Stock's life leading up to her involvement with the FLN, and Riley relies on testimonials, photographs and letters to reveal the critical moments that shaped Prieto Stock's political consciousness. The second storyline centres on Prieto Stock's time in the guerrilla as 'María Luisa' (*nom de guerre*), relying predominately on former FLN compañera Elisa Benavides Guevara's testimony to relate their experiences of living in the safe house. The third narrative takes place in the present day, as the film journeys to the safe house in Nepantla where Benavides recounts the events that took place on the day of the ambush. While *Flor en Otomí* shifts from one narrative frame to another, it is constantly pulled towards the third narrative, the site of the violent ambush.

A salient example of this temporal compression and the film's indexing occurs halfway through the film as Prieto Stock's cousin, Laura, reads from a letter that Dení had sent her in 1970, three years before she went to live clandestinely with the FLN:

> I've had a sort of hazy feeling as though I'm really sick inside. It's like a deep disappointment, but like I'm too lazy to do anything about it. It's so hard to explain. Let me try and to put my thoughts in order. First I started thinking, why the hell I'm studying if in the end I'll probably leave everything and go to the mountains and fight guerrillas and probably get killed in the process.

As Laura reads aloud from the letter in the present day, the camera pans over Prieto Stock's original handwritten text (Figure 3.2), where the

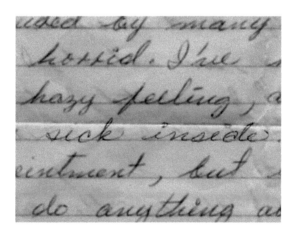

Figure 3.2   Close-up of Prieto Stock's letter to her cousin Laura, centring on the words 'hazy' and 'sick inside'.

phrases 'hazy feeling' and 'sick inside' are in the foreground of the scene. As Laura continues to read the letter, the visuals cut from a black-and-white photograph of a teenage Dení (Figure 3.3), to the text of the letter, as the camera zooms in on the words 'guerrilla' and 'killed' (Figure 3.4). As Laura Stock finishes the letter, the next scene cross-cuts to the yard of the Nepantla safe house, as the camera directs the spectator's gaze skyward.

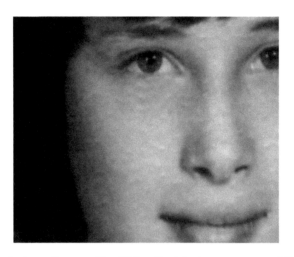

Figure 3.3 A photo of a young Dení Prieto Stock is shown on screen while her cousin Laura reads the letter aloud.

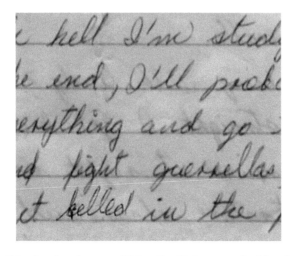

Figure 3.4 Another close-up of Prieto Stock's letter, emphasising the words 'guerrilla' and 'killed'.

By repeatedly cross-cutting to the scene of the ambush in present-day Nepantla, the film evokes this 'seething presence' of the un-representable: the violent repression of the armed insurgencies in 1970s Mexico and the traumatic legacy of Prieto Stock's death. Her death is the seething presence that the film evokes by showing us that it *cannot* be represented, yet the film is able to conjure the spectral qualities that her trauma – and the trauma of this historical epoch – represents. This is clear in the evidentiary editing as Riley blends images of the photograph, the letter and the yard of the safe house (the site of Prieto Stock's death). The quiet stillness of the scenes of the Nepantla house is contrasted with the final words of Prieto Stock's letter, eerily foreshadowing her own death, as well as close-up images of the home's exterior that displays visible bullet holes from the day of the attack (Figure 3.5). The scene of the ambush is always portrayed in the film as tranquil, evoking this sense of haunting as archival photos of the massacre of the FLN members in 1974 are positioned against the calmness of the Nepantla house in 2012.

Figure 3.5   Close-up of the front of the Nepantla safe house, with visible bullet holes in the wall.

This sequence repeatedly centres on Prieto Stock's photograph, each frame providing a closer image of her face. Laura Mulvey articulates the sense of uncertainty that results from photography's allusion to death, or the 'embalmed index'; drawing from Roland Barthes, Mulvey notes that photographs reveal a simultaneous absence and presence in the 'return of the dead' (Mulvey 2006: 60). Mulvey adds: 'The photograph's suspension of time, its conflation of life and death, the animate and the inanimate, raises [. . .] a sense of disquiet that is aggravated rather than calmed by the photograph's mechanical, chemical and indifferent nature' (Mulvey 2006: 60). Thus the combination of material sources used in this sequence reflects this absent presence in the 'conflation of life and death', as the edit cuts between images of Prieto Stock's face, the Nepantla house and text from her original letters. The haunting effect is heightened by Laura Stock providing the voice for the deceased sender of the letter, which in one sense imbues the film with life and animation, yet simultaneously underscores the reality of Prieto Stock's absence.

The convergence of the three narrative arcs is disquieting, as the confluence of these temporalities and archival sources reminds the spectators of Prieto Stock's death. The film evokes the 'sort of hazy feeling' Prieto Stock wrote about, as it attempts to audio-visually track down the spectres of the guerrillas, aware of its limitations in its ability to capture this un-representable subject matter and Prieto Stock's absent presence. What's more, the compression of temporalities in *Flor en Otomí* alludes to the belated impact of trauma in cultural representations of violence. The centrality of absence in the film emphasises the elision of this narrative from the annals of Mexican history and reflects the traumatic and unrecognised legacies of women guerrillas of this era.

Gender and the Cultural Imaginary of Mexico's Armed Struggle

Although *Flor en Otomí* illuminates women's active participation in the elided histories of the armed struggle, the film relays what I believe are contradictory portrayals of femininity and gender. While the first half of the documentary centres on the development of Prieto Stock's political awareness during her adolescence, Riley also dedicates a significant portion of the film to addressing Prieto Stock's romantic relationships. This can be interpreted as a contradiction in the film's intent, as it portrays Prieto Stock as a politically conscious young woman who gave her life for a political cause. A critical limitation emerges in the representation of Prieto Stock as, on the one hand, a politically radical young woman who made her own decisions, and, on the other hand, a pretty teenager preoccupied with romance and dating. Such focus on one's romantic interests is not made central in other biographies or documentaries on male revolutionary figures and *guerrilleros*, and thus we must critically examine Riley's decision to include extensive detail about Prieto Stock's romantic life.

This tension is exhibited in the film's *first* incorporation of Prieto Stock's personal letters addressed to her cousin, Laura. Laura reads a letter sent to her in 1969, where Prieto Stock recounts a new romantic interest, Juan. The next excerpt that Laura reads focuses on the political climate in Mexico as Prieto Stock mentions a political prisoner hunger strike that occurred in Mexico City. Afterwards, Laura shares memories of Prieto Stock, where she notes that 'hanging out with her boyfriends, going to parties' were 'equally big' to Prieto Stock as her political activism.

After Laura Stock reads this first letter, the film introduces a former childhood love interest, Ramón, who discusses the first time he met Prieto Stock. Riley then includes several photographs of Prieto Stock in alluring positions, with one photo of her lying in bed, smiling at the camera, while a sexy soundtrack of a guitar solo backed by trumpets accompanies the photo. Laura then reads passages of Prieto Stock's letter describing her attraction to Ramón, adding that 'Dení was very flirtatious, really enjoyed having attention from all these boys [. . .] she was very small, very pretty, very delicate.' These comments are contrasted with Laura's follow-up observation that Prieto Stock 'was her own thinker [. . .] she wanted to read and understand things'.

These key moments of the film reflect how Prieto Stock's political agency is mitigated by Riley's portrayal of a gender-normative subjectivity. The film's first evocation of Prieto Stock's voice vis-à-vis personal letters is centred on a romantic interest rather than a political memory. In the interview with Ramón, Riley represents Prieto Stock's gender in a way that emphasises a femininity that evokes a teenage frivolity and sexuality rooted in normative assumptions. We must be critical of this particular representation, as Prieto Stock's political commitment is decentred in the film's repeated reference to her diminutive, attractive physical form and multiple romantic interests, which reaffirm existing gendered notions of the *guerrilleras*. It is also important to say that 'typical' teenage girl interests – such as socialising, dating, etc. – are not mutually exclusive from politicised consciousness. I argue here that by making these interests central to the film's narrative, it mitigates the political subjectivity of Prieto Stock.

It is also important to examine the editing techniques of the documentary in its attempt to reconstruct a biography of Prieto Stock. *Flor en Otomí* relies on survivor testimony to reconstruct Prieto Stock's subjectivity.

This contributes to the film's haunting, as Riley utilises the voice of the living recipient of the letter to give voice to the deceased, while the camera centres on images from the original text. Inasmuch as Prieto Stock's personal letters are vital narrative resources in the portrayal of her life, we must focus on which particular excerpts are included in the representation of her subjectivity. These limitations are not only unique to documentary filmmaking, however, as narratives of loss, trauma and death in oral histories must also contend with gaps, contradictions, and many spectres.

Despite the film's limitations, *Flor en Otomí* highlights the central roles women held in Mexico's guerrillas. The film reflects the moments that shaped Prieto Stock's political trajectory and the conscious decision she made to join the FLN, which destabilises the masculinist historiography of the armed insurgency. Prieto Stock's political consciousness is presented in the film and many of the testimonies, and her letters reflect her condemnation of the political climate in 1970s Mexico. Political convictions were her own, and this is reflected in a letter she sends to her family explaining her decision to join the FLN: 'You know that this is not a hasty decision but one made over years. Don't think I'm taking this as a romantic adventure.' While Prieto Stock was likely unaware of the extent of state repression and violence, the film articulates that it was not a 'hasty decision' to join the armed struggle, but rather one based on her political conviction.

What's more, the film questions the tradition of documenting guerrilla activism as a male-centred revolutionary movement, most evident in the iconic, romanticised image of Che Guevara. These revolutionary ideals are typically gendered as masculine, while women's politicised agency is often erased from this history, producing a haunting that is gendered. *Flor en Otomí* relays Prieto Stock's criticism of the gender politics that existed in many male-dominated guerrilla groups. This is evident in a close-up image of Benavides, discussing the machismo that surfaced at times in the Nepantla household. She recounts that the *compañeros* asked the women to wear discreet clothing so they would not appear attractive to them: 'Para María Luisa era ridículo. Le daba risa, y le molestaba . . . Ella llegaba a un momento en que ya no lo aguantaba. Se burlaba, basicamente se burlaba, pero a veces decía, "Mira ya, dejas de decirme nena, dejas de decirnos nenas, porque si no, yo te voy a decir, no sé qué. . ."' [For María Luísa it was ridiculous. It made her laugh and it annoyed her . . . she got to a point where she could no longer tolerate it. She joked about it, laughed it off, but sometimes she would say, 'look, here, stop this girl business, stop calling us girls, because, if you don't, I'll just. . .']. This sequence attests to Prieto Stock's exasperation with masculinist attitudes that were embedded in many guerrillas, and exposes her willingness to contest these gender norms.

The film, then, reflects Prieto Stock's political convictions that defied expectations of some of her *compañeros* as well as the gender norms dictated by the patriarchal Mexican state. Prieto Stock was part of a wider conversation on the legacy of women in Mexico's armed resistance. In the forward to Mexico's *Memoria del primer encuentro nacional de mujeres exguerrilleras*, the organisers state:

> Las mujeres nos integramos a la lucha armada, de muchas maneras rompimos con el rol que la sociedad nos tenía asignado. Dejamos a nuestros padres, a nuestra familia, a veces a nuestros hijos o la perspectiva de una vida cómoda con un esposo que nos mantuviera. Nos integramos a actividades donde sabíamos que podíamos perder la vida. Sabíamos también que teníamos que ser valientes y participar hombro con hombro con nuestros compañeros en las diversas tareas de las organizaciones. (Aguilar Terrés 2007: 18)

> [We women who joined the armed struggle, in many ways we broke with the role society had given us. We left our parents, our families, sometimes our children and in many cases the possibility of a comfortable life with a husband who would support us. We got involved in activities where we knew that we might lose our lives. We knew that we had to be brave and stand shoulder to shoulder with our male comrades, stepping into roles across the organisations.]

These women not only challenged gender norms within the armed movements but their decision to join these groups threatened the patriarchal order of the Mexican state. *Flor en Otomí* positions the protagonist of the film as a *guerrillera* killed by the Mexican army and makes central the unknown gender history and politics of the 'Dirty War'.

The tonal atmosphere of a gendered haunting is established within the first few minutes of *Flor en Otomí*. Returning to the film's opening sequence, Riley includes the *Excelsior* newspaper article that lists Prieto Stock as one of the deceased 'extremists' killed in the ambush. The following scene takes place in the present day as a moving vehicle heads towards the safe house in Nepantla; a woman's voice – Dení's sister, Ayari Prieto Stock –recounts the media coverage of the ambush. The camera's gaze is fixed ahead on the open highway on a clear, sunny day, as Ayari relays the shock upon reading her sister's name listed among one of the deceased in the *Excelsior* article. The scene then cuts to Ayari as she continues her testimony, her face portraying the impact of reliving this trauma. Ayari describes the last conversation she had with her sister:

> Llegó la hora, Dení se levantó, miró a mis padres y les dijo: "Al rato vengo."
> "Acompáñame a la puerta," me dijo. Iban a venir a buscarla, y ella iba a salir de la puerta del garaje a una hora precisa. Asombr. . .asombrosamente mis padres no

se levantaron. Cuando mi hermana volteó y les dijo, "Al rato vengo," fue la última vez que la vieron.

[The time came, Dení got up, looked at my parents and said: 'See you later'. 'Come and see me out', she said to me. They were coming for her, and she had to leave through the garage door at a precise time. Surpr. . .surprisingly my parents didn't get up. When my sister turned around and said, 'See you later', that was the last time they saw her.]

The conflation of the film's three narrative arcs in this sequence not only contributes to this 'hazy feeling' of haunting but also invokes the violence of the past: the site of Prieto Stock's death in the safe house. Ayari's repetition of her sister's final words – 'Al rato vengo' – suspends the narrative of the film in the temporal present of 1970s Mexico City, holding the spectators captive in this moment of frozen time. These words furthermore imply a return as Dení promises her family that she will be back, a promise left unfulfilled as she becomes one of the many victims killed by the Mexican state. By commencing the film in this manner, Riley introduces the haunting nature of Mexico's 'Dirty War' to the spectators and creates an anticipatory tone to the film as we await the return of Prieto Stock and other ghosts of this era. These spectral elements evoked in Prieto Stock's final words are indicative of Derrida's concept of hauntology as articulated in *Specters of Marx*: 'everything begins by the apparition of a spectre. More precisely by the waiting for this apparition' (Derrida 1994: 4). The spectators are unsettled and made uneasy by the impossibility of awaiting Prieto Stock's return. Furthermore, her final words, '[a]l rato vengo', serve as the film's context, as it 'begins by the apparition of a spectre', the spectre of Prieto Stock and other victims of the 'Dirty War'. The opening sequence that announces Prieto Stock's death sets the tone of the film as Riley – and the spectators – must contend with the unrecognised legacy of these (gendered) spectres.

Gendered Ghosts and the Violent Legacy of the 'Dirty War'

It is critical to position the conversations on gender and Mexico's armed struggle within contemporary discussions on the political climate, and the recent neoconservative shift which has conjured the ghosts of the armed struggle. *Flor en Otomí* was released at a politically fraught moment in Mexico's political climate, several months prior to the July 2012 presidential elections. The fraudulent election of Enrique Peña-Nieto signalled the return of the authoritarian rule of the PRI, the party that condoned the use of extra-legal practices which resulted in the torture, disappearance and death of political dissidents during the 'Dirty War'; and the party that sanctioned the raid on the Nepantla FLN safe house which led to the assassination of Dení Prieto Stock, Mario Sánchez Acosta, Anselmo Ríos Ríos and Carmen Ponce Custodio. The film emerged during a time when thousands organised to protest the imposition of Peña Nieto, and *Flor en Otomí* disrupts the PRI's attempt to distance itself from its violent past by making central the haunting caused by the crimes of the PRI regime.

In *Flor en Otomí*, we are confronted not only with the ghost of Prieto Stock (and other victims of the 'Dirty War') but also the absent yet 'seething presence' of the spectres of Mexico's past, as the film incessantly brings the spectator back to these spectres. Although the Mexican state attempts to move away from this past, this merely highlights the relationship between haunting and late capitalism, as Derrida explains:

> At a time when a new world disorder is attempting to instil its neo-capitalism and neo-liberalism, no disavowal has managed to rid itself of all Marx's ghosts. Hegemony still organizes the repression and thus the confirmation of a haunting. Haunting belongs to the structure of every hegemony. (Derrida 1994: 37)

With the return of the PRI in 2012, we see through *Flor en Otomí* and other cultural texts the presence of the ghosts from these repressed pasts. The hegemony of the Mexican state in its imposition of neoliberal economic sanctions in collusion with other structural and historical systems of domination – such as state brutality, *caciquismo* – has had violent repercussions in recent decades, for example with the passage of NAFTA in 1994, the Juárez feminicides, the 1997 massacre in Acteal, Chiapas, and the brutal repression of activists in San Salvador de Atenco in 2006. These incidences, among many others since the demise of Mexico's 'Dirty War', not only showcase contemporary instances of Mexican state violence but also conjure up ghosts of the 'Dirty War'. The film's disquieting, 'hazy feeling' demonstrates that the state has tried, unsuccessfully, to 'rid itself of all . . . ghosts' of this 'bygone era'. Instead, the normalisation of state violence in contemporary Mexico has only served to incessantly bring forth these ghosts of the 'Dirty War', to which Riley alludes in her project.

Despite centring on state crimes that occurred more than thirty years ago, these gaps – such as the lack of identifiers of any testimonial witness, the fragmented narrative structure –not only refer to Riley's specific editing approach but also allude to the legacy of 'Dirty War'-era violence. State-sanctioned violence is a form of gendered silencing and terrorism, as women's narratives remain further marginalised within this barely visible history as they are less likely than their male counterparts to speak out. The theoretical intersection of feminist discourse, Latin American cultural studies and visual culture has allowed us to create a 'hospitable memory' for these gendered ghosts, and to examine the film's representation of Prieto Stock's gendered and political subjectivity.

Returning to Gordon, she notes that haunting implies there is 'something-to-be-done' and this often 'draws us affectively, sometimes against our will and always a bit magically, into the structure of feeling of a reality we come to experience, not as cold knowledge, but as a transformative recognition' (Gordon 2008: 8). *Flor en Otomí* does not provide narrative closure or a redemptive narrative; instead, the film concludes with a final haunting image of the safe house and Popocatépetl volcano before the camera departs in a moving vehicle driving away from Nepantla, as Ayari's voice-over narration reads from Prieto Stock's letter to her family explaining her decision to join the guerrillas. Riley encourages us, as viewers and listeners, to inhabit the role of spectator-investigator, where we are invited to probe the (gendered) historiographical lapses created by Mexico's culture of impunity which give way to a 'transformative recognition' of the political possibilities of documentary film.

Bibliography

Aguilar Terrés, Luz, (ed.) (2007) *Memoria del primer encuentro nacional de mujeres exguerrilleras*, México: S.E.

Amores Perros, film, directed by Alejandro González Iñárritu. Mexico: Altavista/Zeta Films, 2000.

Barthes, Roland (1981), *Camera Lucida: Reflections on Photography*, New York: Hill and Wang.

Castellanos, Laura (2007), *Mexico armado*, Mexico City: Ediciones Era.

Derrida, Jacques (1994), *Specters of Marx: The State of the Debt, The Work of Mourning, and the New International*, translated by Peggy Kamuf. New York: Routledge.

El rumor del incendio, film, directed by Lagartijas Tiradas al Sol. Mexico: Teatro de la Universidad Nacional Autónoma de México, 2010.

Flor en Otomí, film, directed by Luisa Riley. Mexico/USA: Icarus Films, 2012.

Gordon, Avery (2008), *Ghostly Matters*, Minneapolis: University of Minnesota Press.

Hesford, Wendy S., and Wendy Kozol (eds) (2001), *Haunting Violations: Feminist Criticism and the Crisis of the 'Real'*, Urbana, IL: University of Illinois Press.

Montemayor, Carlos (1991), *Guerra en el paraíso*, Mexico: Editorial Diana.

Montemayor, Carlos (2010), *Las mujeres del alba*, Mexico: Random House Mondadori, S.A. de C.V.

Mulvey, Laura (2006), *Death 24x a Second: Stillness and the Moving Image*, London: Reaktion Books.

Nichols, Bill (1983), 'The Voice of Documentary', *Film Quarterly* 36:3, pp. 17–30.

Riley, Luisa. Personal interview. 17 July 2012.

Señorita extraviada, film, directed by Lourdes Portillo. Mexico: PBS/Women Make Movies, 2003.

Who is Dayani Cristal?, film, directed by Marc Silver. UK/Mexico: Pulse Films/Canana Films, 2013.

CHAPTER 4

Stages for an Assassination: Roles of Cinematic Landscape in Jorge Fons' *El atentado* (2010) and Carlos Bolado's *Colosio: el asesinato* (2012)

Maximiliano Maza-Pérez

A cinematic landscape can be interpreted as the filmic representation of a real or imagined space, which complies with a series of cultural functions that allow the aesthetic and ideological assessment of the film as a film discourse. According to Anton Escher (2006), the cinematic landscape is selectively perceived by the audience and can be accepted by it as representative of reality, despite being a production created intentionally. It is not that the landscape represented accurately reflects the way the audience perceives the physical world, but that the receiver trusts the representation. From these considerations, this chapter explores and characterises the functions performed by the cinematic landscape in *El atentado / The Attempt Dossier* (2010) by Jorge Fons and *Colosio: el asesinato / Colosio* (2012) by Carlos Bolado, two Mexican films that address political crimes from distinct aesthetic perspectives. In both films, representational spaces play a pivotal role in the reconstruction of historical events and, at the same time, are key elements that contribute to communicating the uncertainty about these historical moments that form part of an unresolved shared collective memory.

Since the premiere of Luis Estrada's film *La ley de Herodes / Herod's Law* (1999), the treatment of national political issues in Mexican cinema has taken a turn marked by a direct criticism of the abuses of governmental power and corruption among members of the ruling class. Unusually for a Mexican film about politics, Estrada's film dared to show the acronym, colours and logos of the main political parties in the country while openly criticising the abuses committed by the powerful during the presidential rule of Miguel Alemán (1946–52). After many decades of suffering the effects of censorship or self-censorship, Mexican filmmakers began the new century abandoning allusions, innuendos and indirect attacks that were the only way their films could refer to political events and criticise the figures of power.

While *La ley de Herodes* openly addressed the origins of the endemic corruption of the political system that was established in the country after the Partido de la Revolución Mexicana [Party of the Mexican Revolution] (PRM) became the Partido Revolucionario Institucional [Institutional Revolutionary Party] (PRI), the huge success achieved by the film is not solely due to its critical stance towards the institutions and political figures of the past, but because, as stated by Miriam Haddu (2007) and Ignacio Sánchez Prado (2014), its attack is implicitly extended to reach the administrations of Carlos Salinas (1988–94) and Ernesto Zedillo (1994–2000). For Haddu, 'The film's narrative, although set during the Miguel Alemán *sexenio*, continuously alludes to events, scandals and failed social projects that have become associated with Salinas' term in office' (2007: 30). In establishing a parallel between the modernising discourse of the Alemán regime and the advocacy of the benefits of neoliberal capitalism that distinguished the governments of Salinas and Zedillo, Luis Estrada's film offers a deeply pessimistic view of the transformation processes experienced by the country during both presidential terms.

One of the stylistic strategies that predominates in *La ley de Herodes* is the use of the cinematic landscape as an aesthetic device to communicate a critical stance towards those who betrayed the revolutionary ideals and became corrupted by ambition. As a concept emanating from cultural geography, a cinematic landscape can be interpreted as the filmic representation of a space, real or imagined, which is located at the level of staging in a film. In conjunction with framing and editing, the cinematic landscape contributes to creating the spatial dimension of the film, while complying with a number of cultural functions that allow its aesthetic and ideological assessment as filmic discourse. Being selectively perceived by the audience, a cinematic landscape can be accepted as representative of reality, despite being created intentionally as part of the production process (Escher 2006). As mentioned above, it is not necessary that the depicted landscape accurately reflects the way in which the audience perceives the physical world, but that the audience trusts the representation that unfolds before its eyes.

In *La ley de Herodes*, the cinematic landscape of the fictional town of San Pedro de los Saguaros mimics the classic representation of the rural environment of Mexican cinema of the Golden Age (1930s-50s), especially those established by the collaboration between the director, Emilio Fernández, and cinematographer, Gabriel Figueroa, with the aim of demystifying the triumph of the revolutionary epic (see Tierney 2007 and Ramírez Berg 2015). By comparing the similarities and contrasts between Estrada's film and *Río Escondido/Hidden River* (1947), one of the most iconic movies of the Fernández-Figueroa team, Liz Consuelo Rangel (2006: 65) notes the presence of 'blue skies with huge clouds', the appearance of 'saguaros in the foreground' and the presentation of the main characters 'from a very low angle' as three characteristics of Emilio Fernández films found in *Herod's Law* that work in the manner of aesthetic devices fulfilling a critical function. For Rangel,

> [Mientras que] *Río Escondido* crea mitos históricos e idealistas del triunfo de la Revolución y así infunde un sentimiento nacionalista en su audiencia, *La ley de Herodes* [. . .] rompe con las imágenes idealistas y muestra una realidad corrupta que se vivió en aquellos años. (2006: 66)

> [While] *Río Escondido* creates historical and idealistic myths of the triumph of the Revolution and thus instils a nationalistic feeling in its audience, *Herod's Law* [. . .] breaks the idealistic images and displays a corrupt reality that was lived in those years.[1]

Thus the portrayal of the cinematic landscape in *La ley de Herodes* as a stage for the abuse of power contradicts Aurelio de los Reyes' (1987) assessment of the role carried out by the landscape in Mexican cinema, from its origins to the Golden Age, as a vehicle for the expression of a nationalist sentiment. He suggests that, 'quizá la obsesión con el paisaje sea una constante de la producción de aquellos años; paisajismo y nacionalismo fueron términos equivalentes' (1987: 72) [it is possible to say that the obsession with landscape was a constant in film production of those years; the landscape and nationalism were equivalent terms]. In contrast, in *La ley de Herodes*, the nationalist landscape of classic Mexican cinema gave way to a revisionist and critical landscape, which is evident in recent films such as Alfonso Cuarón's *Y tu mamá también* (2001) and Carlos Reygadas' *Japón* (2002).

On the basis of the discussion so far, and considering that *La ley de Herodes* shares an approach evident in a growing number of Mexican films that resort to filmic representation of space as a tool to challenge the nationalist vocation attributed to the landscape in Mexican classic films, this chapter explores and characterises the functions performed by cinematic landscape in two Mexican films that deal with political crimes from very contrasting aesthetic perspectives: *El atentado/The Attempt Dossier* (2010) by Jorge Fons and Carlos Bolado's *Colosio: el asesinato/Colosio* (2012). In both films, the spaces of representation (Soja 1996) play a critical role in reconstructing the narrated historical events, while functioning as key elements that help to communicate the ideological stances of their directors.

El atentado was one of the four films produced with support from the Mexican Film Institute (Instituto Mexicano de Cinematografía, IMCINE), as part of the commemoration of the decade-long (2010–20) Bicentennial of Mexico's Independence and the Centennial of the Mexican Revolution.[2] These are periods that long dominate Mexican politics and whose commemorations are, therefore, necessarily burdened with their recurrence as unresolved hauntings. *El atentado* tells the story of the assassination attempt on the life of President Porfirio Díaz (1830–1915) (Arturo Beristáin) committed on 16 September 1897 by an alcoholic young man named Arnulfo Arroyo (José María Yazpik), who was lynched by a group of people who forcibly entered the police station where he was detained. The strange circumstances of his death led to an investigation which found that his murderers were actually agents of the metropolitan police under the command of General Inspector Eduardo Velázquez (Julio Bracho). The scandal prompted the immediate dismissal of Velázquez, who committed suicide in prison, in an act that heightened the mystery surrounding the case. The film is an adaptation of *El expediente del atentado* [The Assassination File] (2007), a novel written by the Mexican author Álvaro Uribe, which explores the hypothesis of the criminal conspiracy from inside Díaz's cabinet and examines the bonds of friendship between the failed assassin, his murderer and the writer Federico Gamboa (Daniel Giménez Cacho), author of the popular novel *Santa/Santa: A Novel of Mexico City* (1903), who was an officer of the Ministry of Foreign Affairs at the time of the attack on President Díaz and who serves as the main witness of the events depicted both in the novel and the film.

Centred on another political crime, *Colosio: el asesinato* tells the story of an alleged secret investigation aimed at uncovering the truth behind the murder of Luis Donaldo Colosio Murrieta (Enoc Leaño), the PRI presidential candidate, who was assassinated on 23 March 1994 during a campaign rally in Tijuana. In the film, the investigation is entrusted to *El Licenciado* [The Lawyer], an official of the Mexican government with strong resemblance to José Francisco Ruiz Massieu (Odiseo Bichir), former governor of the state of Guerrero and later secretary general of the PRI. *El Licenciado* delegates the operation to Andrés Vázquez (José María Yazpik), a military intelligence officer and trusted ally. The investigation by Vázquez and his team reveal the many inconsistencies in the case and, above all, confirm that the crime is the result of a plot orchestrated from within the government. Finally, the evidence found by the investigators leads to the office of *El Doctor* [The Doctor], José María Córdoba Montoya (Daniel Giménez Cacho), the mysterious character who has ordered the inquiry and whose title and appearance suggest that he is based on the head of the Office of the President and a politician very close to President Carlos Salinas (1988–94).

Although based on events in the public domain, the plot of the film is constructed from facts and situations inconsistent with the circumstances surrounding the assassination of Colosio. In March 1994, Córdoba Montoya did not have any formal authority over Ruiz Massieu, who didn't hold a public post, which would have supplied him with the necessary support to perform an investigation like the one which takes place in the film. Moreover, Córdoba Montoya himself was removed from office a week after the murder of Luis Donaldo Colosio and never again held a public position in the Mexican government (*Revista Proceso* 1995). Inaccurate in such factual detail, *Colosio: el asesinato* nonetheless, uses cinematic landscape to conjure the uncertainty of historiography.

From their opening scenes, both films show spaces of representation which are openly problematised, partly as a result of their intermedial relations. *El atentado* uses the theatre as a means of representing a version of Mexico City which unfolds before the viewer's eyes when the curtain of a *carpa* rises. Literally 'tent' theatre, the *carpa* was 'a popular Mexican theatrical tradition based on vaudeville and improvisation' (Shaw 2005: 125). As a form of popular theatre, the *carpa* has been a space where the popular classes could challenge the powerful through parody and humour. In improvised routines, comics criticised the rich and powerful, either openly or in a slightly veiled way. This opening establishes a liminal space in which the powerful can be attacked, foreshadowing the unfolding events.

As the curtain rises in *El atentado*, the streets and buildings of Mexico City are presented as an expansive backdrop. While this effect is at times clearly fictional, at others the film moves towards a form of documentary realism despite this presentational device. Representational spaces are varied, and their approach is achieved by wide shots and slow tracking shots. In that city painted on cardboard, the characters move as actors in a drama whose ending has already been written, so nothing can be done to change their destinies. The decision to theatricalise the staging of the film contradicts one of the functions that Andrew Higson (1984, 1987) attributes to cinematic landscape, which is to serve as a means to authenticate fiction. Because the film's events are not developed in real places or realistic simulations of such sites, the confirmation of their veracity remains suspended (Figure 4.1).

The strategy of spatial representation used in the first sequence of *Colosio: el asesinato* is diametrically opposed. The film begins with a quotation attributed to Vladimir Lenin, '[t]here are decades where nothing happens; and there are weeks where decades happen'. This quotation

Figure 4.1   Theatricalisation of the staging in *El atentado*.

emphasises the temporal over the spatial and the opening sequence continues with the representation of high-impact events in Mexican political life, such as: the murder of Cardinal Juan Jesús Posadas Ocampo on 24 May 1993; the entry into force of the North American Free Trade Agreement (NAFTA) and the uprising of the Zapatista Army of National Liberation (EZLN), both on 1 January 1994. This appears to be a way of signalling the indeterminacy of historical accuracy; although most of the events are given a date, they are presented without chronological order. This sequence culminates with the assassination of Colosio as the final point of a multi-layered event that transcends its own historical moment.

Notwithstanding the different ways in which *El atentado* and *Colosio: el asesinato* expose their spaces of representation, both films draw on the model of intermedial relationship that Jens Schröter denominates 'transformational intermediality' (2011: 2, 2012: 26) to define the dramatic spaces in which the stories unfold and in which one medium represents another and transforms it 'in such a way that its everyday, normal states of being are defamiliarized' (2012: 27). As a consequence, the qualities or characteristics of the represented medium are exposed as different, even opposed, to those from the representing medium, so that contrast and contradiction cause significant impacts on the functions performed by the cinematic landscape. Thus uncertainty and indeterminacy become central to the narratives.

In the first sequence of *Colosio: el asesinato*, spaces appear enclosed in boxes that occupy only a portion of the screen representing the media coverage of various events of public interest, arranged in a succession of video segments, press photos, political cartoons and magazine covers. Although serialisation underscores both the absence of spatial completeness as well as the lack of temporary order, the fragmentation of the spaces presented in *Colosio: el asesinato* does not negatively impact on its function of displaying them as actual historical sites. On the contrary, the cumulative effect of the sequence helps to authenticate the fiction, since each fragment of space shown contains enough identificatory elements for the viewer to recognise them as representative of the totality of an actual historical location. This is because each fragment corresponds to what Mikhail Bakhtin calls a chronotope or 'the intrinsic connectedness of temporal and spatial relationships that are artistically expressed' (1981: 84). Together, these operate in accordance with the procedures defined by Jean-Michel Adam and André Petitjean (2005) from the perspective of the descriptive analysis of discourse as the matching between the semiotic-discursive macro-operations of anchoring and aspectualisation, that is, naming a place on the basis of one or more of its essential characteristics.

The transformational intermediality raised in the first sequences of both films is reinforced in their central scenes. In *El atentado*, the staging of the attack by Arroyo on Díaz takes place in a setting that represents an area of the Alameda Park in Mexico City as it had been in 1897, with the Moorish pavilion that was located on that promenade painted on the backdrop. Meanwhile, *Colosio: el asesinato* draws upon the mediated staging of the assassination, through the meticulous review of the crime scene's videos carried out by Vázquez and his teammates. The obsessive scrutiny of the images recorded on several videotapes intensifies the fragmentation effect of the main representational space of the story – the dusty terrain of the Lomas Taurinas neighbourhood in Tijuana, Baja California, where Colosio was assassinated. Vázquez's decision not to travel to Tijuana and to entrust the local investigation to a police ally forces both the protagonists and the spectators to reconstruct the facts and imagine the places where they occurred, from a disordered succession of images that are intended to be logical, both in narrative and spatial terms (Figure 4.2).

By resorting to theatrical staging as a point of reference for the significant locations of the action, *El atentado* also meets the metaphorical function attributed by Higson (1984, 1987) to the cinematic landscape. Since the film re-enacts events from national political life that troubled Porfirian society, the cinematic landscape becomes a metaphor for the environment that surrounded the circles of power in Mexico from the late nineteenth century. In *El atentado*, besides the outdoor spaces such as the streets, squares, parks and other public spaces, there are indoor spaces such as

Figure 4.2   The staging of the attack in *El atentado*.

the saloons, *pulquerías* [bars], bedrooms, living rooms, offices, workshops, printing houses, horse-drawn carriages and trains used as locations in a farce that culminates in a tragic ending. The use of the stage takes the form of a play within a play, allowing the main action to stand in contrast to the actions of a couple of *carpa* comedians acting before an audience. Their performances of some key episodes mock the circumstances surrounding the alleged assault. By shifting between spaces and locations the metaphor of the theatre helps illustrate how events leading up to the attack on President Díaz permeated the popular imagination. The *carpa* is a space to play out the public's attitude to the assassination attempt and as a meta-textual metaphor for the film itself. Chris Lukinbeal stresses the importance of metaphors to understand cinematic landscape, stating that '[l]arge metaphors in film structure common ways of seeing the landscape for a social or cultural group. Cinematic landscapes are sites where meaning is contested and negotiated' (2005: 14). The use of the *carpa* as part of the cinematic landscape foregrounds the act of storytelling and invites reflection on class relations during this period.

In *Colosio: el asesinato*, the strategy of spatial representation causes the metaphorical function of the cinematic landscape to be differently realised. In the scenes where Andrés Vázquez and his team review the details of the assassination, the original footage, recorded in the place where Colosio was murdered and attributed to MVS and Argos TV, is cross-cut with images re-created by the filmmakers with the intention of adding points of view – such as close-ups of some of the suspects in the conspiracy – that the original footage does not have. The editing of the audio-visual material adds to the spatial and narrative fragmentation presented in the first sequence of the film in a strategy aimed at building very precise meanings about the guilt of some of the characters involved in the Colosio case (Haddu 2015: 457). These fictional elements incorporated into the film by Bolado transform the images of Colosio's murder into metaphors of the thoughts and emotions of the protagonists of the film and its viewers. In this regard, Haddu points out that

> [t]hese images become crucial witnesses to the event and their scrutiny alludes to hidden plots, unknown participants, and a possible conspiracy against the presidential candidate [. . .]. The extensive examination of the frame-by-frame contents of the PGR footage does indeed lead the main character in the film to piece together the necessary evidence in order to formulate a conclusion that points towards a state-instigated plot to assassinate Colosio. (2015: 464) (Figure 4.3)

Moreover, the cinematic landscape of *El atentado* also serves as spectacle. This role, which Higson succinctly defined as 'a visually pleasurable lure to the spectator's eye' (1984: 3) is the most inherently spatial function of any cinematic landscape, because its value is not defined from a relationship of subordination to a non-spatial element (drama, historical event, character or sociocultural context) but is determined by the affective relationship established between the filmed space and the spectators that through the look seize and re-signify it. Similarly, the cinematic spectacularisation

Figure 4.3 Fragmentation of space in *Colosio: el asesinato*.

of space conveys the director's ideological point of view to the audience, either directly or indirectly, through the eyes of the characters. *El atentado* is told from the perspective of the director Fons, whereby space is projected directly as an artificial environment, flat and without depth, because the events depicted in the narrative are equally artificial and superficial.

As for the role of the cinematic landscape as spectacle in *Colosio: el asesinato* and its relationship to the workings of social memory, the footage of the candidate's murder constitutes a horror show from which it is impossible to look away, because, largely, human beings are fascinated with all that they do not fully understand. Rafael Argullol refers to this power of seduction exercised by tragic images as an 'attraction to the abyss' (2012: 93–4) that belongs to the spirit of Romanticism, and which is located the same way in painting as it is in cinematic images. Thus images of murder in *Colosio: el asesinato* operate according to what Pierre Nora (1989: 12) called *lieux de mémoire*, that is, places of remembrance where people constantly return with the intention of giving meaning to the past. Haddu interprets the morbid repetition of the moment of Colosio's death in the film as a calling up of the 'cultural trauma' suffered by Mexican society in 1994 and attributes it to the need to find an explanation for the tragedy by its repeated viewing,

> [m]irroring the condition of the individual subject that has become traumatized, a collective may find itself re-living and re-examining the traumatic event that has ruptured the social fabric and shattered its last illusions of peace, as was the case of Mexico in 1994. (2015: 462)

Discussing the relationship between cinema, space and memory, Astrid Erll notes that the landscapes and locations of the films function as detonators of collective memory: '[t]his last function of media – to trigger collective remembrance – is performed above all by particular locations or landscapes [. . .] which the mnemonic community associates with specific narratives about the past' (2011: 128). But what kind of narrative about the past is associated with the broad but artificial cinematic landscape of *El atentado*? Which concept of memory is related to the incomplete but realistic space of *Colosio: el asesinato*? The answers to these questions seem to be located in the distinction between Maurice Hallbwachs' (1980) concept of 'collective memory', and the cultural notions of 'communicative memory' of Jan Assmann (2008) and the 'shared memory' of Paul Ricœur (2010).

For Hallbwachs, collective memory grows over time and is the product of the interaction between media and the institutions, starting with the retellings of the past that are shared by a society (see Erll, 2011: 15). Ancient history and the events of an absolute and mythical past, which are foundational to a community and which become traditions, are located in collective memory. The central function of this type of memory, named 'cultural memory' by Assmann (2008: 110), is the formation of cultural identity and is oriented towards the needs and interests of society in the present. By contrast, Assmann's communicative memory consists of everyday experiences shared by the population, which are projected onto a horizon limited by a few generations before disappearing or becoming part of the collective memory. Ricœur claims that shared memory exists in 'un plano intermedio de referencias en el que se realizan concretamente los intercambios entre la memoria viva de las personas individuales y la memoria pública de las comunidades a las que pertenecemos' (2010: 172) [an intermediate level of reference in which the exchanges between the living memory of individual persons and the public memory of the communities to which we belong are concretely carried out]. Based on these concepts, we can distinguish two approaches to the relationship between cinematic landscape and memory in *El atentado* and *Colosio: el asesinato*. With its open references to a distant past, conceived from the imagination created by the theatre and other forms of art such as the landscape painting of José María Velasco (1840–1912), the engravings of José Guadalupe Posada (1852–1913), as well as studio photography and the incipient press photography of the late nineteenth century, the cinematic landscape of *El atentado* points towards the narrative that has leaked into the country's collective memory about the *Porfirian pax* as an age of stealthy deceit, over whose ruins were erected the political institutions that have governed Mexico since the triumph of the Revolution. Meanwhile, in *Colosio: el asesinato*, the lack of a spatial totality is related to the way the film deploys the communicative memory of many Mexicans who remember and share that tragic moment when they were trying to make sense of and give order to the confusion of images that appeared before their eyes.

The inability of audio-visual media to capture the experience of reliving the past is also hinted at in one of the final scenes of *El atentado*, in which Álvaro Mateos (José María de Tavira), reporter for the newspaper *El Imparcial*, shows Gamboa a photograph of the capture of Arnulfo Arroyo, allegedly taken by an American tourist. Together with the snapshot, Mateos gives Gamboa the enlargement of a portion of the image where the attacker supposedly appears, surrounded by several people. Although the enlargement makes it possible to distinguish details that are unnoticeable in the original picture, the only visible part of Arroyo's body is the back of his head. Gamboa hardly pays attention to this primitive technical experiment that attempts to confirm the veracity of the news event by concentrating on the details. For him, it is clear that Arroyo's failed attack is only the first link to a chain of events orchestrated from inside Díaz's cabinet with which he prefers not to get involved.

Using a different strategy in the climactic sequence of *Colosio: el asesinato*, officer Vázquez comes to the same conclusion as Gamboa. On submitting his report to *El Licenciado*, Vázquez and his colleagues stage the assassination of Colosio in an act reminiscent of the theatrical performance in *El atentado*. The stage is a pine forest, a completely different landscape from the arid terrain of Lomas Taurinas. It is a subtle but direct allusion to the place where the crime could have been ordered, *Los Pinos* [The Pines], the official residence of the Mexican president. As in *El atentado*, the strategy is to resort to the re-enactment as a way to make sense of the events. This has a further meta-fictional function. It works as a nod to the audience that *Colosio: el asesinato*, itself, is a re-staging of reality that has only a tentative hold on historical accuracy.

From the analysis of the functions fulfilled by the cinematic landscape in the films *El atentado* and *Colosio: el asesinato*, some significant conclusions emerge. First, the confirmation of the authenticity of the events presented depends not so much on the events being carried out in one boundaried place but on the fragment of space shown being recognised as representative of the whole of a given real historical place. Second, the metaphorical function of the cinematic landscape is completely intentional in both films, achieved by the decision to incorporate very specific scenic elements, such as the theatrical backdrops in *El atentado* or the images cross-cut with the original footage in *Colosio: el asesinato*. Third, the ability of the cinematic landscape to evoke both long-term collective memory and other types of cultural memory is fulfilled through its spectacularisation. Together, these aesthetic strategies help to build the ideological discourse in Fons and Bolado's films.

Conclusion

As discussed at the beginning of the chapter, contemporary Mexican films draw on the stylised cinematographic representation of space as a vehicle to challenge the notion of landscape as a symbol of nationalism, as it was used in Mexican classic films. Likewise, although many of them look towards events and places of the past, at the same time they draw many parallels with the present. Political crimes such as those depicted in *El atentado* were common in Mexico in the first decades of the twentieth century, but they had become unusual until Colosio's murder in 1994.

By 2012, the year when *Colosio: el asesinato* was released, violence in the Mexican political arena had become commonplace again. More than thirty mayors have been murdered since the beginning of Felipe Calderón's presidency in 2006 (*Aristegui Noticias* 2012), two secretaries of state died in suspect plane crashes, and the president himself was revealed to have received death threats during the first months of his presidential term (*Revista Proceso* 2012). However, rumours, lies and multiple versions have prevailed over clear and forceful lines of investigation. The function of the deliberate stylisation and artifice of the *carpa* in *El atentado* and the fragmentary reconstruction of *Colosio: el asesinato* convey the challenges of sifting through political fictions in order to get to the truth.

Notes

1. Unless otherwise stated, all translations are my own.
2. The other films supported under this scheme were: *Hidalgo – La historia jamás contada* [Hidalgo – The Untold Story, formerly *Hidalgo-Molière*] by Antonio Serrano; Luis Estrada's film *El infierno/Hell* and the documentary *La cámara Casasola* [Casasola's Camera] by Carlos Rodrigo Montes de Oca. Three other films set during Independence and the Revolution that did not compete in this call for submissions also received support from IMCINE: *Chicogrande* by Felipe Cazals, *El baile de San Juan* [The Dance of San Juan] by Francisco Athié and *Revolución/Revolution* by several directors. All were released in 2010.

Bibliography

Adam, Jean-Michel, and Petitjean, André (2005), *Le texte descriptif: poétique historique et linguistique textuelle*, Paris: Armand Colin.

Argullol, Rafael (2012), *La atracción del abismo: Un itinerario por el paisaje romántico*, Barcelona: Acantilado Bolsillo.

Aristegui Noticias (2012), '31 alcaldes asesinados durante el sexenio de Felipe Calderón', *Aristegui Noticias*, 30 October. Available at <https://aristeguinoticias.com/3010/mexico/31–alcaldes-asesinados-durante-el-sexenio-de-felipe-calderon> (last accessed 20 February 2018).

Assmann, Jan (2008), 'Communicative and Cultural Memory', in Astrid Erll and Ansgar Nünning (eds), *Cultural Memory Studies: An International and Interdisciplinary Handbook*, Berlin and New York: De Gruyter, pp. 109–18.

Bakhtin, Mikhail (1981), 'Forms of Time and of the Chronotope in the Novel', in Mikhail Bakhtin and Michael Holquist (eds), *The Dialogic Imagination*, Austin: University of Texas Press, pp. 84–258.

Chicogrande, film, directed by Felipe Cazals. Mexico: FIDECINE, IMCINE, and Sierra Alta Films, 2010.

Colosio: el asesinato / Colosio, film, directed by Carlos Bolado. Mexico, Spain, France, and Colombia: Udachi Productions, Alebrije Cine y Video, and Oberón Cinematográfica, 2012.

de los Reyes, Aurelio (1987), *Medio siglo de cine mexicano (1896–1947)*, México: Editorial Trillas.

El atentado / The Attempt Dossier, film, directed by Jorge Fons. Mexico: Alebrije Cine y Video, CONACULTA, and Grupo Santander, 2010.

El baile de San Juan / The Dance of San Juan, film, directed by Francisco Athié. Mexico, France, Germany, and Spain: 8 et Plus Productions, Alejibre Producciones, and Arroba Films S.A. de C.V., 2010.

El infierno / Hell, film, directed by Luis Estrada. Mexico: Bandidos Films, CONACULTA, IMCINE, FOPROCINE and Comisión BI 100, 2010.

Erll, Astrid (2011), *Memory in Culture*, New York: Palgrave Macmillan.

Escher, Anton (2006), 'The Geography of Cinema: A Cinematic World', *Erdkunde*, 60:4: pp. 307–14.

Gamboa, Federico (2014), *Santa*, México: Editores Mexicanos Unidos.

Haddu, Miriam (2007), *Contemporary Mexican Cinema, 1988–1999: History, Space and Identity*, Lewiston, NY: The Edwin Mellen Press.

Haddu, Miriam (2015), 'Political Violence and Fiction in Mexican Film: The Case of Carlos Bolado's *Colosio: el asesinato / Colosio: The Assassination* (2012)', *Journal of Latin American Cultural Studies*, 24:4, pp. 453–73.

Hallbwachs, Maurice (1980), *The Collective Memory*, Chicago: University of Chicago Press.

Hidalgo: La historia jamás contada / Hidalgo / The Untold Story, film, directed by Antonio Serrano. Mexico: Astillero Films, 2010.

Higson, Andrew (1984), 'Space, Place, Spectacle: Landscape and Townscape in the "Kitchen Sink" Film', *Screen*, 25:2–21, pp. 133–56.

Higson, Andrew (1987), 'The Landscapes of Television', *Landscape Research*, 12:3, pp. 8–13.

Instituto Mexicano de Cinematografía (2009), 'Informe del primer semestre de 2009'. Available at <http://www.imcine.gob.mx/OBLIGACIONES/INFORMES/INF_PRIMER_SEM_2009.pdf> (last accessed 30 April 2016).

La cámara Casasola / Casasola's Camera, film, directed by Carlos Rodrigo Montes de Oca. Mexico: IMCINE and Eréndira Producciones, 2010.

La ley de Herodes / Herod's Law, film, directed by Luis Estrada. Mexico: Alta Vista Films, Bandido Films, and IMCINE, 1999.

Lukinbeal, Chris (2005), 'Cinematic Landscapes', *Journal of Cultural Geography*, 23:1, pp. 3–22.

Nora, Pierre (1989), 'Between Memory and History: *Les Lieux de Mémoire*', *Representations*, 26, pp. 7–25.

Ramírez Berg, Charles (2015), *The Classical Mexican Cinema: The Poetics of the Exceptional Golden Age Films*, Austin: University of Texas Press.

Rangel, Liz Consuelo (2006), '*La ley de Herodes* (1999) vs. *Río Escondido* (1947): La desmitificación del triunfo de la Revolución Mexicana', *Divergencias: Revista de Estudios Lingüísticos y Literarios*, 4:1, pp. 61–9.

Revista Proceso (1995), 'En la oscuridad, a la sombra de Salinas, José Córdoba acumuló un poder inédito', 3 April. Available at <http://www.proceso.com.mx/168646/en-la-oscuridad-a-la-sombra-de-salinas-jose-cordoba-acumulo-un-poder-inedito> (last accessed 25 February 2018).

Revista Proceso (2012), 'Revela Calderón que enfrentó riesgo de atentado al inicio de su gobierno', 18 August. Available at <http://www.proceso.com.mx/317449/revela-calderon-que-enfrento-riesgo-de-atentado-al-inicio-de-su-gobierno> (last accessed 25 February 2018).

Revolución/Revolution, Film, directed by Mariana Chenillo, Fernando Eimbcke, Amat Escalante, Gael García Bernal, Rodrigo García, Diego Luna, Gerardo Naranjo, Rodrigo Plá, Carlos Reygadas and Patricia Riggen. Mexico: Canana Films, IMCINE and Mantarraya Producciones, 2010.

Ricœur, Paul (2010), *La memoria, la historia, el olvido*, Madrid: Editorial Trotta.

Río Escondido/Hidden River, film, directed by Emilio Fernández. Mexico: Producciones Raúl de Anda, 1947.

Sánchez Prado, Ignacio (2014), *Screening Neoliberalism: Transforming Mexican Cinema, 1988–2012*, Nashville: Vanderbilt University Press.

Shaw, Lisa (2005), 'Carpa', in Lisa Shaw and Stephanie Dennison (eds), *Pop Culture Latin America!: Media, Arts, and Lifestyle*, Santa Barbara: ABC-CLIO, Inc.

Schröter, Jens (2011), 'Discourses and Models of Intermediality', in *CLCWeb: Comparative Literature and Culture*, 13:3. Available at <http://dx.doi.org/10.7771/1481–4374.1790> (last accessed 25 February 2018).

Schröter, Jens (2012), 'Four Models of Intermediality', in Bernd Herzogenrath (ed.), *Travels in Intermedia[lity]*, Hanover, NH: Dartmouth University Press, pp. 15–36.

Soja, Edward W. (1996), *Thirdspace: Journeys to Los Angeles and Other Real-and-Imagined Places*, Malden, MA: Blackwell Publishing.

Tierney, Dolores (2007), *Emilio Fernández: Pictures in the Margins*, Manchester and New York: Manchester University Press.

Uribe, Álvaro (2007), *El expediente del atentado*, México: Tusquets.

CHAPTER 5

Aliens as Superheroes: Science Fiction, Immigration and Dulce Pinzón's 'The Real Story of the Superheroes'

Catherine Leen

Mexican photographer Dulce Pinzón's 2012 series 'The Real Story of the Superheroes' celebrates Mexican and Latina/o immigrant workers in the United States by radically re-imagining the figure of the superhero.[1] The book that compiles the images from the series features twenty photographs of immigrant workers living in New York, eighteen of whom are from Mexico, while the other two are from Puerto Rico and Ecuador (Pinzón 2012). Pinzón's work is a striking combination of documentary photography and fantasy, as her subjects go about their everyday jobs dressed as superheroes. She was inspired to take the photographs in the wake of the traumatic events of 9/11, when the increased hostility towards migrants in the United States was coupled with an intense celebration of the heroes who attempted to cope with the terrorist attacks. This celebration, in turn, led to a resurgence of the superhero genre.

Pinzón's choice of the visual motif of the superhero raises the paradox that these popular cultural icons are frequently engaged in defending the United States from alien invasions, which are often thinly veiled references to fear of immigrants. This rhetoric has intensified since the 2016 campaign of President Donald Trump, who has persistently vilified immigrants, particularly those from Mexico, and dehumanised them by constantly referring to them as 'illegal aliens'. This chapter contends that Pinzón contests such characterisations of immigrants by presenting Latina/o heroes through the appropriation of a visual language normally synonymous with US hegemony and oppression. Pinzón employs the hybridity inherent in superhero narratives, and which has marked photography in Mexico from its inception, to re-imagine the genre. Moreover, she brings the ghostly figure of the so-called alien into the spotlight, casting migrant workers as transnational heroes who contribute immensely to the economies on both sides of the border. In the United States, they take up poorly paid, often difficult jobs. In Mexico, they support their communities of origin through the sending of remittances. Pinzón's series will be analysed with reference to photographic history, the use of science fiction as political protest, and its relation to a strong tradition of Chicana/o visual culture that reflects on and celebrates hybrid identities.

The Perils of Photography and Pinzón's Superheroes

'The Real Story of the Superheroes' liberates its subjects from their ghostly presence in US society as lowly paid workers whose work is deemed necessary but is undervalued and often rendered invisible. The characters don their superhero outfits as they work in domestic spaces as nannies, in factory spaces as garment workers, in industrial spaces as construction workers, in anonymous kitchens as cooks or in peripheral spaces as delivery boys, sex workers or cleaners. Just as the spaces that Pinzón depicts are often shadowy and liminal, so too does her work cross the boundaries between photographic genres and between Mexico, the United States, and the spaces of diaspora. Her work is a striking combination of documentary photography, portraiture and fantasy. In the alternate universe of Pinzón's photographs, Spiderman is a window washer, Cat Woman a nanny, and Robin a gigolo in Times Square. A small number of the protagonists in the series hold jobs that symbolise authority and even social change, however. Captain America is a real-life police officer, thus reversing the stereotype that the immigrant is always a criminal, while the Birdman is a union organiser.

Pinzón's series conflates at least three main photographic genres: the portrait, documentary photography and tableau photography. The latter would seem to be the antithesis to documentary in that it has been described 'as "constructed" or "staged" photography, since the elements depicted and even the precise camera angle are worked out in advance and drawn together to articulate a preconceived idea for the creation of the image' (Cotton 2014: 9). The images are, on one level, portraits of individuals who are identified as such by the titles that accompany them, which list their name, place of origin, occupation and the amount of money they send home weekly or monthly. Their definition as portraits is complicated, however, by the fact that all but one of the images are full length, so that attention is not necessarily drawn to the face, and many of the subjects look away from the camera, so that at times their features are not seen clearly. By far the most unusual aspect of the images as portraits is that many of the subjects' faces are obscured by masks, thus in a number of cases the sitter cannot be identified. This is a problematic point also in the definition of the photographs as documentary. Although the compositions seem as casual as snapshots, unlike the 'slice of life' portraits by renowned photographer Diane Arbus, whose subjects were inherently dramatic characters such as circus performers, twins or cross-dressers, what lends these photographs their drama is the flamboyant superhero costumes that the subjects don as they go about their everyday lives. There is no suggestion that they habitually do so, however, and so while they are undoubtedly documentary images in that the people and locations are real, they are also carefully staged.

The juxtaposition between the mundane and the extraordinary here in the casting of bodies that do not generally conform to the athletic, muscular build of the prototypical superhero may also suggest an element of ironic detachment from the subjects. A related issue is the possible exploitation of the people portrayed, whose images are used by the photographer in the commercial realm of galleries and publishing houses. Initially, some of the images make for uncomfortable viewing. If the photographs of the aforementioned police officer and union organiser demonstrate how migrants can not only thrive in US society but also play important roles in the legal and justice systems, not all of the subjects enjoy such status. The portraits of the builders, service industry workers, sex workers or nannies in the series are often reveal the most wistful and vulnerable of the sitters. Green Lantern, a superintendent whose real name is Román Romero and who comes from the Mexican state of Guerrero, is seen perched on a roll of fibreglass wrapped in plastic. The open can of Sprite at his feet and the television mounted precariously opposite him suggests that he is taking a break from work in this cramped space, surrounded by construction materials in a half-built room. The scene is illuminated by the harsh, pinkish light emanating from the television set, which creates a rather otherworldly glow. Although his eyes are obscured by his mask, Román's slumped posture, with his chin resting on his gloved hand, and downcast mouth give him a weary, forlorn appearance. Similarly, Batman, a taxi driver called Federico Martinez who sends home $250 a week, looks away from his customer, lost in thought, while she does not give him a second glance. This image crystallises both the invisibility and the loneliness of life for many migrants in the United States.

Pinzón, like her subjects, is an immigrant living and working in New York City. Unlike them, however, she has had the benefit of an extensive postgraduate education that is usually only a possibility for the wealthy in Mexico. She studied media and communications at the Universidad de las Américas in Puebla, and photography at Indiana University of Pennsylvania and the International Center of Photography, New York. In his essay on Mexico City entitled 'Identity Hour, Or What Photographs Would You Take of the Endless City' Carlos Monsiváis (1997) highlights the tendency of photographers to focus on the extremes of wealth and poverty that are immediately noticeable in the capital. He lists what he terms 'the contrasts between rich and poor, the constant antagonism between the shadow of opulence and the formalities of misery' as some of the most common city scenes that are captured on film (Monsiváis 1997: 31–2). Monsiváis's comment on what has been described as the aestheticisation of poverty recalls Susan Sontag's observation that photographers, who have until recently generally hailed from the wealthier echelons of society, have always been fascinated by social inequality:

> Photography has always been fascinated by social heights and lower depths. [. . .] Social misery has inspired the comfortably-off with the urge to take pictures, the gentlest of predations, in order to document a hidden reality, that is, a reality hidden from them. (Sontag 1977: 55)

This gap between the lived experience of photographers and their subjects is thrown into sharp relief by the case of one of the most iconic photographs of poverty in the United States, Dorothea Lange's 'Migrant Mother'. This much-reproduced Depression-era image of a careworn mother surrounded by her children has a rich but contradictory meta-textual history. Lange, as is well known, shot the image in 1936 when she was working as a photographer for the Resettlement Administration, which later became known as the Farm Security Administration. It was one of six shots she took on a brief visit to a pea pickers' camp in Nimpo, California, that was published in the *San Francisco News* as part of an article that same year calling for relief for these poverty-stricken workers. The campaign was a success, and the workers were given aid (Hariman and Lucaites 2007: 53). This uplifting narrative about the transforming power of this photograph of extreme poverty was complicated when the subject of the photograph was interviewed years later. In 1978, a journalist for the *Los Angeles Times* tracked down the woman in Lange's photograph, who had not been named originally, and identified her as Florence Thompson. Thompson's comments contrast sharply with her image as a pensive, passive emblem of poverty. She expresses anger about the commodification of her image and regrets that Lange ever took it, noting that the photographer never asked her name, assured her that the photograph would not be sold and promised to send her a copy, which she did not receive. As Hariman and Lucaites assert, this epilogue exposes the tensions between the successful use of an image and the attitude of its subject: 'we see what happens when the living, named subject of the photograph speaks back in a way that undermines the structure of feeling that the photograph has conventionally evoked'

(Hariman and Lucaites 2007: 61–2). What this case most explicitly high-lights is the difficulties for photographers in negotiating the often unequal exchange between photographers as image makes and curators and their subjects, whose images can be used in ways that they did not anticipate and that they are powerless to control.

Pinzón avoids the problematic and even exploitative encounter between subject and photographer identified by Monsiváis and Sontag and exem-plified in 'Migrant Mother' in a number of ways. Firstly, her photographs are the result of a long-term project that entailed close collaboration with her subjects, whom she clearly knows personally. Secondly, the people behind these highly mediated pictures are either the members of the same trade union for immigrant workers that Pinzón herself belongs to, or her neighbours in New York City. Finally, and perhaps most importantly, she breaks down the traditional distinction and consequent distance between photographer and subject by appearing in the final image in the series, casting off what Lange famously termed the photographer's 'cloak of invisibility' (Gordon 2009: 25). With wry humour, given the fact that, as the photographer, her presence is keenly felt in each image, she portrays herself as a garment worker dressed as the Invisible Woman in the final photograph in the series. If Pinzón initially uses the disjunction between the bodies represented in her photographs and the prototypical images of superheroes to draw the viewer in, her images are not ironic. As Rebecca Wanzo reminds us,

> [t]he costumed superhero is a thoroughly American genre—in the nationalist sense of America that displaces the continents that construct the region. As a sign of America, Superman's chiseled silhouette, white skin and idealisation of the nation became the standard superhero archetype. (Wanzo 2015: 317)

This correlation between masculinity, whiteness and the superhero rele-gates women and people of colour to liminal roles in US popular culture and in society more generally. By clothing her subjects in costumes that immediately suggest supernatural attributes, Pinzón compels the viewer to see the all-too-familiar Latina/o nanny, waiter or construction worker anew. In so doing, she invites them to consider why these bodies have often been seen not as heroes but as villainous others – a deep-seated antipathy stirred up all too successfully by the inflammatory statements of President Trump (Chomsky 2017: 264). By conflating their mundane realities with captions that underline their superhuman work ethic and commitment to their families, Pinzón effectively pays tribute to these workers' remarkable contributions to communities on both sides of the US–Mexico border.

Her work shares a close affinity with that of Nigerian-born British artist Yinka Shonibare, who also conflates the uncomfortable subjects of class and race in his photographs. Like Pinzón, Shonibare uses well-known images as a kind of palimpsest that is radically re-imagined. Inspired by William Hogarth's *The Rake's Progress* (1735), a satirical series of paintings about the debauchery of the rich in contemporary society, Shonibare constructs scenes set in historical interiors and featuring the artist and the other sitters in Victorian costumes. As Cotton observes, in photographs such as 'Diary of a Victorian Dandy 19:00 Hours' (1998), 'The Caucasians are shown to be "colour-blind" to the artist and his skin colour. His place within Victorian society appears to be protected by his guise as a dandy, the declaration of self-fashioning and authenticity being assured through pronounced artifice in manner and dress' (Cotton 1998: 56–7). It is unlikely that the viewers of Pinzón's photographs would not be struck by the casting of Latina/o subjects as heroes rather than villains or aliens given the tropes of the science-fiction genre in the United States. Nonetheless, in the images themselves, the figures that surround the superhero protagonists do not seem to find this situation remarkable and their costumes clearly identify them as heroes recognisable as such, not only through their dress but through their unflagging work ethic and loyalty to their families at home.

Science Fiction as Metaphor and Metonym

Another potentially contentious issue is that Pinzón's choice of the visual motif of the superhero raises the paradox that these popular cultural icons are frequently engaged in defending the United States from alien invasions, which are often thinly veiled references to fear of immigrants. This seemingly dubious choice is explained by Pinzón herself, who notes that she was inspired to use the motif of the superhero to represent Mexican migrant workers when she saw a Spiderman costume in a shop in Mexico City, reminding her of the huge popularity of superheroes on both sides of the border. In her artist's statement, she comments further that:

> After September 11th, the notion of the 'hero' began to rear its head in the public consciousness more and more frequently. The notion served a necessity in a time of national and global crisis to acknowledge those who showed extraordinary courage or determination in the face of danger, sometimes even sacrificing their lives in an attempt to save others. (Pinzón 2012: np)

This observation has also been made by numerous critics and journalists, and undoubtedly the superhero genre has seen a notable resurgence since the traumatic events of 9/11. Superheroes such as Spiderman, the Fantastic Four, and Superman crowded onto cinema screens, and new characters such as the protagonists of Brad Bird's *The Incredibles* (2004) suggested that being a superhero was fun for all the family. Explanations for this revival in the popularity of the superhero in US culture are numerous and varied. Comic writer Mark Millar believes that people needed diversion and entertainment to make the grim reality of the chaos, insecurity and economic devastation that ensued from the terrorist attacks bearable: 'There's always peaks and troughs and when things are VERY bad ... a world war, September 11th, the financial crisis, people look for more of an escape and a way to have a good time (cited in Mosby 2013: 317). Other critics have suggested that human powers were found wanting before and after the attacks and that only superheroes could be relied upon to defend North America in the future. Commenting on the previous failed attempt on the World Trade Center and the subsequent attack on September 11th, Sharon Packer notes that, 'If such an event could occur, not once, but twice, then surely we need a superhero to sweep down from the sky and do the job better than the FBI, the Armed Forces, and the Special Services' (Packer 2010: 48–9).

The post-9/11 scenario for Mexican and Latina/o migrant workers was also traumatic, as suspicion of immigrants increased dramatically. This heightened antipathy led to a change in the focus of the US–Mexico border control to include the prevention of terrorism, despite the absence of any link between the perpetrators of the attacks and Mexico. Fernando Romero describes this new agenda as follows:

> Since the terrorist attacks, numerous bills pertaining to national security and immigration have changed the way the United States, a country often referred to as a nation of immigrants, receives foreign visitors and migrants. September 11, 2001, marked a major turning point for the US–Mexico border, because now in addition to illegal immigration, drug trafficking and the many other issues surrounding the border region, it has become an important element of the U.S. War on terrorism. (Romero 2008: 73)

The increased militarisation of the US–Mexico border has forced those who attempt to enter the United States without documents into harsher and harsher terrain, most notably the desert of Arizona, where the likelihood of surviving the week-long walk to the United States is extremely low as would-be migrants can only carry enough water to last for two days. For those who do survive the crossing, the traditional notion of cyclical migration, whereby migrant workers remained in the United States for a period and returned home, is no longer a possibility, as if do they reach the United States, they cannot risk journeying back and forth.

The post-9/11 scenario, which combined veneration of the superhero with increasing hostility towards immigrants, led Pinzón to rewrite the superhero narrative to pay homage to migrant workers routinely referred to as 'illegal aliens' irrespective of whether or not they are undocumented. Notably, this is not an issue that her photographs explicitly address, as she wishes to celebrate migrants whether or not they are documented. The Spiderman image, which is the first in the series, sets the scene for those that follow as it presents the superhero incongruously engaged in the mundane, poorly paid labour of cleaning windows as he hangs outside the exterior wall of a high-rise building. As we have observed, Pinzón provides a caption for this and the other photographs that identifies her subject by name and state and country of origin. The Spiderman image powerfully establishes Pinzón's stated objective of celebrating workers, who despite having no superpowers labour in extreme conditions to support their families and communities. It also addresses the question of the invisibility of these workers. Although the image would initially not appear to refer explicitly to an immigrant worker, as the protagonist's face is obscured by a mask, in fact it is the wearing of this mask that communicates the idea of the migrant worker's invisibility. Moreover, he is depicted as at once part of and apart from the commerce represented by the office building, as he literally hangs outside it. The vertical wall of the building divides the frame in half, thus reinforcing the idea that the migrant worker is not really a part of the city that they inhabit because of their subaltern status but also because the amount of money they send home means that they cannot enjoy the attractions of New York, a notoriously expensive metropolis. The backstory to this image reinforces the sense of isolation experienced by the migrant worker, just as Spiderman was envisaged by the creator of the comic book in which he first appeared in 1962 as a kind of everyman, a nerdy teen called Peter Parker. In a chapter in the comic book entitled 'Midtown High's Only Professional Wallflower', Parker is depicted as isolated because of his rejection by the cool students at his high school. Notably, in this image we see a wall again act a physical and metaphorical division, this time between Parker's outcast teen and his future alter ego (Morrison 2012: 94). Unusually for a superhero, Spiderman is also a suitable figure with which to start the series as he has a strong Latino connection. He was re-imagined in 2011 as Miles Morales, who was of Cuban and African-American descent. Jesus Trivino noted that this was not Spiderman's first Latino incarnation, explaining that '[i]n 1992,

Marvel developed 2099, a comic series set over 100 years in the future, and introduced Spiderman 2099, Mexican and Irish geneticist Miguel O'Hara' (Trivino 2013: np).

The Spiderman image then, both in its visual impact and in the combination of the superhero backstory with the caption, suggests that the migrant worker lives in an in-between world that is characterised by Chicana theorist Gloria Anzaldúa as *nepantla*. Anzaldúa coined this term by adapting the Nahuatl word for 'the space between two bodies of water, the space between two worlds. It is a liminal space, a space where you are not this or that but where you are changing. You haven't got into the new identity yet and haven't left the old identity behind either' (Anzaldúa 2007: 237). Anzaldúa uses this term to describe the tensions and difficulties experienced by Mexican-Americans and Latina/os in the United States, who negotiate two different cultures but struggle to be truly accepted by either. Pinzón's conflation of this theory with the appealing concept of the superhero means that the figures in her photographs are not outcasts like Parker, but rather unsung defenders of the family who become aspirational figures on both sides of the border.

In their use of the science-fiction trope of the superhero, the images also reference a long tradition in Mexican and Chicana/o art of subverting the stereotype of the 'illegal alien' by using themes and figures related to science fiction. Contemporary Mexico has a strong graphic tradition dating back to the work of José Guadalupe Posada (1852–1913). As Montserrat Galí i Boadella maintains, Posada transformed the use of the otherworldly and even surreal image of the skeleton from part of a religious practice related to the rituals of death to 'a reflection on the living, their defects, weaknesses, and vices. Fundamentally the *calaveras* [skulls] do not deal with death, and still less with metaphysical speculation, but rather with the satire and mockery of the living' (Galí i Boadella 2008: 57). The inventive hybridity of Posada's work is reflected in later superheroes such as Kalimán. Created in the early 1960s by Mexican Rafael Navarro Huerta and Cuban expatriate Modesto Vásquez González, *Kalimán* sold weekly for twenty-six consecutive years (Fernández L'Hoeste 2009: 57). The character is clearly related, as his name indicates, to the goddess Kali, and he is notably peaceful. He never kills, respects all of nature's creatures, can communicate with animals and morph into any other form. He also has a young Egyptian companion called Solín, who has been compared to Batman's Robin (Fernández L'Hoeste 2009: 58). While the ramifications of this complex melange of references are too complex to unpack here, the mere existence and popularity of this character suggests that Mexican superheroes are the product of a cultural engagement that embraces diversity. Moreover, Kalimán's engagement with various belief systems is entirely in tune with Mexico's long tradition of religious syncretism (Fernández L'Hoeste 2009: 62). More recently, the link between superheroes and political activism in Mexico was revived through the figure of Superbarrio, a grassroots activist who represented people left homeless or in substandard housing as a result of a 1985 earthquake. Dressed as a masked wrestler, Superbarrio effectively represented this issue to politicians (Levi 2001: 347).

This tradition of incorporating diverse, intercultural superhero motifs into Mexican popular culture has been employed to great effect by performance artist and writer Guillermo Gómez-Peña to subvert the demonisation of the Mexican migrant. Gómez-Peña's *Codex Espangliensis: From Columbus to the Border Patrol* (2000) is an elaborate text produced in collaboration with Enrique Chagoya and Felicia Rice. Inspired by pre-Hispanic codices, it opens from left to right and contains texts in various languages and images that range from pre-Columbian gods to comic-book superheroes. While partly a satirical examination of the ubiquitous influence of US culture on the world, which is reflected in Superman's battles against pre-Columbian deities, the text has the serious message of asserting the richness of Latin American culture through a text no less elaborate than the original codexes, which like it, present a radical rewriting of history. Filmmaker Alex Rivera, who noted that Gómez-Peña's work has had a profound influence on his own career, also used the tropes of science fiction to create a trailer for the alien invasion film *Independence Day* in 1997, which he transformed into *El día de la independencia*. In this spoof trailer, Rivera takes the stereotype of the 'illegal alien' to its logical extreme by casting sombreros as space ships that destroy the White House by spraying it with hot chili sauce. Rivera, in turn, has collaborated with the Chicano cartoonist Lalo Alcaraz, whose cartoons have been collected in volumes such as *La Cucaracha* (2004a) and *Migra Mouse* (2004b). The latter volume re-appropriates the image of Mickey Mouse, often considered a shorthand for US cultural hegemony, to satirise the Immigration and Naturalisation Service (INS), commonly known by Spanish speakers as 'La migra'. Alcaraz has created memorable science-fiction parodies such as an alternative version of *Star Wars* (George Lucas, 1977), and the Mexterminator, a satirical portrayal of Arnold Schwarzenegger, who is best known for playing a ruthless cyborg with a human appearance in the 1984 film *The Terminator* (James Cameron, 1984). As is well known, Schwarzenegger is himself an immigrant, who spoke in terms that are as fantastic as his science-fiction alter ego about his feeling that the United States was his real home in his autobiography *Total Recall*:

> I'd fantasize sometimes: What if my mother had gotten frisky at the end of the war, and my father wasn't really Gustav Schwarzenegger but, in fact, an American GI? That could explain why I always had the powerful feeling that America is my true home. Or what if the hospital where she gave birth to me was actually in an American-occupied zone? Wouldn't that count as being born on US soil? (Schwarzenegger 2012: 464)

Despite his own background, when Schwarzenegger became governor of California in 2003, he displayed little empathy for other immigrants and pursued fervently anti-Latino policies.

The continuation of such policies in contemporary North America has led the decidedly innocuous character of Dora the Explorer to be targeted as part of the debate on US immigration policy. Dora, a young girl who speaks Spanish with a North American accent, is beloved by children who follow her adventures and learn some Spanish in the process. Arizona's notoriously racist bill SB 1070 allows authorities to demand proof of legal residence in the United States from anyone suspected of being undocumented, makes it illegal to employ an undocumented worker or even transport them in a car, and requires state employees, including teachers, to report anyone they suspect of being undocumented. The bill consistently refers to undocumented immigrants as aliens and has been the subject of heated debate since it was signed into law in 2010 (Cisneros 2013: 112–13). After SB 1070 became law, the children's television channel, Nickelodeon, was drawn into this debate as the network was inundated with calls and emails demanding to know Dora the Explorer's national origin and legal status in the United States. The channel refused to comment on either issue (Tareen 2010: np). In the wake of the incident, a fake mug shot was created by opponents of the Arizona law, ridiculing the fact that hysteria about immigration had led to criminal accusations against a fictional cartoon character. Supporters of SB 1070 in turn adopted this image, however, to suggest that the threat from so-called illegal aliens was such that US children were not safe from the dangerous foreign influence supposedly represented by Dora.

What distinguishes Pinzón's work from these parodies of stereotypes of the immigrant is that the hybrid characters she creates are positive and aspirational, thus distancing them from previous satires of the 'illegal alien' that undoubtedly call into question negative stereotypes but may have had the unfortunate unintended effect of reinforcing the association between undocumented workers and so-called illegal aliens. Pinzón's work also references the strong graphic art tradition in Mexican culture. This reference is most clearly suggested by the one Mexican superhero featured in the series, El Chapulín Colorado, who is himself a humorous parody of the US superhero genre. Like the comic super-agent Maxwell Smart, El Chapulín Colorado is a hapless, bumbling character who only ever manages to avert disaster through a series of slapstick adventures that unexpectedly turn out for the best. Apart from the fact that El Chapulín Colorado does not conform to the athletic, muscular physical archetype of the US superhero, he is also rather dim-witted, and his catchphrases, such as '¡Más agil que una tortuga! [Fitter than a tortoise!] and '¡Más noble que una lechuga!' [Nobler than a lettuce!], are less than inspiring. What is most notable about this character in terms of Pinzón's images is that she uses it to signal the fact that Mexico and the United States, despite having an undoubtedly conflictive history, also share a long tradition of transnational cultural exchange.

The intercultural nature of Mexico's superheroes is strongly reflected in the history of Mexican photography, whose development was shaped in part by the presence in Mexico of such internationally renowned photographers as Edward Weston, Tina Modotti, Henri Cartier-Bresson and Paul Strand, all of whom lived and worked there in the 1930s (Debroise 2001: 143). Strand, a US photographer who became chief of the department of photography and cinematography in the Mexican Secretariat of Public Education, suggested that successful photographic portraits of people 'make others care about them by revealing the core of their humanness'. (Jeffrey 2008: 120) Similarly, Trish Ziff observed that so many images of Mexico have been taken by non-Mexicans that it can be difficult to find images that, as she puts it 'see beyond the exotic' (Ziff 1990: 10). Despite the seemingly fantastic costumes of her subjects, Pinzón's project shares these humanising objectives. Pinzón's series manages to fulfil both Strand's idea of communicating the humanity of the subject and Ziff's idea of transcending the theatrical but othering vision of Mexico. Pinzón does this by picturing her subjects in costumes that initially seem exotic but in fact suture the Mexican worker into the family of the US superhero, thus paradoxically emphasising their humanity by casting them as extraordinary figures with superhuman powers.

The Chicana/o Art of Hybridity: From Wonder Woman to the Virgen de Guadalupe

The image in the series that is most identifiable as a portrait is that of Wonder Woman, María Luisa Romero, a native of the Mexican state of

Puebla who works in a laundromat and sends home $150 a week. This is one of the few images where the subject's face, which is distinctly non-European, is seen in detail. María Luisa's gaze does not confront the viewer, however, as it is directed beyond the frame of the photograph. Her wistful yet resolute looking is intimately connected to time, a theme further underlined by the presence of a clock in the background. It has often been noted that every photograph is a kind of memento mori that freezes a particular time in its frame, but as John Berger asserts, the viewer must give it meaning by expanding this isolated moment: 'An instant photographed can only acquire meaning insofar as the viewer can read into it a duration extending beyond itself. When we find a photograph meaningful, we are lending it a past and a future' (Berger and Mohr 2016: 89).

The choice of costume here is far from incidental. Wonder Woman was created in 1941 by William Moulton Marston, a psychologist who invented the polygraph and was the author of the academic text *The Emotions of Normal People*. Wonder Woman began her life on the all-female Paradise Island as the daughter of the Queen of the Amazons (Saunders 2011). When air force pilot Captain Steve Trevor's plane crashed on the island, she fell in love with him and returned with him to the United States as an immigrant, a land she adopted and pledged to defend. Wonder Woman's extraordinary wisdom is matched by her superhuman strength and she is, in the original version of her story, a gay icon. Marston frequently pictured Wonder Woman lassoing or otherwise physically restraining her opponents, a physical subjugation that produced in both parties what he rather quaintly terms 'pleasant captivation emotion' (Saunders 2011: 44). Wonder Woman's unique catchphrase 'Suffering Sappho!' further underlines these tendencies. She was adopted as a feminist icon by *Ms.* magazine, on whose cover she appeared in 1972 with an essay by Gloria Steinem (Saunders 2011: 36–46). What is striking about Pinzon's portrayal of Wonder Woman is that it is not immediately obvious as a version of the superheroine, given that she stands in a static pose far removed from Wonder Woman's physicality and seems lost in thought.

In the photograph of Wonder Woman, the past is clearly Mexico but the subject's present and perhaps uncertain future lie in the United States. While it may seem to be a cliché in itself to immediately associate an image of a Mexican woman with the Virgen de Guadalupe, I would also interpret this portrait as part of an artistic tradition that re-imagines the Virgen de Guadalupe as a border-crossing superheroine. Not only is the Virgen de Guadalupe the patron of Mexico, and therefore a link to the sitter's past, but María Luisa's striking face, cloak and motionless posture recall traditional representations of the patron saint known as the 'brown virgin'. The idea that Pinzón's image represents another version of the Virgen de Guadalupe is suggested not only through the connections with these famous images by Chicana artists but also through Mexico's tradition of religious syncretism. Mexican and Chicana/o art has long explored the mixture of pre-Columbian and Catholic emblems that remains an integral part of religious worship in Mexico and the Mexican diaspora. This hybridity and the unproblematic mixing of the sacred and the secular, if not the profane, in Mexican culture is most notable in the best-known Mexican superhero, El Santo. As his name suggests, this figure, who started his career as a wrestler, has divine properties, and many of his film exploits depict him warding off threats to Mexico. His contemporary counterparts include Fray Tormenta, who was the inspiration for the Hollywood film *Nacho Libre* (Jared Hess, 2006). This wrestler was a real-life priest who used the money he earned from his matches to support his parish. To return to Pinzón's image, her Wonder Woman is certainly a feminist icon in the mould of the US superheroine, but her calm, pensive pose is decidedly reminiscent of the original image of the Virgen de Guadalupe, an image that has traditionally had a strong political as well as religious resonance.

Re-appropriating the Virgen de Guadalupe has such a strong tradition in feminist Chicana art that the artist Alma López and the writer and academic Alicia Gaspar de Alba (2011) have devoted a book to the subject (López and Gaspar de Alba 2011). This tradition started with Ester Hernández's 1974 pen-and-ink drawing entitled 'La Virgen de Guadalupe Defendiendo los Derechos de los Xicanos' [The Virgin of Guadalupe Defending the Rights of the Chicanos]. Pinzón's image is also reminiscent of another series of portraits produced in the 1970s by Yolanda López. López famously re-imagined the Virgen de Guadalupe through images that featured her mother and grandmother stitching the cloak of stars that adorns the Virgin's figure, as well as a self-portrait of the artist jogging. By recasting the cloak in the domestic sphere of the seamstress, López simultaneously relates it to the lives of real women and celebrates female manual labour. Her image of herself, which portrays her in an active pose more like the superheroine than the Virgin, has also been circulated widely as a photograph, which has clear parallels with Pinzón's Wonder Woman.

Like the Virgen de Guadalupe, this hybrid Wonder Woman bridges the *nepantla* or in-between space mentioned by Anzaldúa through her self-sacrifice, a virtue synonymous with the patroness of Mexico, but also by her strength and endurance. While we do not know whether she is a mother or not, she and the other subjects in the series all adopt a parental

role through the remittances that they send home to support their families. Moreover, like the Virgin, the migrants presented in this series form a
kind of bridge between home and the United States through their contact
with their loved ones and the money their labour allows them to send.

Conclusion: Fake News, Real Heroes

One of the most damaging aspects of President Donald Trump's attacks
on migrants, and Mexicans in particular, is that he distorts the reality of
their situation. In addition to his frequent remarks about building a 'beau-
tiful' wall that Mexico will pay for, despite clear opposition to this notion
from Mexico, he has also made pronouncements about preventing 'illegal'
immigrants from accessing public benefits (Ye Hee Lee 2017: np). This
idea that Mexicans and other immigrants are a drain on public resources
harks back to the Great Depression, when migrants were scapegoated and
even deported from the United States as they were blamed for the nation's
economic woes (Gutiérrez 1995: 72). Trump paints a misleading picture
of migrants as criminals who are a burden on the state, when in fact the
vast majority of migrants, including Pinzón's subjects, are extremely
hard-working law-abiding people. The title of Pinzón's series takes on a
new significance in the contemporary United States, as it stresses that she
is telling the real story behind the hysteria and falsehoods that charac-
terise much reporting about migrants. Moreover, as Mata notes, Pinzón
overturns the convention of carefully concealing the true identity of the
superhero by providing factual information about her subjects:

> The descriptive label works to unmask the superhero and identify her/his alter
> ego while stripping his/her labor of the level of secrecy under which it normally
> functions. While some of the individuals remain masked because of the nature of
> the hero costume, these individuals are not anonymous. Pinzón's emphasis on the
> identities of these workers rejects the imperialist practice of capturing images of
> nameless bodies of colour. No longer nameless faces, they are real people, with real
> names, real lives, and real communities. (Mata 2014: 135)

It is in the paradoxical juxtaposition of the fantastic and the real that
Pinzón captures the individuality of the subjects she celebrates and most
successfully bridges the gap between photographer and subject and
between subject and viewer.

In her subversive yet humorous and appealing photographs, Pinzón
manages to celebrate her subjects while raising uncomfortable questions about marginalisation and racism. Her approach is not didactic or
judgemental, however, and so does not preclude a positive response to

the images on the part of US audiences. By re-imagining superheroes as migrant workers, Pinzón uses a visual language that is immediately familiar and appealing to US audiences. She persuades them to contemplate images that ultimately reassert the idea of family, albeit in a transnational context where the term may describe members of a diaspora united by a union rather than the nuclear family, which has been ruptured by neoliberal global economic imperatives. Her activism celebrates real heroes and elevates them to the status of the contemporary sci-fi icons, a fact confirmed by the title of the series, which does not explain why these people are superheroes but rather purports to tell us their real story, thus challenging alarmist anti-immigrant narratives. Through her radical re-appropriation of US pop-culture icons, she creates hybrid figures with whom both Latinos and non-Latinos can identify, thus presenting the situation of the workers in a new light that may lead to increased empathy with them and which strongly asserts their humanity.

Note

1. The images from the series can be seen on Pinzón's web page, available at www.dulcepinzon.com.

Bibliography

Alcaraz, Lalo (2004a), *La Cucaracha*, Kansas City: Andrews McMeel Publishing.

Alcaraz, Lalo (2004b), *Migra Mouse: Political Cartoons on Immigration*, New York: Akashic Books.

Anzaldúa, Gloria (2007), *Borderlands / La frontera: The New Mestiza*, San Francisco: Aunt Lute Books.

Berger, John, and Mohr, Jean (2016), *Another Way of Telling: A Possible Theory of Photography*, London: Bloomsbury.

Chomsky, Noam (2017), *Who Rules the World?*, New York: Penguin Random House.

Cisneros, Josue David (2013), *The Border Crossed Us: Rhetorics of Borders, Citizenship and Latina/o Identity*, Tuscaloosa: University of Alabama Press.

Cotton, Charlotte (2014), *The Photograph as Contemporary Art*, London: Thames & Hudson.

Debroise, Olivier (2001), *Mexican Suite: A History of Photography in Mexico*, Austin: University of Texas Press.

Fernández L'Hoeste, Héctor (2009), 'Race and Gender in "The Adventures of Kalimán"', in Héctor Fernández L'Hoeste and Juan Polete (eds), *Redrawing the Nation: National Identity in Latin/o American Comics*, New York: Palgrave Macmillan.

Galí i Boadella, Monsterrat (2008), 'José Guadalupe Posada: Tradition and Modernity in Images', in José Lebrero Stals and Ramón Reverté (eds), *Posada: Mexican Engraver*, Seville: Centro Andaluz de Arte Contemporáneo, pp. 45–62.

Gómez-Peña, Guillermo, Enrique Chagoya, and Felicia Rice (2000), *Codex Espangliensis: From Columbus to the Border Patrol*, San Francisco: City Lights Publishers.

Gordon, Linda (2009), *Dorothea Lange: A Life Beyond Limits*, New York: W. W. Norton & Co.

Gutiérrez, David C. (1995), *Walls and Mirrors: Mexican Americans, Mexican Immigrants and the Politics of Ethnicity*, Berkeley: University of California Press.

Hariman, Robert, and John Louis Lucaites (2007), *No Caption Needed: Iconic Photographs, Public Culture, and Liberal Democracy*, Chicago: University of Chicago Press.

Jeffrey, Ian (2008), *How to Read a Photograph: Understanding, Interpreting and Enjoying the Great Photographers*, London: Thames & Hudson.

Levi, Heather (2001), 'Masked Media: The Adventures of Lucha Libre on the Small Screen', in Gilbert M. Joseph et al. (eds), *Fragments of a Golden Age: The Politics of Culture in Mexico Since 1940*, Durham, NC: Duke University Press.

López, Alma, and Alicia Gaspar de Alba (eds) (2011), *Our Lady of Controversy: Alma López's Irreverent Apparition*, Austin: University of Texas Press.

Mata, Irene (2014), *Domestic Disturbances: Re-Imagining Narratives of Gender, Labor, and Immigration*, Austin: University of Texas Press.

Monsiváis, Carlos (1997), *Mexican Postcards*. London: Verso.

Morrison, Grant (2012), *Supergods: Our World in the Age of the Superhero*, London: Vintage.

Mosby, John (2013), *Gods, Monsters and Mutants: How the Superhero Movies Came of Age in the Twenty-First Century*, Scotts Valley, CA: JM2 Publications.

Nacho Libre, film, directed by Jared Hess. USA/Mexico: Paramount Pictures, 2006.

Packer, Sharon (2010), *Superheroes and Superegos: Analyzing the Minds Behind the Masks*, Santa Barbara, ABC-CLIO.

Pinzón, Dulce (2012), *The Real Story of the Superheroes*, Barcelona: RM Verlag.

Romero, Fernando (2008), *Hyper-Border: The Contemporary U.S.-Mexico Border and its Future*, New York: Princeton Architectural Press.

Saunders, Ben (2011), *Do the Gods Wear Capes? Spirituality, Fantasy, and Superheroes*, London: Continuum.

Schwarzenegger, Arnold (2012), *Total Recall: My Unbelievably True Life Story*, New York: Simon & Schuster.

Sontag, Susan (1977), *On Photography*, New York: Penguin.

Star Wars, film, directed by George Lucas. USA: LucasFilm, 1977.

Tareen, Sophia (2010), 'Dora the Explorer: Illegal Immigrant?', *Associated Press*, 21 May. Available at <http://www.nbcnews.com/id/37279132/ns/us_news-life/t/dora-explorer-illegal-immigrant/#.U1fLCfldWtI> (last accessed 10 January 2017).

The Incredibles, film, directed by Brad Bird. USA: Pixar Animation Studios, 2004.

The Terminator, film, directed by James Cameron. UK/USA: Cinema '84, 1984.

Trivino, Jesus (2013), '10 Superheros You Never Knew Were Latino', *Latina*, 3 May. Available at: <http://www.latina.com/entertainment/movies/super heroes-you-never-knew-were-latino> (last accessed 10 January 2017).

Wanzo, Rebecca (2015), 'It's a Hero? Black Comics and Satirizing Subjection', in Frances Gateward and James Jennings. (eds), *The Blacker the Ink: Constructions of Black Identity in Comics & Sequential Art*, New Brunswick, NJ: Rutgers University Press, pp. 314–33.

Ye Hee Lee, Michelle (2017), 'President Trump's claim about immigrants "immediately" collecting "welfare"', *Washington Post*, 4 August. Available at <https://www.washingtonpost.com/news/fact-checker/wp/2017/08/04/president-trumps-claim-about-immigrants-immediately-collecting-wel-fare/?utm_term=.1b009dcc4e40> (last accessed 10 August 2017).

Ziff, Trish (1990), *Between Worlds: Contemporary Mexican Photography*, New York: New Amsterdam Books.

CHAPTER 6

#YoSoy132 as a Continuation of the 1968 Legacy

Jessica Wax-Edwards

The 1968 Tlatelolco massacre, where government-led troops violently supressed student protesters, represents a persisting hauntological narrative in Mexican history. This clash between students and the state exposed, and came to exemplify, the authoritarian hegemony of the Partido Revolucionario Institucional's [Institutional Revolutionary Party] (PRI) seventy-one years in power. The ongoing official absence of government accountability for the unjustifiable violence perpetrated against these peaceful protesters, however, remains a source of societal trauma that continues to corrode public trust in the political apparatus as a whole.

After a twelve-year hiatus, the 2012 presidential elections threatened, and ultimately realised, a return of the PRI to executive power. During the presidential campaigns, a mass student-led protest known as #YoSoy132 emerged to contest the candidacy of the former PRI governor Enrique Peña Nieto as well as the impartiality of the news media in reporting on this public dissent. The emergence and popularity of the #YoSoy132 movement in the face of ongoing political impunity testifies to the residual effects of unresolved historical suffering in contemporary Mexican society. As will be explored in this chapter, under Peña Nieto's governance in the year 2006 protestors in the town of Atenco were brutally repressed by police, resulting in numerous human rights violations. The state's role in this repression, and notably the part of the PRI, recalls that of the 1968 government and foregrounds an unchanged governmental response of brutality in the face of protest.

This chapter will explore the links between the legacy of the events of 1968 and the #YoSoy132 student movement, with specific reference to the graphic art produced by students of both. My visual analyses of cultural legacy will be informed by the notion of spectrality and haunting as introduced by Jacques Derrida in the *Specters of Marx* (1994). As argued by Derrida (1994: 175), the study of hauntology is borne out of a 'concern for justice'. In the sections below, this chapter will explore the contexts of recent historical injustice that characterised and coloured the 2012 general presidential elections. These injustices, seen in the 2006 repression of Atenco and a historical trend for controversy relating to elections in Mexico, provide further examples of the ruptures and ghosts that fuelled the emergence of the #YoSoy132 movement and the graphic artworks produced alongside it. This chapter will examine the visual parallels that exist between the artistic outputs of the 1968 and 2012 student protest movements and, specifically, the role of graphic art in disseminating and articulating civil dissent. In this vein, this chapter seeks to address the extent to which the graphic art produced by #YoSoy132 members is influenced by the art of the 1968 protestors and the complex memory of that violent repression.

Contexts: Atenco

The town of San Salvador Atenco in the Estado de México, a state bordering the Federal District, was governed in the year 2006 by President of the Republic Enrique Peña Nieto. On 3 and 4 May 2006, the people of Atenco fell victim to the conditions of violent state repression that resulted in numerous human rights violations, and the memory of the attack persists in the public imaginary.[1] In this section, I will provide a brief overview of these events as a means of contextualising the controversy of Peña Nieto's campaign for the presidency.

During the early hours of the morning on the 3 May 2006, a group of sixty flower vendors were prevented from setting up their stands in a public market in Texcoco by state police; those who resisted suffered violent responses from the officers. The group called to the Frente de los Pueblos en Defensa de la Tierra (FPDT) [People's Front in Defence of the Land], who in the years 2001–2 successfully protested government plans to build an airport terminal on their farmland. Since this victory, the FPDT has become a symbol of resistance in the collective memory (Castillo 2007: 121). The FPDT responded by blockading the motorway between Lecheria and Texcoco just as they had done in 2001. Police were sent to remove the blockade but their unsuccessful attempts at repression quickly escalated to full-blown violent conflict. By 3pm on the same day, the confrontation had resulted in many wounded and one dead, 14-year-old Javier Cortés Santiago; it would later come to light that Javier had been killed by a bullet fired by the police (Suprema Corte de Justicia de la Nación 3/2006: 6–9). As tensions and conflict escalated, the national television media repeatedly propagated images of an unconscious police officer being kicked between the legs and called on the government to deploy more aggressive police action (Gibler 2011). In the early hours of the following day such police action was implemented: special forces in the *Policía Federal Preventiva* [Federal Preventive Police] (now known simply as the *Policía Federal* [Federal Police]) supported by state police and the ASES (members of the *Agencia de Seguridad Estatal* [State Security Agency]), numbering approximately 3,500 officers, entered the town of Atenco in what was known as *Operación Rescate* [Operation Rescue]. During the operation officers brutally beat residents and violently raided houses, indiscriminately arresting anyone they encountered, allegedly in search of the supposed leaders of the conflict (Zamora Lomelí 2010: 66).

The violent government-instigated action in San Salvador Atenco on 3 and 4 May 2006 was the cause of profound public outrage. Mexican critic Elena Poniatowska, whose book *La noche de Tlatelolco* [the Night of Tlatelolco] (1971) was the only published testimonial account of the 1968 massacre for twenty years, described the events in Atenco as, 'algo que nos duele mucho' [something that hurts us a lot] (Rodríguez 2006).[2] The 2006 violence persists in public memory as an example of authoritarian repression and unresolved collective trauma. This is attested to by the sundry cultural responses of various filmmakers that seek to contend with the societal impact of the events, including the Canal 6 de Julio documentary entitled *Atenco: romper el cerco* [Atenco: breaking the siege] (2007) and Kyzza Terrazas' award-winning fiction feature *El lenguaje de los machetes* [Machete language] (2011).

In the words of the writer and activist Humberto Robles (2010/11: 131), 'El caso Atenco es un caso paradigmático de terrorismo de Estado, de criminalización de la lucha social y del triunfo de un pueblo en resistencia' [The Atenco case is a paradigmatic case of state terrorism, the criminalisation of social struggle and the triumph of a people in resistance]. As Robles identifies, the PRI's treatment of protestors in Atenco is both reflective and a perpetuation of its notoriously authoritarian dealings with protestors in 1968. Indeed, the repetitious continuation of these unresolved traumas is witnessed again six years later in the mass student protests against Peña Nieto's presidential campaign. The 2012 protests attest to the irreversible effects of extreme police aggression and its lingering impact on the public psyche. As such, the next section of this chapter will explore the strategy of the Peña Nieto's presidential campaign and its historical implications in light of the impunity.

Election Campaigns and the Return of the PRI to Power

Having located Enrique Peña Nieto's highly contested presidential campaign within the contexts of the violent repression in Atenco, in this section

I will elaborate on the further controversies surrounding the candidate's electoral bid. This section will examine the historical trend of polemic associated with presidential elections as a means of contextualising the events of the 2012 elections.

Election campaigns in Mexico are frequently the site of controversy, protest and social upheaval. The foundation of Mexico's current political system, the 1910 Mexican Revolution, was borne as a result of electoral crisis.[3] Such crises have plagued presidential elections into Mexico's present, as Antonio Ugues (2010: 499) argues, 'anyone familiar with the history of Mexican politics knows [that] electoral competition pre-1988 was merely a façade'. The 1988 presidential elections in particular, where the PRI candidate Carlos Salinas de Gortari ran against frontrunner opposition candidate Cuauhtémoc Cárdenas, are widely held to be fraudulent (Ugues 2010: 497–8). On the evening of the elections Cárdenas was leading the polling count but following an unexpected malfunction of the electoral computers, Salinas was announced the winner later that night. It was only in the year 2000 that an alternative political party, the Partido Acción Nacional (PAN) [National Action Party] succeeded to executive office. In the following elections in the year 2006, the negligible margin of victory (0.56%) between the PAN candidate Felipe Calderón and the Partido de la Revolución Democrática (PRD) [Party of the Democratic Revolution] candidate Andrés Manuel López Obrador led to mass protest, societal polarisation and widespread accusations of electoral fraud (Maihold 2006: 170–1).

Artistic responses to these historical instances of political crisis have been varied. Documentary cinema, in particular, has provided an instrument to interrogate and contend with these narratives of political instability and corruption. The documentary production company Canal 6 de Julio sourced its name from the date of the 1988 Mexican presidential elections and continues to play a vital role in exposing abuses of power and their impact on social structures in Mexico. This includes producing a documentary investigating the events of the 2006 conflict in Atenco entitled *Atenco: romper el cerco* [Atenco: breaking the siege] (2007) (Traverso and Wilson 2014: 198). The 2006 elections provoked multiple documentary responses including Luis Mandoki's box-office hit *Fraude: México, 2006* [Fraud: Mexico, 2006] (2007) and Lorenzo Hagerman's *0.56%: ¿Qué le pasó a México?* [0.56%: what happened to Mexico?] (2010).[4]

The 2012 general elections fit neatly into Mexico's historical pattern of a divisive and controversial process of presidential appointment. Following a twelve-year absence from high office, the PRI was poised to return to Los Pinos and from the start of his campaign in March 2012

Peña Nieto led the polls as the presidential favourite (Olmeda and Armesto 2013: 248). Although Peña Nieto was marketed as the young face of a new and modernised PRI, his detractors perceived him as a political puppet for the authoritarian PRI of the past (Olmeda and Armesto 2013: 248–9). This derisory viewpoint was partly influenced by the leading candidate's heavily mediatised campaign and the accompanying allegations that he had received favourable coverage and support from Mexico's largest television network Televisa (Arsenault 2012).

As will be explored in the following section, the evolution of the #YoSoy132 movement was directly linked to both Peña Nieto's handling of the Atencan protest and the media and government's occlusive and misrepresentative response to candid civil dissent.

Emergence of the #YoSoy132 Student Movement

The 2012 student movement known as #YoSoy132 arose as a direct result of perceived media bias and the threat of continued political impunity. This section explores the emergence of the movement, its crucial links to historical trauma and social media and its rise to becoming one of the most important social actors in recent Mexican history.

On 11 May 2012, PRI candidate for the presidency Enrique Peña Nieto was invited to address students of the Universidad Iberoamericana, a private Catholic university in Mexico City known as La Ibero. During the lecture students held signs and yelled criticisms that protested Peña Nieto's candidacy as well as his role in the brutal repression of citizens in the town of Atenco (Nuñez Albarrán 2012: 255). Peña Nieto publicly defended his actions to the students by stating that 'Fue una decisión que asumo personalmente para restablecer el orden y la paz, lo hice en el uso legítimo de la fuerza que corresponde al Estado. [I personally accept responsibility for a decision undertaken to restore order and peace, I did so using the legitimate use of force that corresponds to the state] (Garcia 2012). This justification for the state's use of brutal force to subdue protest as a means of restoring order recalls the circumstances of the repression that led to the massacre of student protesters at Tlatelolco square in 1968. Peña Nieto's actions as governor, along with this rationalisation of those actions, align his campaign with the authoritarian politics of the past. Notably, two days later, the PRD candidate López Obrador compared Peña Nieto's rhetoric to that of former president Gustavo Díaz Ordaz in the wake of the 1968 Tlatelolco massacre (Figueiras Tapia 2012: 56). This familiar response to state violence highlights how the unresolved nature of historical injustice continues to impact and shape the present socio-political climate. Through

its persistent haunting, the ghost of this past violence plagues and destabilises the present. As such, Peña Nieto's words only served to incite the
audience further and he was obliged to leave the stage via the backdoor,
taking refuge in the university bathrooms from the mass of student protesters that pursued him (Garcia 2012).

In an attempt to discount the validity of the incident, representatives
of the PRI and the media responded by labelling the protesters as '*porros*'
[idiots], '*acarreados*' [people transported to a polling station by the gov-
ernment], '*ajenos*' [outsiders] or members of the opposition PRD party
planted to sabotage the event (Vite Pérez 2016: 671). Such an action by
the PRI to discredit the legitimacy of protestors recalls similar efforts by
Luis Echeverría and Gustavo Díaz Ordaz to label protesters as dangerous communists during the 1968 student protests (Figueiras Tapia 2012:
13). Indeed, it was ultimately this attempt to mislabel the students and
redirect public attention to the political opposition that spawned the student movement (Figueiras Tapia 2012: 48). Since the events of October
1968, there exists a tense and inauspicious relationship between the PRI's
political power and the university community in Mexico (Figueiras Tapia
2012: 39). The combination of continued political impunity embodied by
Peña Nieto and the return of the PRI, explored in the previous section of
this chapter, and the further efforts to silence dissent by the right-wing
party stoked an outrage in the students that would fuel the movement. The
campaign's recourse to a duplicitously palliative approach to opposition,
namely undermining the legitimacy of dissenting voices instead of effectively addressing the cause of discontent, further aligned Peña Nieto's ide-
ology with the despotic PRI of the twentieth century.

To protest this nefarious misrepresentation of events, the students
of La Ibero took to social media. Social media networks have proved a
potent means of disseminating and communicating opposition outside of
traditional media channels. Since 1994 the *Ejército Zapatista de Liberación
Nacional* [Zapatista Army of National Liberation] (EZLN) has used the
internet alongside other media to publicise the plight of indigenous peoples (Goggin and Albarrán Torres 2014: 31) while, in more recent years,
many studies have shown the importance of online activism during the
Arab spring (2010–11) (Lotan 2011; Al-Kandari and Hasanen 2012;
Dahdal 2012; Noueihed and Warren 2012).

On 14 May 2012, students uploaded a video to YouTube that featured contributions from 131 different protestors present at the event.
In the video, each participant states their names and student number and presents their student identification to the camera, confirm-
ing their identity and their legitimacy as individuals enrolled at the

university (Vite Pérez 2016: 671). The students' audio-visual response to the media's smear campaign was shared extensively on social media sites such as Facebook and Twitter and garnered widespread attention (Kavanaugh, Sheetz, Sandoval-Almazan, Tedesco and Fox 2016: 597). Students from other universities and citizens outside of these academic circles showed their support and solidarity with the 131 Ibero students using the hashtag #YoSoy132. This name began to trend on Twitter and ultimately became a powerful moniker for the movement (Gómez García and Treré 2014: 503. #YoSoy132 effectively used social media to circulate information, channel political disillusionment and mobilise a previously disaffected and overlooked youth in mass protest. Though the movement originated in La Ibero, the students' rejection of the old regime of power and their demand for the democratisation of the media brought together individuals from various academic institutions such as the Universidad Nacional Autónoma de México [Mexico's National Autonomous University] (UNAM), the Universidad Autónoma Metropolitana [Autonomous Metropolitan University], the Instituto Tecnológico y de Estudios Superiores de Monterrey [Monterrey Institute of Technology and Higher Education], and the Instituto Politécnico Nacional [National Polytechnic Institute] as well as wider society.

Overall in June 2012, the movement organised twenty-two protests of varying size and significance across Mexico (Figueiras Tapia 2012: 84–7). While the long-term political impact of the movement is still difficult to assess, in the year 2012 #YoSoy132 succeeded in foregrounding issues such as a need for greater media democratisation. This, as one example, altered the way TV networks broadcast the presidential debate and aided greater access to knowledge (Gómez García and Treré 2014: 501). The rest of this chapter will now focus on the artistic outputs of those involved in the #YoSoy132 and its links to the 1968 student protests.

Artistic Responses – Frente Gráfico/Artistas Aliados

Having established the origins of #YoSoy132 and its wider socio-political implications, this section will home in on the artistic outputs associated with the movement and their dialogic relationship with the protest art of 1968. My analyses will focus on the graphic art produced by the Frente Gráfico [Graphic Front] and explore to what extent their work is influenced by the artistic responses associated with the 1968 student movement. I will examine how members of the Frente Gráfico articulate the effects of political violence witnessed in institutional impunity and the silencing of oppositional voices.

One of the first offline protests organised by #YoSoy132 on 23 May 2012 saw thousands of students convene at the Estela de Luz, an architectural symbol of government opacity and corruption.[5] From this central monument, the students marched to the offices of Televisa in Chapultepec. It was at this early event that students at the different participating universities worked together to produce *mantas* [banners], posters and other visual and textual signs to accompany the rally (Olivares 2014).[6] The artistic branch of the #YoSoy132 movement, known collectively as Artistas Aliados [Allied Artists], emerged as a result of this initial march. Art, and in particular graphic art, has a longstanding symbiotic relationship with political protest in Mexico. Before the advent of social media, art served as a medium to challenge systems of power and spread alternative information (Escuela de Cultura Popular Revolucionaria Mártires del '68 2013). Graphic art in the form of murals, posters and stickers has accompanied all manner of civil protest in contemporary Mexican history ranging from the 1968 student movement to the various calls for support from the EZLN (Escuela de Cultura Popular Revolucionaria Mártires del '68 2013).

The Artistas Aliados comprised many different schools and art forms and was thus further sub-divided into different fronts focusing on specific cultural disciplines. The graphic artists organised themselves under the name Frente Gráfico and began to produce posters and stickers to share during later marches, meetings and assemblies. The formation of the Frente Gráfico, as well as other artistic fronts, brought a universal language to the movement.

During the many protests the Frente Gráfico produced four separate collective graphic series. According to the front's wordpress blog, each series was an open call to collectives and individuals interested in producing stencils, posters, and stickers on a particular theme (Frente Gráfico 2012). The sections below will focus on a selection of works from two of these series.

'Contra la violenta imposición, pacífica movilización'

The first series from the Frente Gráfico focused solely on the production of stickers and was created under the theme, 'Contra la violenta imposición, pacífica movilización' [Against violent imposition, peaceful mobilisation] (Frente Gráfico 2012). The title of this first series alludes to the oppressive nature of state control in the face of peaceful protest in Mexico's past and at the time of production. This mantra for peaceful civil mobilisation in the face of systemic violence could be applied to the events at Tlatelolco in 1968, at Atenco in 2006 and equally with #YoSoy132 in 2012. This series is particularly interesting given the many visual themes it touches upon, such as different historical motifs that represent peaceful protest.

One graphic (Figure 6.1) produced by the collective and credited to Adriana Lucía Izquierdo depicts a hand-drawn image of an upright rifle that is constricted by the vines of a flower. Out of the gun's barrel emerges the Mexican flag and next to the gun the series' slogan, 'Contra la violenta imposición, pacífica movilización', is scrawled informally in a childlike style. The imagery here is simple and easily read. Flowers have long been a symbol of peaceful protest referenced for instance by Allen Ginsberg in his essay 'Demonstration or Spectacle as Example, as Communication or How to Make a March/Spectacle' (1965). Ginsberg suggests protestors construct barricades from flowers and advises the use of other non-violent emblems such as flags and children's toys. Though floral imagery was particularly prevalent internationally in the 1960s in what is known as the 'flower power' age, particularly in the 1967 protests against the Vietnam War, such imagery was not typical of the graphic language used by protestors in Mexico in 1968. Instead, in the context of the 2012 elections, the symbol of the flower recalls the victims of Atenco. As previously examined, the original outburst of dissent that resulted in the use of force by the state was provoked when state police prevented flower sellers from setting up their stands in a public market in Texcoco. Thus the image of the flower here carries a dual meaning in its representation of peaceful protest, drawing on both historic and contemporary examples of non-violent civic remonstration. In this capacity the flower is a recurring theme in the series.

In another graphic produced by the front, credited to Mariana Ortiz, a disembodied hand presents a bunch of daisies to the viewer. The image is digitally rendered and here the slogan is split to convey the message more clearly. While the image of the flowers is aligned with the second part of the mantra 'pacífica movilización', the first part 'contra la violenta imposición' appears alongside the image of a television with a glaring face on its screen. Though under the same banner, the entire tone of the image is different to Figure 6.1. While the image of the gun in Figure 6.1 points directly up in a neutral manner and is repurposed as a flagpole, the imagery this second graphic is direct and assaulting. The face on the screen stares aggressively at the viewer, while the flowers are presented in a fist at the foreground of the frame. Similarly, the text appears in bold block capitals that visually assault the reader. Thus while the focus in the first image is on the power of peaceful protest, the second seeks to denounce the systemic violence of an undemocratic media directly. The glaring face personifies the television, and by extension the media, and subverts the notion of passive viewership through its own hostile gaze. These visual references to

Figure 6.1 Graphic by Adriana Lucía Izquierdo.

media bias and indeed the very issue of a government-influenced news media hark back to problems of censorship at the time of the Tlatelolco massacre. In 1968 President Díaz Ordaz's government exercised total control over newsprint, meaning the repression was minimally represented in the news and particularly in a visual capacity (Glanville 2012). Following the violence, agents from the *Secretaría de Gobernación* [Ministry of the Interior] reportedly raided Mexico's City's newsrooms demanding and destroying all materials, visual and written, relating to the incident (Doyle 2003). Much like the events of 1968, the political crisis of 2012 was one of political legitimacy. Both governments attempted to maintain control by exerting physical force over citizens and manipulating media representation of their actions. While 1968 is widely viewed as a watershed moment that revealed the truly autocratic nature of PRI rule, the ongoing public discontent witnessed in the 2012 protests demonstrates an extension of this struggle into Mexico's present political climate. That is to say that due to the unresolved nature of this past conflict, there exists a dialogic relationship between the past and the present; the 1968 repression represented an untreated historical wound that continues to surface and affect the present. This persevering trauma is reflected in the Frente Gráfico's artwork, where the issues depicted represent the same problems as present forty-four years after this critical turning point.

Just as the victims of government violence in 1968 have been side-lined or diminished by the media as well as by the extant political impunity, so too does this legacy of erasure persist in the present. As Derrida (1994: xviii) argued, hauntology represents an ethical responsibility to restore and repair the memory of the victims of the past, those, 'who are not present, nor presently living, either to us, in us, or outside us'. Spectrality therefore presents an opportunity to promote this forgotten legacy with a view to ending the cycle of trauma and positively impacting the future outcomes. Figure 6.2, credited to Ana Paula Tello of the Frente Gráfico, highlights the hopeful aspirations of those involved in the movement through its digital depiction of an olive tree growing out of the screen of a television set. Much like the flower vines in Figure 6.1 that are drawn as constricting the rifle, in this image the roots of the olive tree engulf the defunct device. It is unclear whether the television screen has shattered as a result of compression by the roots or if the tree has burst out from within it, but, regardless, the imagery alludes to a still-broken media system that the students are confronting and overcoming with peaceful protest. Thus Figure 6.2 achieves an optimistic tenor through its depiction of this nascent youth movement which is growing, even blossoming, out of the foundations of a traumatic past and a still fragile present.

Contra la violenta
imposición,

pacífica
movilización.

Figure 6.2   Graphic by Ana Paula Tello.

While the first three images analysed above display clear links with societal disillusionment with the media and political violence, they are not directly related to the artwork produced in protest at the 1968 massacre. The graphics in this series that could be seen to allude to 1968 use slightly different imagery to the previous three examples. One of the most iconic symbols of the 1968 repression was the image of the dove. The Tlatelolco massacre occurred ten days before the start of the 1968 Summer Olympics held in Mexico City. Since its commencement, the Olympics has represented a truce period, where citizens and athletes from around the world can assemble and participate in these games of peace (International Olympic Committee 2009). This truce is symbolised by the figure of the dove (International Olympic Committee 2009). During the preparations for the Olympics in Mexico, the image of the dove was plastered around the city in the form of decals in shop windows (Byrne 2014). Following the violent repression of protesters in Tlatelolco square, students would subvert this image of peace by spraying a red spot on the bird that dripped down like blood. The vandals' *détournement* of the symbol through the use of spray paint foregrounded the brutal violence that these strategically promoted 'games of peace' sought to obscure. In 1968, the Mexican state was attempting to showcase its modernity to the world and present itself through the Olympics as a democratic and developed country. However, the smooth running of this event ultimately came at the expense of protestors' lives and the criminalisation of dissent. In her contribution to the Frente Gráfico's first graphic series, Mónica Olivares re-appropriates the icon of the dove, alluding to the present-day relevance of this historical tragedy (Figure 6.3).

This monochrome digital representation of a dove taking flight marries the notions of past and present merging in graphic visual representation. The tail end of the dove grows from long and prolific roots that stretch towards the bottom right corner of the frame while the beak of the dove carries a white flag with the numbers 132 depicted in olive branches. The image suggests a journey from Mexico's literal historical roots through to a peaceful future via the vehicle of the dove. The slogan frames the dove figure which, as a potent icon of peace and recalling the 1968 protests can equally be seen as a vehicle of memory. The dove therefore, in Figure 6.3's rendition, creates a bridge between peaceful protest in Mexico's present and its past. To this end the imagery of the Frente Gráfico once again presents a hopeful outlook for Mexico's political future. By incorporating the themes and symbols of the past into its artwork, the Frente Gráfico is in part recuperating the voices and legacies of those oppressed in 1968. This act, in turn, provides a means

Figure 6.3 Graphic by Mónica Olivares.

of repurposing these lost, erased and unheard stories as an aegis against further injustice in the future.

El gobierno que tenemos y el gobierno que queremos

A further graphic series entitled 'El gobierno que tenemos y el gobierno que queremos' [the government that we have and the government that we want] was commissioned by the Frente Gráfico on 21 August 2012. Similar to their first call for contributions, the series includes both digital and hand-rendered graphics which were submitted to be reproduced as posters and stickers. Among this group of images, there are two contributions in particular that stand out for their visual allusion to the iconic protest imagery of 1968. The spectral discourses articulated in these graphics, through their recourse to the image-making of 1968, indicate rifts in memory and highlight the fragile state of power relations between the elected authority and its citizens as a symptom of ongoing impunity and repression.

The first is a stencilled poster featuring red text written on a plain white background. From top to bottom the poster reads, 'México 2012 / Yo Soy 132 / Re.Evolucion / Esta es tu lucha' [Mexico 2012 / I am 132 / Re.Evolution / It is your fight], while the words '2012' and '132' are flanked by the text 'soy paz / soy luz' [I am peace / I am light] and 'x tu país / x tu raíz' [for your country / for your root], respectively. The upper half of the image, which features the words 'México 2012', uses a three-line geometrical structure that was originally devised by the designer Lance Wyman as an integral part of the branding for the 1968 Summer Olympics. As Wyman explains of the design:

> It started when I realized the single lineal geometry of the five-ring Olympic logo could be central to constructing the number 68, the year of the event. The resulting three-line structure of the 68 numbers became the typography for the word 'Mexico', and the logo was born. (Byrne 2014)

Through this simple geometric style, Wyman made the five Olympic rings central to the entire branding of the event. In his design, the word 'Mexico' elides with the figure '68' out of which emerge the rings. To this end, the word 'Mexico' and the number '68' become prototypical of the rings themselves. However, following the Tlatelolco massacre, protesters of the violence used this branding as part of their own dissenting graphic art, seen in *mantas*, posters and stickers. This in turn subverted the meaning of the design by relating its visual components, as well as the event, country and year, to the forceful subdual of students. This transmuting of visual cultural artefact is also observed with regards to the collective memory of the events of October 1968. Just as Wyman's design was linked to the repression so this time period is now remembered as representative of hostile authoritarianism and not, as was originally hoped, a triumphant moment of political modernity.

While this image does not incorporate the title of the Frente Gráfico's series in its text, its appropriation of the three-line typography provides a powerful visual call-back to the government's previous violent transgressions. Simply via the use of this iconic typography, and submitted under the topic 'El gobierno que tenemos y el gobierno que queremos', the image is able to align the country's current political regime with that of its brutal past. In 1968 Mexico's hosting of the Olympics represented the country as modern to the rest of the world as, too, had the transition to democracy in the year 2000; the Frente Gráfico's red-and-white stencil image attempts to undermine these supposed political advancements by constructing a visual bridge between 1968 and 2012 that suggests the same oppressive regime is still in power. This desire for political change is represented visually by contrasting the three-line motif that reads 'Mexico 2012' on the top half of the page with a weighted, or filled-in, version of this motif on the bottom half that reads, 'Yo Soy /132/Re.Evolucion/Esta es tu lucha'. Thus the aims of the movement and the current state of the nation are contrasted via the use of font style and weighting. The image does not simply appropriate this iconic motif from 1968 but instead, through its use alongside a slightly altered version, creates a dialogue between the trauma of the past and the insufficiencies of the present. By juxtaposing these typographies, the artist asserts that the Mexican government in the year 2012 is a continuation of the government responsible for the 1968 repression and that, by contrast, the #YoSoy132 movement represents a new and more hopeful political avenue.

The second image from this series that bears further analysis due to its allusions to the art of 1968 is the final image under consideration. Beyond Wyman's notorious Olympic designs, the students of 1968 used other imagery to convey their disillusionment with the political forces in power at the time. Unlike the Artistas Aliados which boasted artists from a variety of institutions, in 1968 the students hailed mainly from the Escuela Nacional de Artes Plásticas [National School of Visual Arts] and Escuela Nacional de Pintura y Escultura [National School of Painting and Sculpture]. Staff members at these art schools, who had themselves participated artistically in notable protest movements of the past, contributed to the production of graphics (Flaherty 2012: 3). One faculty member in particular, Adolfo Mexiac, allowed students to reinterpret his own work and from this his print *Libertad de expresión* [Freedom of expression] (1954) became an iconic image during the protests (Flaherty 2012: 3). The print, originally created in support of the plight of indigenous peoples in Chiapas, features the face of a young man whose mouth in constrained by a padlocked metal chain. For its repurposing in 1968, the students added the words 'Libertad de expresión' alongside the 'Mexico '68' typographic symbol, highlighting the hypocrisy of these supposed games of peace. In this image, from the Frente Gráfico, the artist adopts the iconic elements of Mexiac's print while modernising its content and simultaneously subverting its subject. Unlike the scratched texture of the original linocut image, this image is digitally rendered with smooth shading and colouring. In place of the anguished young man, the graphic features the proud face of Peña Nieto. The candidate's mouth is gagged by a black banner that reads '#YoSoy132', while at the top of the image the words 'Nos toca callarlos' [it is our turn to silence them] are printed in a bold white font. While in Mexiac's images the victim is silenced by the heavy chains of an oppressive regime, in Frente Gráfico's image it is the political system, as represented by the PRI candidate Peña Nieto, who is being muzzled. Similarly, instead of chains Peña Nieto's mouth is constricted by the movement's hashtag, which functions as an allusion not only to the power of the student movement but also to the pivotal role of social and alternative media as a platform for counter-narratives that challenge hegemonic control.

As with the previous image considered, the reinterpretation of artwork associated with the 1968 movement seen with Mexiac's image indicates a conscious dialogue with the struggles of this political period. While the influence of Mexiac's image is immediately clear to the viewer, the inversion of the power struggle represented in the Frente Gráfico's version suggests a dynamic engagement with the ghosts of the past. The image simultaneously acknowledges the history of political repression that has affected protestors in Mexico for decades while subverting previous artistic responses to it. As the header 'Nos toca callarlos' suggests, the tables have turned and it is the responsibility of and moment for the members of the 2012 student movement, as well as those citizens that support it, to challenge governmental authority. The image distinguishes #YoSoy132 as the keystone for overcoming systems of subjugation and propagating voices of dissent. Thus Mexiac's image has the dual quality of calling upon the memory of civil opposition in 1968 while supplanting this imagery with a more active message. Here, the proponents of the #YoSoy132 movement are the ones taking control and deciding who speaks and who is heard. The ideological discrepancies between this image and its original referent create a destabilising quality that points to the unresolved trauma of the events of 1968.

Conclusion

The events surrounding the 2012 general presidential elections fit aptly into Mexico's tumultuous electoral history. Once again the chronic issues of PRI-instigated repression and the lack of accountability for violence, seen in the candidacy of Enrique Peña Nieto, were met with public protest and outrage, evidenced by the #YoSoy132 student movement. Ultimately, despite the PRI's return to power, the success of the student protests can be observed in their ability to mobilise large numbers of citizens both online and on the streets across the country.

In 2012 as in 1968, graphic art played a key role in articulating civil discontent with hegemonic control and the media apparatus. These works produced by the Frente Gráfico demonstrate an engagement with historical instances of state brutality seen in the silencing of dissent and the violent subdual of protestors. The palimpsest nature of the Frente Gráfico's output, which builds on the art produced in 1968, points to a persisting narrative of trauma in the collective memory that remains unresolved at a socio-political level.

As observed in this chapter, Jacques Derrida's notion of hauntology provides a useful framework for the study of unresolved trauma in Mexico's contemporary history. The search for political justice witnessed in the 2012 student protest movement highlights the ongoing need to address socio-historical fissures in Mexico's past. It is clear from the above analyses that the spectre of repression continues to mould and collide with Mexico's present. Equally, in keeping with the notion of hauntology, the Frente Gráfico's artwork represents an effort to fulfil an ethical obligation to the victims of past repression by attempting to heal societal ruptures and restore memory. The visual output of the 2012 students' movement is thus borne from and unavoidably influenced by the memory and unresolved trauma of the 1968 Tlatelolco massacre. To this end, the Frente Gráfico seeks to expose and challenge the political violence of Mexico's past, present and potential future.

Notes

1. The repression in Atenco was one of the key motivations for the student protests against the candidacy of Enrique Peña Nieto in the electoral race of 2012. In May 2013 the repression was the subject of a social media campaign known as 'Recuerdo Atenco' (I remember Atenco), triumphing the role of memory in recuperating the power of collective organisation. See Hernández Castillo (2013).

2. Unless otherwise stated, all translations are my own.

3. During his thirty-five-year regime, politician Porfirio Díaz was unable to implement a democratic system of presidential succession. In the year 1910, this failure resulted in electoral fraud and a subsequent revolt that would ultimately oust Díaz from power and instil a new phase in Mexican politics.

4. Upon its release *Fraude: México 2006* (2007) was the most successful documentary feature to screen in Mexican cinemas and earned over $12 million pesos in 2007. For more details see MacLaird (2013).

5. The Estela de Luz is a monument in Mexico City that was originally constructed in 2010 as part of Mexico's bicentennial commemorations but was ultimately not finished ahead of the celebrations in the year 2011. Given the excessive and largely unaccounted for expense of its construction, the monument is viewed as a symbol of the corruption of the PAN government in power at the time of erection. For more information see Islas Weinstein (2015) and Avilés, Garduño and Méndez (2013).

6. My interview with Mónica Olivares, a participant at the protests and student artist at the UNAM's Escuela Nacional de Artes Plásticas (ENAP), 9 April 2014.

Bibliography

0.56%: ¿Qué le pasó a México?, film, directed by Lorenzo Hagerman. Mexico: Compañia Productora Lynn Fainchtein/FOPROCINE, 2010.

Al-Kandari, Ali, and Mohammed Hasanen (2012) 'The Impact of the Internet on Political Attitudes in Kuwait and Egypt', *Telematics and Informatics*, 29:3, pp. 245–53.

Arsenault, Chris (2012), "Profile: Enrique Peña Nieto", *Al Jazeera*, 24 June. Available at <https://www.aljazeera.com/news/americas/2012/06/2012614 10114116811.html> (last accessed 3 January 2018).

Atenco: Romper el cerco, film, directed by Nicolás Défossé and Mario Viveros. México: Canal 6 de Julio y Promedios de Comunicación / Canal 6 de Julio en DVD, 2007.

Avilés, Karina, Roberto Garduño, and Enrique Méndez (2013), 'Estela de luz la corrupción en cadena', *La Jornada*, 21 February. Available at <https://www.jornada.com.mx/2013/02/21/politica/002n1pol> (last accessed 3 January 2018).

Byrne, Emmet (2014), 'Radiant discord: Lance Wyman on the '68 Olympic design and the Tlatelolco massacre', *Walker Art*, 20 March. Available at <https://walkerart.org/magazine/lance-wyman-mexico-68–olympics-tlatelolco-massacre> (last accessed 3 January 2018).

Castillo, R. Aí (2007), 'State Violence and Gender in San Salvador Atenco, Mexico', *Chicana/Latina Studies*, 6:2, pp. 118–29.

Dahdal, S. (2012), 'Social Media and the Arab Spring: The Historical Context and the Role of Aljazeera Satellite Station', in Peter Parycek and Noella Edelmann (eds), *Conference for E-Democracy and Open Government (CeDEM)*, Vienna: Druckerei Berger.

Derrida, Jacques (1994), *Specters of Marx: The State of the Debt, the Work of Mourning, and the New International*, translated by Peggy Kamuf, New York and London: Routledge.

Doyle, Kate (2003), '"Forgetting is not justice": Mexico bares its secret past', *World Policy Journal*, 20:2, pp. 61–72.

El lenguaje de los machetes, film, directed by Kyzza Terrazas. Mexico: IMCINE/FOPROCINE, 2011.

Escuela de Cultura Popular Revolucionaria Mártires del '68 (2013), 'From the Blowout to the Movement: Mexican Political Action in Print', *Creative Times Reports*, 2 October. Available at <http://creativetimereports.org/2013/10/02/from-the-blowout-to-the-movement-mexican-political-action-in-print-after-tlatelolco> (last accessed 3 January 2018).

Figueiras Tapia, Leonardo (ed.) (2012), *El movimiento estudiantil en el proceso electoral 2012 in del 131 al #YoSoy132: Elección 2012*, México: Comunicación y Política Editores.

Flaherty, George F. (2012), 'Appropriation and Parody in Mexico City Student Movement Graphics, 1968', *Contested Games: Mexico 68's Design Revolution*. University of Essex Art Gallery: pp. 1–3.

Fraude: México, 2006, film, directed by Luis Mandoki. Mexico: Contra el Viento Films, 2007.

Frente Gráfico (2012), 'Contra la violenta imposición, pacífica movilización', Facebook.com/FrenteGrafico, 28 July 2012, Available at <https://www.facebook.com/pg/FrenteGrafico/photos/?tab=album&album_id=45068 2061632104> (last accessed 15 September 2017).

Garcia, Jacobo G. (2012), 'Peña Nieto pagó a importantes periodistas mexicanos para que hablaran bien de él', *El Mundo*, 11 May. Available at <https://www.elmundo.es/america/2012/05/11/mexico/1336765581.html> (last accessed 15 September 2017).

Gibler, John (2011), *México rebelde: crónicas de poder e insurrección*, translated by Juan Elías Tovar, Mexico City: Random House Mondadori.

Ginsberg, Allen (1965), 'Demonstration or Spectacle as Example, as Communication or How to Make a March/Spectacle', *Berkeley Barb*, 19 November. Available at http://self.gutenberg.org/articles/Flower_power (last accessed 28 May 2020).

Glanville, Brian (2012), 'Murder in Mexico', *Index on Censorship*, 41:2, pp. 70–5.

Goggin, Gerard, and César Albarrán Torres (2014), 'Political and Mobile Media Landscapes in Mexico: The Case of #yosoy132', *Continuum: Journal of Media and Cultural Studies*, 28:1, pp. 1–15.

Gómez García, Rodrigo and Emiliano Treré (2014), 'The #YoSoy132 Movement and the Struggle for Media Democratization in Mexico', *Convergence*, 20:4, pp. 496–510.

Hernández Castillo, Rosalva Aída (2013), 'Recuerdo Atenco: La memoria como resistencia'. Available at < https://www.jornada.com.mx/2013/05/05/opinion/015a1pol> (last accessed 5 May 2013).

International Olympic Committee (2009), 'Olympic movement promotes peace worldwide', Olympic.org, 23 May. Available at <https://www.olympic.org/news/olympic-movement-promotes-peace-worldwide> (last accessed 15 September 2017).

Islas Weinstein, Tania (2015), 'A Eulogy for the Coloso: The Politics of Commemoration in Calderón's Mexico', *Journal of Latin American Cultural Studies*, 24:4, pp. 475–99.

Kavanaugh, Andrea L., Steven D. Sheetz, Rodrigo Sandoval-Almazan, John C. Tedesco, and Edward A. Fox (2016), 'Media Use During Conflicts: Information Seeking and Political Efficacy During the 2012 Mexican Elections', *Government Information Quarterly*, 33:3, pp. 595–602.

Lotan, G. (2011), 'The Revolutions Were Tweeted: Information Flows During the 2011 Tunisian and Egyptian Revolutions', *International Journal of Communication*, 5, pp. 1375–405.

MacLaird, Misha (2013), 'Documentaries and Celebrities, Democracy and Impunity: Thawing the Revolution in Twenty-First-century Mexico', *Social Identities: Journal for the Study of Race, Nation and Culture*, 19:3–4, pp. 468–84.

Maihold, Günther (2006), 'México: La elección en disputa: Retos para el nuevo gobicrno de Felipe Calderón", *Iberoamericana*, 6:24, pp. 167–72.

Noueihed, Lin, and Alex Warren (2012), *The Battle for the Arab Spring: Revolution, Counter-Rrevolution and the Making of a New Era*, New Haven and London: Yale University Press.

Nuñez Albarrán, Ernesto (2012), *Crónica de un sexenio fallido*, Mexico: Grijalbo.

Olmeda, Juan C., and María Alejandra Armesto (2013), 'México: El regreso del PRI a la presidencia', *Revista De Ciencia Política (Santiago)*, 33:1, pp. 247–67.

Robles, Humberto (2010/11), 'Atenco: Un caso de terrorismo de estado', *Papeles De Relaciones Ecosociales y Cambio Global*, 112, pp. 131–40.

Rodriguez, Ana Monica (2006), 'Como sucedió en 1959, persiste hoy un enorme descontento: Poniatowska', *La Jornada*, 10 May. Available at <https://www.jornada.com.mx/2006/05/10/index.php?section=cultura&article=a05n-1cul> (last accessed 15 September 2017).

Sprinker, Michael (2008), *Ghostly Demarcations: A Symposium on Jacques Derrida's Specters of Marx*, London: Verso.

Traverso, Antonio, and Kristi Wilson (eds) (2014), *Political Documentary Cinema in Latin America*, London and New York: Routledge.

Ugues, Antonio (2010), 'Citizens' Views on Electoral Governance in Mexico', *Journal of Elections, Public Opinion & Parties*, 20:4, pp. 495–527.

Vite Pérez, Miguel Ángel (2016), 'Mexico, the Construction of Enemies through Social Protest: Some Reflections', *Critical Sociology*, 42:4–5, pp. 661–77.

Wax-Edwards, Jessica (2014), 'Interview with Mónica Olivares, a participant at the protests and student artist at the UNAM's Escuela Nacional de Artes Plásticas (ENAP)', 9 April 2014.

Zamora Lomelí, Carla Beatriz (2010), 'Conflicto y violencia entre el estado y los actores colectivos – un estudio de caso: El frente de pueblos en defensa de la tierra en San Salvador Atenco, estado de México, 2001–2009', PhD thesis, El Colegio de México. Available at <https://ces.colmex.mx/pdfs/tesis/tesis_zamora_lomeli.pdf> (last accessed 28 May 2020).

CHAPTER 7

Loss and Mourning in Documentary: Tatiana Huezo's *Ausencias* (2015)

Miriam Haddu

Before making this docu [sic], my first premise was to discover what violence-generated fear can do to people. It's a fear that paralyzes; a kind of sickness of the soul that impedes you from getting on with life, from evolving. (Tatiana Huezo in De la Fuente 2015)

Tatiana Huezo's short film *Ausencias* [Absences] (2015) is a story that follows the emotional journey of Lourdes Herrera de Llano (who also refers to herself as Lulú in the film), a mother from Saltillo, Coahuila whose son Brandon and husband Esteban Acosta Rodríguez were kidnapped and disappeared on the morning of the 29th August 2009 as they drove two family members to Monterrey airport. The case was covered widely by both local and national media, which saw the event as evidence that crime and violence now also included the kidnappings and disappearance of children, exemplified in the abduction of Brandon. As Marcela Turati (2012) writes in *Proceso* magazine:

Atrás quedaron los días en que la delincuencia respetaba a las familias, sobre todo a los niños, quienes ahora en el fragor de la guerra calderonista contra el narcotráfico y las pugnas por el control de las plazas son la parte más vulnerable de la población. Y ello no sólo por el riesgo de quedar atrapados en el fuego cruzado o de recibir una bala perdida, sino porque ahora se les secuestra y desaparece como a los adultos. (Turati 2012)

[Gone are the days when crime used to respect families, and especially children, who now, in the heat of the Calderonist war against drug trafficking and the struggles to control the *plazas*, remain the most vulnerable part of the population. And this not only because of the risk of getting caught in the crossfire or receiving a stray bullet, but because they [children] are now kidnapped and made to disappear like adults.][1]

Previous reports had included the finding of abandoned children in public spaces, after their parents and relatives had been kidnapped (Riveles 2011).

However, the difference in this case was that Brandon, a young boy of eight, had become the victim of organised crime (Figure 7.1).

In her documentary *Ausencias* it is Lourdes' personal tragedy that Huezo chooses to focus on. Guided by a series of rhetorical questions that drive the narrative, the documentary explores the themes of absence, grief and loss. How does one cope after the enforced removal of a family member – a beloved, or one's child? How to focus the emotions, sense of absence and bereavement? And, how do these factors manifest themselves in the day to day of life, after the event? These are some of the questions that Huezo attempts to examine with her film, by focusing on Lourdes' story. Despite the personal angle, however, Lourdes' ordeal in the film is symbolic of a much wider national state of trauma that is characterised by a sense of loss, disempowerment and the politicisation of grief as a responsive action. Huezo continues exploring these topics in her next film, *Tempestad* (2016), a documentary that follows the lives of two women who are victims of the social instability and violent conflict affecting Mexico. In *Tempestad* we share in the pain of a mother's separation from her child, whether it be conducted through enforced imprisonment in a narco-run jail, or through kidnapping and disappearance. Absence as a prolonged state of grief runs throughout both of Huezo's recent films. In *Ausencias*, Lourdes' narrated experiences following the disappearance of her son and husband offer insights into her private grief and profound moments of despair. Lourdes' narrative helps to shed light on the many lives and personal stories that have been affected by widespread violence, which involve kidnappings and enforced disappearances. Furthermore, such crimes of abduction have been on the rise in Mexico, reaching unprecedented levels during the drugs crisis.

Huezo's *Ausencias*, therefore, articulates a concern with the nature of violent discourse dominating the media, public streets and private spaces in Mexico. And it is these private spaces of mourning and loss, as examples of affected experience after an enforced disappearance has occurred, that constitute the focus of this chapter's analysis. According to the Mexican periodical *El mundo*, between the years 2006 and 2010 (which coincides with the period in which Esteban, along with his son and brothers, disappeared) 18,491 cases of kidnappings and enforced disappearances were reported to the authorities (Veiga 2011). At the time of the film's release, the number of disappeared victims in Mexico according to the Amnesty International Annual Report for 2015–16 stood at 27,000, and more recent figures suggest closer to 40,000 disappeared, with some commentators pointing towards a much higher number of

Figure 7.1 *Ausencias* (2015) film poster.

cases that remain unreported for fear of repercussions from organised crime, as Riveles notes:

> [. . .] las victimas de desaparición forzada no confían en el sistema de justicia, ni en los ministerios públicos, ni en la policía y ni en las fuerzas armadas; la impunidad es un patrón crónico y presente en los casos de desapariciones forzadas, y no se han realizado los esfuerzos suficientes para determinar la suerte o paradero de las personas desaparecidas, para sancionar a los responsables ni tampoco para brindar reparaciones. (2011: 106)

> [[. . .] victims of enforced disappearance do not trust the justice system, or the public ministries, or the police or the armed forces; impunity is a chronic and present pattern in cases of enforced disappearances, and sufficient efforts have not been made to determine the fate or the whereabouts of missing persons, [so as] to punish those responsible or to provide reparations.]

The unprecedented increase in narco-violence in Mexico and the dominance of crime syndicates within the public sphere, in combination with a sense of impunity for the violations committed, aided by the allegations of corruption at the heart of local and national government, have all contributed towards shaping the nation's socio-political landscape almost beyond recognition. Added to this fact, the high number of enforced disappearances in Mexico has fuelled a climate of fear which in turn has fed the sense of insecurity and a lack of safety, of which Huezo speaks in the opening quote to this chapter. Inviting comparisons with the Southern Cone's traumatic experiences of kidnap, torture and disappearance conducted during the Argentine military Junta (1976–83), and also following Augusto Pinochet's coup d'état in Chile in 1973, respectively, Mexico at the time of writing continues to grapple with the complexities and consequences of targeted abductions, unmarked mass graves and the status of 'unknown' in relation to thousands of officially reported victims of the conflict. Referred to in the media as '*levantones*', the crime of kidnapping in Mexico has reached unprecedented levels, impacting the sense of national stability and instilling a sense of terror and uncertainty in the victims' families, who in turn are condemned to a prolonged and undefined state of mourning.

Levantones

En México la palabra 'levantón' tiene una connotación semejante a lo que en Argentina se conoce como desaparición forzada. Al levantón suele seguirlo una muerte. Es un secuestro por el que no necesariamente se pide rescate: inmigrantes, turistas, empresarios, campesinos y narcos o policías asesinados en ajustes de cuentas engrosan las estadísticas de este delito en un país militarizado (Veiga 2011).

[In Mexico the word '*levantón*' has a connotation similar to what in Argentina is known as an enforced disappearance. The snatching is usually followed by a death. It is a kidnapping for which rescue is not necessarily requested: immigrants, tourists, businessmen, peasants and drug traffickers or police officers are killed in the settling of scores that swell the statistics for such a crime in a militarised country.]

Perhaps the case that encapsulates the sentiment of public indignation (at the sense of impunity enjoyed by many of the criminals who carry out the enforced abductions) is that of the 43 missing students from the Ayotzinapa Normal School, located in the city of Iguala in Guerrero. The case is one that has caught media attention both nationally and internationally, and has come to exemplify the failed rhetoric of economic prosperity and how the PRI did not have a handle on national security, despite promising to achieve this on their return to power. Enrique Peña Nieto's first eighteen months in office was dominated by a PR campaign that announced economic growth and heralded a new era spearheaded by the newly sworn-in president. Evidence of this can be seen in Peña Nieto's early 2014 appearance on the cover of *Time* magazine accompanied by a story that announced him as the leader of what many termed the economic 'Aztec tiger', heralding him as responsible for 'saving Mexico' (see Berggruen and Gardels 2013; Hapak 2014). However, that same image of a proud-looking young president would soon become debunked when many on social media platforms took to satirising the *Time* magazine cover, replacing the same with an adjusted image of Peña Nieto as the Grim Reaper, complete with the tagline 'Slaying Mexico'. Just a few months later, the scandal of the 43 Ayotzinapa disappeared students would confirm criticisms that Mexico continued to struggle with narco-related instability and institutional corruption, despite the efforts of the Peña Nieto PR campaign which had worked hard to prove the contrary.

On 26 September 2014, according to official reports, the 43 students had taken several buses to Mexico City to commemorate the anniversary of the 1968 Tlatelolco massacre. During their journey, local police intercepted the buses with more than ninety students on board and a confrontation ensued. A small number of students were able to escape, and 43 were detained by the police. Details of what happened during and after the clash remain unclear, but investigations have concluded that once the 43 students were in custody, they were handed over to the local *Guerreros Unidos* (United Warriors) crime syndicate and allegedly murdered. Furthermore, Mexican newspapers reported that Iguala's mayor at the time, José Luis Abarca Velázquez, and his wife María de los Ángeles Piñeda Villa had masterminded the abduction in an effort to avoid discrediting

Piñeda Villa's forthcoming candidacy for mayor. On the night of the disappearance, Abarca Velázquez had organised a gathering of colleagues and supporters at an event designed to unofficially launch Piñeda Villa's bid for mayor. The couple, it is alleged, were concerned with the possibility of unruly disruption to their celebrations, caused by the student protestors. According to media reports, on 26 September, upon hearing of the student buses' movement northbound and fearing their imminent arrival, Abarca ordered the police to intercept the journey, and to halt the students' progress (Tuckman 2014). This led to an altercation when the police encountered the buses, giving way to a violent clash with armed police firing at the passengers. This resulted in five dead, several wounded, and 43 captured and taken into custody. The whereabouts of the 43 detainees remains unknown, and the students have not been seen since. In the weeks following the disappearance of the students, both Abarca Velázquez and Piñeda Villa went into hiding but were found and arrested in November that same year in Itztapalapa, Mexico City. They are both at the time of writing serving prison sentences for a number of charges including money laundering, criminal misdemeanour and illicit enrichment (Martínez 2014).

Since 2014 the crime of the 43 disappeared has provoked a wave of mass demonstrations galvanising members of the public beyond the affected areas of Guerrero, who have united to protest against the perceived government impunity and the rise in mass abduction and enforced disappearances, all of which have become commonplace in recent years. Furthermore, the hashtag #Ayotzinapa has gathered momentum in the years since the event, attracting media attention and criticism for Peña Nieto's government and its official response to the crimes. Peña Nieto's administration took more than ten days to acknowledge the incident and to offer condolences to the families of the disappeared. When the president finally visited the city of Iguala in 2016, two years after the actual event, it was seen as an attempt to rectify the mishandling of the tragedy on behalf of the PRI administration (Associated Press 2016). Furthermore, the Ayotzinapa case has highlighted a significant flaw in the institutional position against organised crime and, in particular, the authorities' response to the increasing levels of mass kidnappings and disappearances. The proclamations of governmental corruption and the sense of indignation at the unprecedented levels of insecurity and crime in Mexico have coincided with the rise in large-scale demonstrations on the nation's streets and the emergence of protest *caravanas* (rallies) (such as those coordinated by the families of the missing 43) which in turn have moved beyond national frontiers and into the US, gathering support and highlighting their plight as a consequence. Echoing the protest movement instigated by the poet Javier Sicilia following the kidnapping and killing of his son in March 2011, which became known as the Movimiento Por la Paz con Justicia y Dignidad [Movement for Peace with Justice and Dignity], and which also saw the coordination of a peace caravan that travelled north and into the US, the #Ayotzinapa demonstrations and media coverage have highlighted the growing discontent felt by the public and, in particular, the politicisation of grief enacted by the families of the victims. United by their sense of loss and indignation at the lack of investigative progress made on their cases, families of the victims have turned to social media platforms to voice their protests and have formed collective groups that seek to bring to justice those responsible for the crimes committed against their loved ones. These include the Movimiento por Nuestros Desaparecidos en México [Movement for Our Disappeared in Mexico] (MNDM), the Campaña Nacional Contra la Desaparición Forzada en México [National Campaign Against Enforced Disappearance in Mexico], Grupo Guerrero de Reacción Inmediata de Desaparecidos [Guerrero Group for Immediate Reaction of the Disappeared], Nuestras Hijas de Regreso a Casa [For the Return of Our Daughters Home], and Fuerzas Unidas por Nuestros Desaparecidos en México [United Forces for Our Disappeared in Mexico] (Fundem), among many others. Perhaps most crucially of all, the families of the victims seek to unveil the truth behind what happened to their next of kin, which in turn would allow for closure of the cycle of grief and would offer them the space to finally mourn their loss.

In Huezo's documentary, the protagonist, Lourdes, reflects on her current condition of perpetual mourning. She describes herself as being in an in-between emotional space, where she is unable to move on to alternate stages of grief, and thus process the loss of her loved ones because, as she puts it, she lacks their physical bodies to mourn. Each death, however harrowing, is accompanied by various stages of mourning, which assist in the processing of the traumatic experience of losing a loved one. Societal rituals such as funeral ceremonies, aid in the visualisation and performance of loss and allow for the processing of grief to take place. However, when there is the lack of a body or a corpse to confirm the death, the sufferer is left with a sense of emotional vacuum, and the process of mourning is problematised. In *Ausencias* Lourdes remembers how she was able to mourn the death of her father, who had passed away several years earlier, and how his funeral and subsequent gravestone had allowed her the space to grieve and to process her loss. However, in her current condition Lourdes is deprived of this process and is unable to grieve the physical loss of her husband and son, and yet the small sense of hope due to the lack of confirmation of their deaths keeps her in waiting for their return. The memorialisation of the deceased, furthermore, in the form of tombstones and graveyards allows for the demarcation of a life once lived and offers the mourner the space for reflection and recognition of their loved one's presence, albeit posthumously. As María Soledad García observes:

> Los epitafios, las placas, las lápidas y los panteones se establecen como señales de la muerte para quien visita y recuerda (más allá del vacío y ausencia que deviene con la muerte). El cementerio, y particularmente la sepultura, proporcionan el reconocimiento del cuerpo, y en consecuencia, de la muerte. Pero ¿qué sucede si no hay cuerpo? ¿Qué sucede si no hay marca de vida en la muerte? (2002: 12)

> [Epitaphs, plaques, tombstones and pantheons are established as signs of death for those who visit and remember (beyond the emptiness and absence that comes with death). The cemetery, and particularly the grave, provide recognition of the body, and consequently, of death. But what happens if there is no body? What happens if there is no mark of life in death?]

What does happen when there is no body to grieve, as María Soledad García suggests above, is a profound state of prolonged mourning that maintains the sufferer in an almost pathological condition of melancholy. In his famous essay 'Mourning and Melancholia', Freud (1917) posits that the process of mourning after the death and loss of a loved one is comparable to the phenomenon of melancholia/depression. In his analysis Freud explains that both conditions have a similar outward effect on the subject due to their similar environmental influences. Furthermore, the inhibition of the ego, and the disinterest displayed in relation to the external world, is manifest in conditions both of mourning and melancholia in equal measure. However, despite their apparent similarities, both melancholia and mourning remain fundamentally different responses to loss. During the grieving process, normal grief eventually eases when the sufferer emotionally detaches from the lost person or object and replaces sorrow with other emotions. If this process fails to evolve, however, severe depression may develop, which can manifest itself in self-destructive tendencies. Furthermore, within the condition of mourning, Freud observes that the sufferer deals with the grief of losing a specific love object in the conscious mind. In melancholia, however, a person grieves for a loss that they are unable to comprehend fully or identify, and thus the process takes place in the unconscious mind. The act of mourning, therefore, is considered a healthy and natural process of grieving a loss, while melancholia is considered a potentially pathological condition. In addition, Freud observes that melancholia develops when the feelings of sorrow are inappropriate to the context, gradually becoming internalised. This process leads to the melancholic subject identifying with the lost object or loved one on an unconscious level, paving the way for a process that, according to Freud, leads to the loss of ego. Therefore, despite their similarities, the conditions differ in that mourning is recognised as a normal process while melancholia is considered an abnormal pathology with links to suicidal tendencies that may require clinical intervention.

In this way, the lack of a body or corpse in the case of the thousands of disappeared (and presumed dead) victims of the *levantones* in Mexico problematises the process of grief for the families affected by loss, reducing them to a state of emotional limbo, unable to grieve fully yet clinging onto the uncertain hope of their loved ones' return. This continued sense of hope paradoxically prolongs the condition of mourning in the sufferer, exacerbating the notion of absence of those who have been lost. As García (2002) notes, the non-forgetting of those who have been disappeared, undertaken by those who lie in wait for their return, condemns the latter to what she terms '*un duelo eterno*' [an eternal [state] of mourning]:

> No olvidar reclamar la desaparición como estrategia de continua espera y continua muerte. Convivir entre la memoria y el olvido quizá sea el único duelo eterno que podamos realizar ante el cuerpo desaparecido. (2002: 13)

> [Not forgetting that the consequence of disappearance is a state of continuous waiting and continuous death. Living between memory and oblivion may be the only eternal grieving we can perform before the missing body.]

Therefore, those who are left to deal with the after-effects of the *levantón* are condemned to exist within this state of emotional in-betweenness, positioned within the sites of memory and forgetting. As García's (2002) suggestion above confirms, this emotional in-between space is where the sufferer is placed when confronted with the reality of a disappeared body, a lack of physical body and a lack of body of proof (of death). Such a stalling within the processing of grief, aided by the lack of corporeality, paves the way for the victims' families to remain in a state of profound depression, unable to mourn in a healthy way and running the risk of developing the condition of melancholia. These states of emotional in-betweenness, of profound despair and of the engulfing sense of absence, are aspects that drive the narrative of *Ausencias*, where Huezo sets out to explore how the impacted family members cope with this loss and sense of absence as exemplified by Lourdes' story. Commenting on filmic responses to the cases of disappearances in Argentina from the time of the Junta, Paula Rodríguez notes a commonality between the spaces of memory, the traumatised condition and the all-pervasive sense of the past in the present, noting that:

> Los filmes sobre la desaparición de personas se reconocen por un pasado que no cesa. Este vaivén entre dos tiempos obedece a lo propio de los acontecimientos de extrema violencia, a lo traumático de las situaciones límite y también a la condición de la desaparición forzada como una de estas situaciones. (2006: 174)

> [Films about disappearances of people are marked by a repeating past. This to-and-fro between two time periods responds to the specifics of the experience of extreme violence, to the trauma of situations at the limits and also to the repercussions of forced disappearance.]

And it is this process of attempting to make sense of the trauma and its meanings for the present that we see as the crux of Lourdes' internal journey, as she reflects on her personal history while continuing to explore the labyrinths of memory, a process that Rodríguez names a form of 'memoria airada' [irate memory] involving 'una estrategia de transmisión de lo traumático a la memoria' [a transmission strategy of the traumatic to memory] (2006: 173). This type of memory remains pivotal to an understanding of collective traumas because 'la memoria airada es una forma de representación cultural. Se trata de una estrategia de inscripción de lo traumático en la producción cultural y en las prácticas fílmicas' [irate memory is a form of cultural representation. It is a strategy that involves the inscription of the traumatic into cultural production and film practices] (2006: 177) and maintains, therefore, a dialogic relationship with its context of production. In terms of the use of *memoria airada* in the shaping of filmic narratives, Rodríguez comments that

> la memoria airada: por un lado, [contiene] la reelaboración del pasado realizada desde el presente, atisbos de rememoración y del trabajo de recuerdo. El otro aspecto que coexiste es el núcleo de la memoria airada, la memoria identificada con la querella que se diferencia de la rememoración

> [irate memory: on the one hand, [contains] the reworking of the past made from the present, [providing] glimpses of remembrance and the workings of memory. Existing alongside this is the core of the irate memory, a memory identified with the grievance which differs from the recollection] (2006: 177)

And it is this practice described by Rodríguez that primarily maintains the function of re-evaluating the past from the position of the present within the context of grief. Reading *Ausencias* within the spectrum of a re-visitation of the past through the use of memory and language conducted in the present, as Rodríguez's example above suggests, reveals a process that relies on the use of the image as playing a crucial role in the processing of a personal trauma, seen in the home movies and photographs displayed in the documentary. This notion in itself provides Huezo's film with layers of meaning that work mimetically with the context of their making, reflecting a much wider problematic and national condition.

Ausencias

Running to twenty-seven minutes, *Ausencias* explores Lourdes' emotional world, now without the presence of her husband Esteban and younger son Brandon. The camera is often positioned to one side, below, or focused on another object as Lourdes speaks in a voice that delivers her tale with composure as we learn of the horrors of her story. The film opens with a montage sequence of home movies, containing scenes of family gatherings, birthday parties and afternoons spent in the park. The first sounds we hear are those of children laughing, set against a blank screen. We then see our first image, of Dayana (Lourdes and Esteban's eldest child) as a small girl, speaking to an off-screen character (possibly Esteban). Images of smiling children, proud parents and family harmony fall into sequence. These opening scenes reveal family video recordings and a discussion about the process of taking family photographs. Each parent takes it in turn to pose in front of the camera with their children. First in this sequence is an image of Lourdes standing with her children on either side, yet before we even see her physically on the screen we hear her voice, as she asks her husband to 'take the photo'. We then see a flashback to a younger, smiling Lourdes with her children, posing for the camera. In this opening scene Lourdes gives Esteban instructions as to how best focus the lens, and which angle is better suited for a photograph. This commentary on how to take a photograph is accidently being captured by Esteban's camera, and rather than focusing on the preparation for the snapshot, Esteban is actually recording the event. These sequences recall Walter Benjamin's observations that within the imprints of time that result from the snapshot taken by a camera, we observe

> the countless movements of switching, inserting, pressing and the like, [that] the 'snapping' of the photographer has [. . .] the greatest consequences. A touch of the finger now sufficed to fix an event for an unlimited period of time. The camera [gives] the moment a posthumous shock, as it were. (Benjamin 1992: 171)

Thus the process of taking a family portrait is highlighted within the film's opening sequence and underlies its narrative concern, an important point that I will return to in my analysis below. Once Lourdes begins her narration, we realise that these family portraits are all that remain as traces of a past family life, once the father and son have disappeared. The family pose for a framed moment in front of the camera, and the grainy, colourful and warm-textured images contrast with the current day scenes in the documentary's timeline that portray a stark change in the reality of Lourdes' existence. Next we view a family gathering for Brandon's birthday, which is filmed by Esteban. In this scene Lourdes is framed next to her son, lavishing him with loving gestures and smiles. And it is at this point that Lourdes' voiceover can be heard for the first time, introducing her son Brandon and referring to him as her 'clone'. This early statement by Lourdes will be the first of several instances during the voice-over narration where she will refer to herself in the third person, as if demonstrating temporary emotional detachment from the images of the past and the anguish of her ordeal in the present timeframe. Furthermore, the birthday home movie scene is where we learn of the mother's difficult pregnancy with Brandon and the dangers it posed for her health, since she fell pregnant so soon after her previous caesarean.

During the next home movie element of the film's opening sequence, we are invited to observe an intimate moment of relaxation shared between a father and his two children. In this scene all three are lying down, with the camera held above them and at a slight angle. Both children are embracing their father and Dayana is talking about how she plans to stay with her parents forever, even when both she and Brandon are old. The scene is a touching portrayal of family connivance and the joy shared by both parents as they revel in the company of their young children. This is the only scene in which the camera frames Esteban close up; he is shown to be quietly smiling at his daughter's words, and he glances over occasionally at the camera. The scene marks a poignant moment in the film when viewed retrospectively, since we later learn of his disappearance, making these home movies touching testimonials to a life once lived. In the home movies Lourdes' voice (as filmmaker of this segment of the home movie) is overrun by the reflexive voice-over presence of the current, re-collecting and sorrowful Lourdes, as we go on to discover in the scenes that follow.

In the first scene of the documentary to be set in the present day, and which is placed directly after the family home movies, spectators are transported to a dark, solitary room with what looks like a bed at the centre of the frame. At first it appears that what we are viewing in this scene is simply an empty bed, but then the sudden stirring of a body underneath the covers changes this interpretation. There is silence, apart from the sound of a dripping tap heard in the background. The movement under the covers acts as a self-reflexive technique whereby the spectator is reminded of the voyeuristic tendencies of the camera. It feels odd and intrusive to be watching somebody sleeping alone in their room, and the reasons behind the filming of this scene remain unclear. One explanation could be that its role is that of providing a contrast with the family-filled home movie sequences we just viewed. Aesthetically the ambience has changed, and we are presented with grey, black, and blue hues that visually frame the scene in a dreary colour pallet that contrasts with the warm grainy textures of the home movies. This sleeping body turns out to be Lourdes herself, who is alone and in an empty, cold-looking room. We notice that she's wearing warm clothes in bed (a red sweater) and the room is predominantly dark with the only light emanating from the early-morning sun's reflections on the wall. Aesthetically, the choice of colours in this scene gives the setting a cold, almost prison-like feel, which aims to represent externally the sense of emotional isolation and despair felt by the protagonist. Such bleak images are juxtaposed with shots of the morning sun reflected onto the leaves of a tree outside, which rhythmically sway with the wind and catch the sunlight flickering on and off their surfaces. Then the *mise-en-scène* reveals a close-up of a woman's feet, featuring painted toenails resting on a carpeted floor. The camera lingers here, partly to reveal that the protagonist has risen from her slumber, and partly to introduce us to the main female subject of the film.

Lourdes in this scene cuts a solitary figure in the room, which is empty of possessions apart from the bed. There is an indication that the emotional imprisonment in which Lourdes currently finds herself is mimetically conveyed by her surroundings. Her first words in this scene – the first uttered in the present context of the narrative – are 'la ausencia te duele' [absence hurts], reflecting the film's title and thematic focus. Thus the first scene with Lourdes in the present timeframe is a reflection on absence and loss. She describes the experience as a type of 'silence' that has arrived and remained. Accordingly, this scene is shot in silence, apart from her voiceover. From this moment on the spectator becomes aware of a triadic structure to Lourdes' characterisation in the documentary. We have the Lulú (Lourdes) of the past home movies, where a carefree and smiling young woman is presented and is surrounded by her family. Then we have the contrast of the present Lourdes, who is the main subject of the documentary's narrative, and who invites us into her current world of uncertainty, loss and pain. And third we have Lourdes/Lulú's voiceover, which acts as a bodiless presence throughout the narrative, linking the past with present events and inviting the spectator to share in her inner turmoil. These vocal interactions reflect on the events of the past, and their traumatic effect for the present, alongside Lourdes' current journey of unending grief, reminding us of García's (2002) observation in relation to the condition of families of the disappeared as being one of 'eternal mourning'. The separation of perspectives also provides a certain distance between the narrator Lourdes and the protagonist Lourdes on whom the former reflects, and refers to in the third person, often naming her Lulú, as if she were an alter ego.

Returning to the home movies shown at the beginning of the film, it is easy to see how these recordings, which contain images of the family taking snapshots, are significant since they highlight the photograph's crucial role as both pictorial testimony which constitutes performance of memory and as palpable, visible relic of the past. Family photographs and family albums in particular adhere to the construction of what Annette Kuhn (2007: 284) refers to as 'repositories of memory'. These visual repositories of memory frame our understanding of what is no longer physically present in the documentary's current timeframe, and are crucial to our engagement with the film's exploration of the notion of absence. At this point in the discussion we are reminded of Roland Barthes' observations on the relationship between death and the photographic image, whereby the traces of mortality present in the photograph are accentuated due to the absence now prevailing in the present. As the author observes, every 'photograph is a certificate of presence' (1980: 87), and in the case of Lourdes' experiences of loss, a confirmation of an existence. Although the Acosta family's disappearance comes without the confirmation of their demise, their prolonged physical absence arouses a sense of continued mourning, as we observed above, much in the manner of a recent death. In his *Camera Lucida*, Barthes discloses what he sees as photography's primary role, in that the photograph 'does not necessarily say *what is no longer*, but only and for certain *what has been*' (1980: 85). Watching these home movies within the documentary, and observing the discussions taking place about how to take a photograph, in addition to the final framing of the film with an image of a smiling Brandon, emphasises the importance of photography for both recording, preserving and also maintaining a sense of confirmation of a life once lived, an existence that has taken place. Moreover, photographs work in conjunction with a notion of memory in that they act as testimonies of the past, but in addition can reconfigure understandings of a cultural context and setting. Furthermore, the use of family photographs to interpret the past takes on the form of a visual palimpsest that offers possible historical readings. These insights provide new layers of meaning when applied to the case of the missing victims of Mexico's drug wars. In this context photographs are used and displayed publicly by the

families of the victims as visual emblems of their loved one's disappearance, as memorials, and as markers of protest, re-visualising those who
have become invisible. Such collective spectral images of the disappeared
subject return to haunt the public imaginary and challenge the official discourse on the context of violence in Mexico. What is more, they do so in a
manner that resists forgetting, and brings to the fore the importance of the
family album for articulating notions of memory and cultural awareness,
as Kuhn observes:

> Personal and family photographs figure importantly in cultural memory, and
> memory work with photographs offers a particularly productive route to under-
> standing the social and cultural uses and instrumentalities of memory. (2007: 283)

Kuhn's insights offer a framework from which to read the images contained
within *Ausencias*, and specifically the role played by the photographic
image in the process of memorialisation. What is more, connecting both
sets of films intertextually, that is, the diegetic home movies and Huezo's
documentary, is the fundamental role that memory plays in guiding the
viewer. The use of memory as a narrative vehicle is assisted in the film
through the concept of the family photographs and home movies, as well
as Lourdes' own recollections of the events that led to the disappearance
of her loved ones. The physical presence of both Esteban and Brandon in
these opening images, therefore, reinforces the idea of their current physical absence, and alludes to what Rodríguez sees as a process that engages
'imágenes [con que] se muestra la ausencia que se transforma en *metonimias
del trauma*' [images (with which) absence is shown that are transformed
into *trauma metonyms*] (2006: 173). In her article on the work of Argentine
filmmaker Lita Stantic, and in particular the notion of latent trauma in
films about the enforced disappearances during Argentina's 'Dirty War',
Rodríguez explores the relationship between trauma, memory and representation. The type of memory manifestation that she identifies, namely
the aforementioned *memoria airada*, constitutes 'una forma subjetivada de
la memoria colectiva sobre lo traumático' (2006: 171) [a subjective form
of collective memory concerned with the traumatic], and in her analysis
the author examines how this use of memory frames the filmic discourse
of Stantic's *Un muro de silencio* [A Wall of Silence] (1993). Stantic's first
film observes the traumatic expressions of the illegal crimes of Argentina's
military Junta upon the individual (and the national psyche), which
include, among other reports, the torture and enforced disappearances of
thousands of civilians. These past events have shaped the *memoria airada*
of Argentina's 'Dirty Wars' and its casualties. What is more, Rodríguez

suggests that this type of memory, though existent within the wider collective, nevertheless remains repressed and not fully explored:

> consideramos la memoria airada como una forma de la memoria atribuida a un colectivo social que supone olvidos y silencios, así como las huellas del registro de lo imaginario que no están plenamente integradas al orden simbólico. (2006: 175)

> [we consider irate memory as a form of memory attributed to a social collective that involves forgetfulness and silence, such as traces of registering the imaginary that are not fully integrated into the symbolic order.]

Thus the Argentine example of the enforced disappearances during the military Junta's reign of terror, and the nation's filmic responses to the processing of this national trauma on the screen, is a case that can be used comparatively when attempting to read Mexico's ongoing current crisis. Films about enforced disappearances, the struggle to find justice and the impact of military and narco-violence on society are finding their way onto the screen in Mexico, and in particular are becoming more common within the documentary genre. Such films focus on the topic of violence and enforced disappearances from both sides of the border. Examples include Natalia Almada's *El velador/ The Night Watchman* (2011), Luis Ramírez Guzmán y Federico Mastrogiovanni's *Ni vivos ni muertos* [Neither Dead Nor Alive] (2014), Matías Gueilburt's *Antes que nos olviden* [Before They Forget Us] (2014), Katya Adler's *Mexico's Drug War* (2010) and Matthew Heineman's *Cartel Land* (2015), to name but a few.

Perhaps applicable to our readings of the opening sequence of Huezo's *Ausencias* is Rodríguez's suggestion that the role of images in the creation of a sense of *memoria airada* is crucial, and the transference of these concepts of image-making, collective memory and national traumas onto the screen is one that can provide challenges for the filmmaker because of the power of *memoria airada* to convey the affective experience of loss.

In the case of *Ausencias*, Huezo's challenges lie in how to convey such deep emotions of loss and mourning by visual means. How does the filmmaker share the protagonist's inner world and re-create that sense of absence around which Lourdes' life revolves? One of the fundamental obstacles in representing the disappeared is their lack of physical presence, and the question of how to convey a sense of absence, because, as Bill Nichols observes:

> Documentary film operates in literal compliance with the writ of *habeas corpus*. 'You should have the body' – without it the legal process comes to a standstill. 'You should have the body' – without it the documentary tradition lacks its primary referent, the real social actor(s) of whose historical engagement it speaks. (1987: 9)

This lack of physicality, as Nichols posits, is replaced by photographs, home movies, testimonies and witness accounts, forming an overall picture of the disappeared. Drawing on a close reading of the documentary *Roses in December* (Ana Carrigan and Bernard Stone, 1982) which traces the life and disappearance of Jean Donovan in El Salvador through archival news footage, interviews, home movies and diary readings, Nichols ponders on the problems that arise from attempting to represent the disappeared subject. Although focusing mainly on Donovan's story, *Roses in December* also tells the story of the three nuns who were with Donovan at the time of her demise, and who were also murdered by a government death squad in El Salvador. In terms of the film's subject matter, Nichols observes that the 'film does offer, however, an exemplary demonstration of how the human body can be represented through a weave of materials that stand in for a person who is dead' (1987: 10). And it is these materials, seen in the form of photographs, home movies, snapshots and diaries, that ultimately piece together an understanding of this missing 'character' in the film *Roses*. This same reading of *Roses* and of the missing subject can also be applied to *Ausencias*, where the re-creations of both Esteban and, in particular, Brandon come about through the piecing together of pictorial and verbal materials that describe, visualise and re-create the lost subjects. Furthermore, given the structure of this documentary which begins and ends with a photographic image, and the narrator's reliance on the role of memory to document and reveal the events of the past, in addition to its non-linear narrative sequence, it is also possible to view *Ausencias* in its entirety as constituting what Kuhn (2010) classifies as a 'memory text'. In terms of structural characteristics, Kuhn observes that in memory texts:

> [. . .] time rarely comes across as continuous or sequential: for example, events may have a repetitive or cyclical quality ('we used to. . .'), or may telescope or merge into one another in the telling so that a single recounted memory might fuse together a series of possibly separate events, or follow no obviously logical or temporal sequence. The memory text is typically a montage of vignettes, anecdotes, fragments, 'snapshots' and flashes that can generate a feeling of synchrony: remembered events seem to be outside any linear time frame or may refuse to be easily anchored to 'historical' time. In the memory text, events often appear to have been plucked at random from a paradigm of memories and assembled in a mode of narration in which causality is not, if apparent at all, a prominent feature. (Kuhn 2010: 299)

The structural processes of *Ausencias* that rely on the use of memory and memory materials (such as home movies and photographs) to narrate the events of the past, and reveal the condition of the present, align the documentary with the characteristics of the memory text as described by Kuhn (2010) above. Furthermore, this narrative fluidity, with timeless sequences and the intermixing of imagery with voice-over reflections, assigns to *Ausencias* a poetic quality that encourages the viewer to engage visually with the image being framed, and emotionally with the audio-narration. The mimetic interaction between the content of the voice-over narration and the aesthetic dimension of the film, seen in the camera's fascination with forms, light, shadows, colours, textures and sounds, illustrates the performative aspect of the film's quality. Furthermore, *Ausencias* delivers what Kuhn notes to be a main feature of the memory text, namely the 'abrupt shifts of scene and/or narrative viewpoint', because:

> [. . .] memory texts have more in common with poetry than with classical narrative. In the memory text [. . .] structure and organization seem to be of greater rhetorical salience than content. The metaphoric quality, the foregrounding of formal devices, the tendency to rapid shifts of setting or point of view all feed into the characteristically collagist, fragmentary, timeless [. . .] quality of the memory text, which by and large possesses an imagistic quality [. . .] Significantly, all of these attributes have to do with performance: the memory text embodies a particular approach to, or type of, performances of memory. (2010: 299)

As we shall see below, it is at the point when Lourdes begins to delve into her memory and recollect the traumatic moment when Esteban and Brandon went missing that the film aesthetically changes. At this point in the narrative the diegetic and extra-diegetic soundscapes become more oppressive, audibly engulfing her words and mimicking her despair in an attempt to represent the inexpressive pain of a mother's loss.

Representing the Inexpressible

In the scene that follows the opening shots of Lourdes asleep in her room and the sequence of home movies, we view Lourdes positioned in front of the camera with her back to the spectator. She is on the phone, and at first it is not clear who she is speaking to (Figure 7.2).

It soon becomes apparent, however, that Lourdes is in the process of leaving a voicemail for an unknown recipient. Later we learn that her absent husband's mobile phone, which she keeps topped up with credit, is still active. This enables Lourdes to make these daily phone calls to an unknown potential listener at the other end, whom she hopes might heed her pleas and grant her the return of her son and husband. This is the only point in the narrative in which we see a distinct and palpable vulnerability in Lourdes, as her voice cracks at the mentioning of Brandon's name as

Figure 7.2   Lourdes on the phone in a scene from *Ausencias* (2015).

she leaves her daily message. We witness her silently weeping, away from
the camera's focus, while imploring her son's invisible abductors to let him
go. Due to the polite, restrained and courteous manner in which Lourdes
speaks on the phone, at first it seems as though she is speaking to a government bureaucrat or official investigating the case of her missing husband
and son. It is therefore all the more poignant and tragically powerful to
learn that Lourdes is in fact leaving a voicemail for their kidnappers, in the
belief that one day she may appeal to the better nature of those who have
taken her son and husband away from her. This daily ritual paradoxically
restores a sense of order and control over a situation that has become in
Lourdes' words 'a living nightmare'. It also demonstrates the extent of
Lourdes' unreserved hope in finding her loved ones again, and for their
safe return. And, perhaps more importantly, it shows Lourdes' belief in
the inner goodness of people, since with her messages she attempts to tap
into the human instincts of the kidnappers and arouse a sense of parental empathy or shared experience. Her final words to them, 'I need my
son so that I can live', summarise what Huezo had observed in Lourdes
when she first began interviewing her as a potential documentary subject
(Bautista 2015). In an interview in the Mexican periodical *El financiero-
Huezo recalls hearing Lourdes' voice for the first time and being struck
by its haunting, almost absent quality, as if the speaker were only half living (Bautista 2015).

The camera in this scene then focuses on the blank walls as Lourdes
begins to tell us her story, which, she informs us, began four years prior

to the making of the film. We learn of how Esteban, her in-laws, Walberto and Gerardo (Esteban's brothers), and son Brandon set off one morning for Monterrey airport to see one of the brothers off back to Los Angeles, where he then lived. The party of five left at 6:50am, with Esteban promising to return by midday since he had to be at work for 1pm. While Lourdes relates these details, the camera focuses on bare derelict walls, and on puddles of water in the room, which constitute bleak, damp, unwelcoming exterior visuals. As the story of Esteban and his family members' kidnapping becomes more emotive and harrowing, the external visuals of the walls darken, the cracks on the surfaces are heightened and framed, insects are traced as they crawl up a wall's surface, a rusty nail is framed, an orifice resembling a bullet hole is focused on, and the general lighting of the room fades considerably. These filming techniques remind us of Kuhn's (2010) observations above on the poetic value of the memory text in that the images in these scenes act as a form of visual pathetic fallacy, with their increasing bleakness and dark compositions mirroring the depths of despair felt by the protagonist as she recalls her experiences of the days immediately following the abduction.

Lourdes continues with her story and informs the spectator that at 4pm Walberto's wife had phoned to say that her husband had not arrived at the airport in Los Angeles. They were told that out of the eighty-two passengers all but one had boarded the plane from Monterrey to LA that morning. As the narrative/voiceover progresses, the imagery on the wall worsens. The rising damp is framed as visually engulfing the wall, the painting is shown to be peeling, the images are of rotten and cold matter, and the wall looks stained and dilapidated. At this point Lourdes reveals the extent of her anxiety on the day of their disappearance and its intensification as they make their way to the authorities to declare Esteban and his party missing. She recalls how when they arrive at the district attorney's office the weather turns cold and grey, and then it begins to rain heavily, highlighting the connection between her inner turmoil and her environment. As if to accentuate this emotion the camera frames a close-up of a deep crack in the wall and an unfilled, dark hole. These symbolic images constitute an externalisation of Lourdes' emotional universe, which has been shattered by the sudden loss of her husband and son. These same explorations, moreover, conducted by the camera of a decaying exterior wall, serve as a visual exercise in the filmic approximation to the traumatic experience. The ordeal suffered by the protagonist in turn is externalised and visually relayed through the camera's framing of matter, object and texture. The element of light plays a major role in the documentary in that the dancing shadows on the wall that we saw earlier now turn to darkness, while the oppressive tones of the colour palette heighten the sense of anxiety and powerlessness felt by the protagonist as she fears the worst for her loved ones. Thus in these scenes each image changes and worsens mimetically with Lourdes' words as she describes her ordeal, and the soundscape similarly matches this uncertainty and sense of danger as we hear chattering voices, distant planes flying overheard, footsteps, doors closing, and the far-off sound of gunshots, all sounds that do not directly correspond with the dark images being framed but are present to provide a sense of foreboding, confusion and despair.

As if by way of contrast, as the narrative progresses the imagery brightens, and we view Lourdes venturing beyond the dreary interiors, stepping into daylight and the outside world. We see how social activity continues to take place outside of the family home, where Lourdes' solitary figure is framed against a busy, cosmopolitan cityscape. In these scenes she is either driving her car in an overcrowded road, sitting quietly contemplating the world from a café window, or standing watching a group of young boys, roughly her son's age, as they gather in the park, chattering among themselves. These scenes serve to remind us of how the everyday, and the mundane, continues, and how despite the tragedy inflicted on the family, life goes on. In these scenes Lourdes is deliberately shot as an outside observer; her moments in the car reflect her constant search for her loved ones and we are told how the fleeting view of a car similar to the one her husband was driving on the day of the abduction sets her heart racing and her mind alert. Her sense of hope and longing is resolute, and she sees the possibility of reunion at each street turning. When we finally view Dayana (Lourdes' eldest child) again she is almost a young woman, on the cusp of adulthood. We witness her continuing with her passion for swimming (mentioned by the voiceover at the beginning of the film), and we see the close bond between mother and daughter (Figure 7.3).

Lourdes' voiceover reveals the tumultuous feelings of guilt, love and gratitude for her daughter. During the dark days following her husband and son's disappearance Lourdes abandoned herself to her feelings of despair and entered a state of profound depression. She confesses to being unaware of her daughter's needs and neglectful of her duty as her mother. Once again Lourdes' voice cracks under the strain of her remorse, and she confesses that she will never forgive herself for temporarily forgetting her daughter. Then one day, we are told, the sunlight shone through the window and its reflection was caught on Dayana's face. It was at this point, Lourdes' voiceover recollects, that she understood that the little girl was her reason for living. At this point in the narrative, and as if to mimic Lourdes' memory, Dayana is framed bathed in sunlight, as she smiles while

Figure 7.3   Lourdes and her daughter, Dayana, in one of the final scenes of the film.
A still from *Ausencias* (2015).

waiting for her turn to dive into the swimming pool. Thus the past memory as narrated by Lourdes' voiceover and the present as seen on screen
are brought together. The darker moments of the film, with the bleakness of the abandoned rooms and derelict walls, are replaced by sunlight,
the chatter of children by the pool, and an image of a proud Lourdes
watching on as her daughter swims lengths in the water. The film ends
on this note, and the last character we see is Dayana leaving the pool and
walking away from the camera. These sunlit instances bring a sense of
relief from the trauma and frame the ending of the film with a notion of
hope – hope that Lourdes may find some peace and solace in her daughter, and hope that Dayana may grow up to become a commendable young
woman, scarred by the events of the past, but strong and secure in the care
of her mother. The profound sadness provoked by Lourdes' story lingers
long after the closing credits have ceased, and yet Huezo's choice to end
the narrative in the present day, with a brightly lit scene and a more serene
Lourdes watchful of her daughter's achievements, offers a sense of hope, as
far as is possible given the context of uncertainty. This sense of hope in the
film's ending in turn mirrors the hopeful position maintained by the thousands of families of these victims of *levantones* – families who lie in waiting
for their loved ones to return, and who until that day comes, continue to
campaign nationally and internationally. These families of the victims of
violence in Mexico, whose loved ones have been taken from them, work

hard to make sure that the disappeared are not forgotten, that they remain visual despite their disappearance. Key to this process of resistance is the role of the photograph and, in particular, the centrality of the family portrait within the struggle for visibility and accountability. Thus the idea of the immortality of the image is encapsulated in the closing frame of the film, which aptly ends with a photograph of a smiling Brandon.

Note

1. Unless otherwise stated, all translations are my own.

Bibliography

Antes que nos olviden, film, directed by Matías Gueilburt. USA: FICG, 2014.

Associated Press (2016), 'Enrique Peña Nieto visita ciudad donde desaparecieron 43 estudiantes', *El Universo*, 24 February. Available at: <https://www.eluniverso.com/noticias/2016/02/24/nota/5425365/enrique-pena-nieto-visita-ciudad-donde-desaparecieron-43> (last accessed 28 May 2020).

Ausencias, film, directed by Tatiana Huezo. Mexico: FICM, 2015.

Barthes, Roland [1980] (1993), *Camera Lucida*, London: Vintage.

Bautista, Eduardo (2015), 'Documentar el vacío de los desaparecidos, el reto de *Ausencias*', *El Financiero*, 21 January. Available at: <https://www.elfinanciero.com.mx/after-office/documentar-el-vacio-el-reto-de-ausencias> (last accessed 28 May 2020).

Benjamin, Walter [1939] (1992), 'On Some Motifs in Baudelaire', in *Illuminations*, London: Fontana.

Berggruen, Nicholas, and Nathan Gardels (2013), 'The rise of the "Aztec tiger"', *The Wall Street Journal*, 26 April. Available at: <https://www.wsj.com/articles/SB10001424127887324474004578443272628571346> (last accessed 28 May 2020).

Cartel Land, film, directed by Matthew Heineman. USA: The Orchard, 2015.

De la Fuente, Anna Marie (2015), 'Morelia: Mexico's Tatiana Huezo on Voices, Abduction, Prison', *Variety*, 26 October. Available at: <https://variety.com/2015/film/festivals/morelia-tatiana-huezo1201627300–1201627300/> (last accessed 28 May 2020).

El velador, film, directed by Natalia Almada. Mexico: Icarus Films, 2011.

Freud, Sigmund (1963), 'Mourning and Melancholia', in *The Standard Edition of the Complete Psychological Works of Sigmund Freud*, London: Hogarth Press.

García, María Soledad (2002), 'Ansia de cuerpo: Presencia y vacío en la representación del cuerpo desaparecido', *Desde El Jardín De Freud*, 2: pp. 12–18.

Gudiño, Alma (2016), 'Cereso varonil de saltillo cumple con normas internacionales de la ONU', *Excelsior TV Noticias*, 24 February. Available at: <https://www.youtube.com/watch?v=QPOsTTK0dD0> (last accessed 28 May 2020).

Guindal, Carlota (2016), 'Humberto Moreira, el expresidente del PRI, trabajaba para el cartel de los Zetas', *El Español*, January 21. Available at: https://www.elespanol.com/espana/20160121/96240415_0.html (last accessed 28 May 2020).

Hapak, Peter (2014), 'Saving Mexico', *Time*, 24 February. Available at: <http://content.time.com/time/covers/europe/0,16641,20140224,00.html> (last accessed 28 May 2020).

Kuhn, Annette (2007), 'Photography and Cultural Memory: A Methodological Exploration', *Visual Studies*, 22:3, pp. 283–92.

Kuhn, Annette (2010), 'Memory Texts and Memory Work: Performances of Memory in and with Visual Media', *Memory Studies*, 3:4, pp. 298–313.

Lakhani, Nina (2013), 'The Disappeared: At Least 26,000 People Have Gone Missing in Mexico's Drugs War', *Independent*, 19 October. Available at: <https://www.independent.co.uk/news/world/americas/the-disappeared-at-least-26000–people-have-gone-missing-in-mexicos-drugs-war-8884385.html> (last accessed 28 May 2020).

MacLaird, Misha (2013), *Aesthetics and Politics in the Mexican Film Industry*, Basingstoke: Palgrave Macmillan.

Martínez, Jan (2014), 'Iguala Mayor and his Wife Arrested in Mexico City Over Missing Students', *El País*, 4 November. Available at: <https://english.elpais.com/elpais/2014/11/04/inenglish/1415120929_564306.html> (last accessed 28 May 2020).

Mexico's Drug War, film, directed by Katya Adler. UK: BBC, 2010.

Nichols, Bill (1987), 'History, Myth, and Narrative in Documentary', *Film Quarterly*, 41:1, pp. 9–20.

Ni vivos ni muertos, film, directed by Federico Mastrogiovanni. Mexico: Grijalbo, 2014.

Redacción (2009), '"Levantados" cuatro miembros de la familia acosta', *Zócalo*, 1 September. Available at: <https://www.zocalo.com.mx/new_site/articulo/Levantados-cuatro-miembros-de-la-familia-Acosta> (last accessed 28 May 2020).

Redacción AN (2016), 'En España, investigan vínculos de Humberto Moreira y "los Zetas"', *Aristegui Noticias*, 21 January. Available at: <https://aristeguinoticias.com/2101/mexico/en-espana-investigan-vinculos-de-humberto-moreira-y-los-zetas> (last accessed 28 May 2020).

Riveles, José (2011), *Levantones, narcofosas y falsos positivos*, Mexico City: Grijalbo.

Rodríguez, Paula (2006), 'Estrategias de lo traumático y la "memoria airada" en "un muro de silencio"', *Signo y PensamientoI* 25:48, pp. 171–84.

Roses in December, film, directed by Ana Carrigan and Bernard Stone. New York: First Run Features, 1982.

Smith, Paul Julian (2014), *Mexican Screen Fiction: Between Cinema and Television*, Cambridge: Polity Press.

Tempestad, film, directed by Tatiana Huezo. Mexico: Cinefilm, 2016.

Tuckman, Jo (2014), 'Mexican Mayor Charged with Murder Linked to Students' Disappearance', *The Guardian*, 14 November. Available at: <https://www.theguardian.com/world/2014/nov/14/mexican-mayor-jose-luis-abarca-charged-murder-students> (last accessed 28 May 2020).

Turati, Marcela (2012), 'Las bandas también levantan y desaparecen niños', *Proceso*, 28 June. Available at <https://www.proceso.com.mx/312519/las-bandas-tambien-levantan-y-desaparecen-ninos-2> (last accessed 28 May 2020).

Veiga, Gustavo (2011), 'El levantón, un cruento método narco', *Página12*, 21 February. Available at <https://www.pagina12.com.ar/diario/elmundo/4-162761-2011-02-21.html> (last accessed 28 May 2020).

CHAPTER 8

Teresa Margolles' Work with Space: Ruins, Resonances and the Echo of the Absent

Julia Banwell

The Mexican neo-conceptual artist Teresa Margolles' (b. 1963) artistic career now spans three decades, from the 1990s to the present. An artist of great standing in the international contemporary art world, she has shown her work in solo and group exhibitions worldwide. This chapter will explore the ways in which Margolles draws attention to gender-based violence in a selection of her works. Discussion will focus on the artist's use of space and emptiness, and issues around agency in the performance of bodies and of ruins.

Margolles is a multi-media and a transmedia artist. Her work employs multiple modes of expression to tell different stories, and also offers different material perspectives, including photography, sculpture and video to mine experience for relics of death and grief. She began her artistic career during the 1990s as a member of SEMEFO, a collective that took its name from the organisation that collects corpses and transports them to the morgue in Mexico (see Gallo 2004 for further detail on the early part of Margolles' career). The morgue was for a number of years her principal locus of operation, and corpses, body parts and bodily residues such as fat and blood were depicted in and incorporated into her artworks. As a qualified forensic technician, Margolles occupies a dual position as scientist and artist, and brings the material of death into the public realm, exposing the direct link between violence and absence, and also highlighting the systemic social inequities that affect treatment of the body after death. Many of the corpses featured in her works belonged to individuals whose families could not afford to bury them. Such corpses often end up as medical study cadavers or buried in a *fosa común* [mass grave],[1] a fate that would not befall the corpse of a person who benefits from economic and social privilege. The artist's access to the restricted space of the morgue has afforded her a 'privileged perspective' (Bacal 2015 263) from which to survey the brutalising effects of violence on individual bodies and on wider society: a single violent death causes bodily disintegration, and multiple deaths destabilise the fabric of society's body. Margolles gathers and documents evidence from this perspective, selecting artefacts and fragments to share through her work, which shows the direct relationship between violence and absence.

This has been the impetus behind Margolles' use of her art as a means by which to confront the viewer with unpalatable truths by forcing close proximity with the effects of the systemic violence that disproportionately affects people marginalised on the grounds of gender, sexuality and economic status - or a combination of these factors. In the series of five photographs *Autorretratos en la morgue* (1998), Margolles appears beside corpses in a morgue. The most emotionally affecting of the images is the one in which the artist in her dual role as mourner-activist and forensic technician (the latter signified by her white coat and thick rubber gloves) holds the badly damaged body of a girl in her outstretched arms, and looks directly into the camera, which is positioned at a high angle. The added poignancy of this image stems from the symbolic power of a child's death; the idea of a life cut short before blossoming into adulthood carries great weight and provokes an especially sharp sense of grief and injustice. The camera is positioned more closely to the subject of this image, bringing the child's body and the artist into direct physical contact and also drawing the viewer into greater intimacy with both. The other images in the series are long shots in which bodies are shown on metal trolleys with the artist standing beside them, arms folded. There is a gendered dimension to this positioning of the artist who engages with death as mourner for a community since women have traditionally embodied the role of carriers of collective pain, acting as professional mourners in funeral processions, adding their wails to the weeping of the deceased's loved ones. Here, the dead, and in other works, the living participants, are a vehicle for shared expression. Many artists who explore physical and emotional trauma in their works do so via performance of their own bodies: Marina Abramović, Mona Hatoum and Ana Mendieta are three prominent examples. Margolles, however, rather than inhabiting and performing pain enacted in or onto her own body, offers a photographic lament that mourns the pain experienced by others and brings it into collective experience. This series evidences Margolles' interest in showing the reality of death, rather than constructing narratives in which she is placed at the centre. Though she does – unusually – appear in these photographs, she draws the viewer's attention not to herself but to the cadavers beside or in front of her; we look at *them* first, watched over by the artist's unnerving, unwavering gaze.

Margolles' work across diverse forms of expression reveals the artist's fascination with traces and remains, the lingering evidence of trauma,

injustice, and institutionalised violence that lets marginalised people metaphorically fall through the cracks, rendering them invisible. The artist in
this context functions as an archaeologist of trauma, uncovering evidence
of crimes and atrocities and presenting material evidence to be witnessed.
Central to her activity in the public realm is a sense of the artist as activist,
one who calls to awareness through actions that incorporate fragments of
lives and deaths via the inhabiting of derelict and liminal spaces in careful,
deliberate positioning of the body and its residues as a challenge to the
dynamics of violence that threaten and destroy them.

More recently, and particularly since 2005, Margolles' work has moved
out of the morgue, a shift that reflects the increase in violence related to
the narcotics trade, the so-called 'War on Drugs' and the visibility of death
and bodies in public spaces (see Watt and Zepeda 2012). The increase in
the presence of death outside of the morgue has made necessary this shift
into public locations, and the growing engagement of performance by living participants attests to the urgency of the need to respond and resist
the dehumanising effects of such apparently ubiquitous extreme violence.
The artist's interest in traces is what ties together all of her works, in
disparate geographical locations, with dead and living bodies, materials
that acquire other meanings through contact with remains. In Margolles'
work, fragments and residues constitute material memories of past lives of
bodies, and objects can take on a metonymic function, standing in place of
the absent in a manner at times reminiscent of Doris Salcedo's work with
everyday items, space and absence.

The Ruin, Space and Power Dynamics

Margolles has a long-held focus on the northern Mexican city of Ciudad
Juárez, which became notorious as a location for extreme violence associated with the drug cartels and organised crime that has gone unchal-
lenged by a judicial system riddled with corruption. Furthermore, during
the so-called 'War on Drugs', the level of crime and violence actually rose
despite increased spending on security (Watt and Zepeda 2012: 187). The
city has come to be particularly associated with gendered violence, which
has caused the disappearances of hundreds of women and girls since the
early 1990s and particularly following the implementation of the North
American Free Trade Agreement in 1994. When - if - missing girls and
women are found, 'they are disfigured beyond recognition and often
beheaded' (Gygax 2018: 221). Despite the extreme and prolific nature of
this violence that specifically targets women and girls, very little is done
by municipal and national authorities to bring any perpetrators to justice.

As Chiapas University of Arts and Sciences researcher Mercedes Olivera explains, 'feminicide is a mechanism of domination, control, oppression, and power over women' (cited in Vicario 2018: 122).

Local and international attention has been drawn many times to these crimes, yet scant regard is shown by those in power to the experience of women in Ciudad Juárez. They live and work in precarious conditions and many reside in neighbourhoods with no street lighting. They travel long distances to work in the *maquiladoras*, the factories that assemble a range of technological appliances and where tens of thousands of young women, many of whom moved alone from other parts of Mexico, work long hours for little pay (see Bowden 2010; Watt and Zepeda 2012: 157–61).

The *feminicidios*, however, are not the only form of gendered violence perpetrated in Mexico. The 'Glitter Rosa' march in August 2019 (La Verdad Juárez 2019) drew attention to the 'victimisation' of a teacher who accused four university lecturers of rape (see La Jornada 2019). This protest echoed other protests in Mexico City and elsewhere, which called for a halt to the criminalisation of women who reported police officers for the same crime. The geographical distribution of these marches shows the ubiquitousness of gendered violence and the lack of action to prosecute it under the misogynistic, *machista* culture evidently rife at all levels of the authorities supposed to protect citizens from injustice and abuse.

In Ciudad Juárez, the bodies and body parts of murdered women and girls are often found at locations in the desert that have come to be used as dumping grounds (Vicario 2018: 123). Margolles documents some of these locations directly, for example in the earth sculpture *Lote Bravo* (2005), which takes its name directly from one such place. The artist visited the location and collected up earth to make adobe bricks. This earth, shaped into rectangular bricks that have the same dimensions but are all slightly different, acts not only as a signifier of the place where it was found but as a repository or store for the traces of death: the tiny, invisible particles of blood, hair, clothing left behind after a body or a part of a body has been collected and taken to the morgue. Vicario (2018) explains Margolles' process: 'She collected this material from more than a hundred locations and had the brick maker blend this into the raw clay before being formed and dried by the desert heat' (Vicario 2018: 123–9).

The action of making the bricks was documented *in situ* in photographs which have then been displayed, while the bricks themselves form an installation. Owing to their number and form, they may be used to build a wall in the gallery space or stood on end in a formation reminiscent of blank headstones. In this layout, they become sentinels, silent witnesses, and defiant memorials to these unnamed women. Margolles also produced a video, *Lomas de Poleo, Anapra y Cerro del Cristo Negro* (2005), which documents the artist's journey through the body dumping locations named in its title.

Margolles carried out these forensic investigations at considerable risk to her own safety. She engaged local activists and investigators and began to compile information about characteristics common to missing women, such as their ages and any features that may have marked them out as potential targets. Her 'grass roots approach' (Vicario 2018: 122) saw her travelling late at night.

Against this backdrop, Margolles' artistic protests and calls to awareness take on particular resonance. Her works hold up a lens through which she invites the viewer to examine the trauma inflicted by the epidemic of gendered violence. The continuing inaction on the part of the authorities, as well as the actions of those who abuse and persecute cis and transgender women, are held up for scrutiny, and exposed for their cruel neglect and the violence they inflict on disenfranchised and marginalised individuals. Her inclusion of people oppressed by systemic violence, and their agency in occupying spaces where they claim visibility against the power dynamics that exploit and devalue them, provide evidence of the crimes against them and wrest their lived experience from the fog of collective amnesia and into the public consciousness, where it is re-located as a testimony of uncovered trauma. As a highly acclaimed transnational artist, Margolles finds herself in a position conducive to being an effective loudspeaker.

More recently, Margolles has tackled the ruination of parts of Ciudad Juárez as the epicentres of its nightlife fall to a tide of gentrification under which demolition precedes reconstruction and the repurposing of ground. In Ciudad Juárez, demolition of buildings in the city's historic centre and the construction of new attractions expected to re-boost tourism were marketed as a 'new face' for the city (according to a 2013 report cited by Jonquères 2018: 249). Jonquères explains that: 'To carry out this plan, the city council demolished hundreds of homes, dance halls and canteens. Throughout this process only five historically important buildings were left standing' (Jonquères 2018: 249, 252).

The city council manifested its vision of progress in a way that excluded local residents, academics and other experts from participating (see Jonquères 2018: 252). The violence was not just inflicted on the spaces, it also impacted marginalised subjects through the removal of the places they occupied and worked in. This final destruction concluded the process of effacement that had been ongoing for some time, during which the trans community in Ciudad Juárez had 'watched most of the places that protected them disappear, exposing them to harassment by the police' (Jonquères 2018: 249).

As a way of drawing attention to this erasure, one of Margolles' recent projects in Ciudad Juárez focuses on the experience of trans women who worked in nightclubs in a part of the city scoured by demolition. Trans people, and sex workers, are subjected to disproportionate levels of violent abuse that forms part of a system of unequal power relations.

Pistas de baile [Dance Floors] (2016) is a series of photographs in which transgender sex workers pose on fragments of dancefloors from nightclubs they used to work in, which have now been demolished. The visibility in these images of individuals belonging to a societally, systemically oppressed group directly challenges the demolition of the buildings and the marginalisation of the people who inhabited them. This work is one of many in which the artist raises consciousness via images that stand as memorials to the destroyed buildings, to the murdered people, and to groups and individuals who are subjected to systemic oppression. Margolles' presence as artist-creator of these images exists alongside that of the participants who pose defiantly in them (Figure 8.1).

The women stand in the burning heat of the day, present and visible against the obliterating tide that has swept away the places where they

Figure 8.1   *Pista de baile del club 'Centro Lagunero'* [Dancefloor of the club 'Centro Lagunero'], 2016.

worked. For each image, Margolles poured water onto the tiled dance-floor. The water not only washed away the sand that covered the floor but also highlights the area, its wetness drawing the eye to the figure's shock-ing pink high heels and the small patch of patterned floor that stands out against a derelict backdrop. The photographs are named after the night-club that stood on the now vacant spot of land. The poured water, though, challenges the finality of the demolition: a fragment remains, and it is inhabited once more by a person who inhabited the place that used to stand there. The ephemerality of the water, which in the 50°C heat is soon to evaporate, attests to the ebbs and flows of construction and destruc-tion in the contemporary city, and exposes the neoliberal power dynamics that aggressively wash away the places and the lives of marginalised and oppressed individuals. Water, with its connotation of cleansing and purifi-cation, makes the dancefloors look smooth and mirror-like; in some of the images, partial reflections of the shoes and legs of some participants are visible, and in others, their shadows stretch away behind or beside them as if they, too, stand defiantly and mark their presence on the land that was their territory.

The *Pistas de baile* explore the dynamics of oppression in one aspect of the sexual economy of Ciudad Juárez. The photographs document the impact of power enactment and the further marginalisation of already vic-timised people. Gendered violence is complex and multi-layered, played out in every sphere of private and public life, and here, in this specific context, we see the active persecution of one of the most vulnerable social groups; they have been treated as mere collateral in the push–pull of power in the border region, subjected to unspeakable violence in a con-text in which hatred and repression of women and girls continues with vehemence. Through her work, Margolles makes them visible and evokes the history of the spaces they worked and inhabited. Tragically, 'the indi-viduals [pictured in these images] have all died since being photographed' (Vicario 2018: 129). Consequently, the photographs as objects constitute a material life after death, not the 'life of the corpse' itself but the repro-duced images of people now departed. They memorialise not only the places depicted, but those who occupied them; a double-layered haunting of space and body.

Though photography, like memory, shows only fragments and is inher-ently selective, Margolles' photographs of ruins (Figure 8.2), like ruins themselves, stand as reminders, memorialising and signifying that which went before, and which fell to the ravages of time or violence. Ciudad Juárez is but one of many cities worldwide in which subcultures are squeezed out of city centre locations by gentrification. So while Solnit

Figure 8.2   *Pista de baile del club 'Rodarte'* [Dancefloor of the club 'Rodarte'], 2016.

is correct in her observation of a similar process in San Francisco that '[R]uins are evidence not only that cities can be destroyed but that they survive their own destruction, are resurrected again and again' (Solnit 2011: 151), the ruins Margolles photographs will be built over as opposed to reconstructed, and nothing will stand as a reminder of how the space was used before, or who used it. These ruins will not survive to be Simmel's positive reminders of the life that dwelled there, a palpable 'immediately perceived presence' or the 'present form of a past life' (Simmel [1911] 2011: 23). Margolles' photographs act as remnants of the past. They will not be cherished monuments to the past. It will be as though the past of these spaces never existed: invisibility precedes forgetting. However, the stripping away of collectively useable space and the visibility it grants is contested. The images themselves, and the individuals depicted therein, resist institutionalised forgetting, enforced invisibility.

Margolles' extensive repertoire of work in Ciudad Juárez foregrounds the life of the ruin and of the wasteland, the abandoned, the derelict, the disused, the forgotten and deliberately erased. Her photographs of demolished spaces preserve them evidentially in the collective memory - as well as in the memories of the people who frequented them since via their display they are now seen by others. The 'life of the corpse' (Görner and Kittelman 2004: 41) that was the driving conceptual force behind the early part of Margolles' career has become the aesthetic of the ruin, the archae-ology of waste. The spaces used in performance have been chosen because they are the front line in the tidal surge that threatens and sweeps away structures inhabited by people who are positioned as marginal to the neo-liberal agenda. These spaces, and the traces of violence they contain and signify, can therefore be reconfigured as loci of defiance against the gentri-fication of areas deemed unsavoury, unregulatable, not suitably profitable.

For Theodor Adorno: 'works of art are after-images or replicas of empirical life' (Adorno [1970] 1986: 6). Artworks can consequently be seen as trace evidence as well as the constructed artefacts they clearly are. In the *Pistas de baile* photographs, participants stand on sections of the dancefloor that the artist has marked with water. The building, the night-club itself, has been demolished, and eventually this piece of floor will be ripped up or built over, and disappear. The images capture a moment in time before total destruction and subsequent recreation and catalogue the deaths of these structures and spaces in the same way that other works cat-alogue the deaths of individuals, capturing them and thrusting them into visibility, or at least a new corporeal presence, albeit without subjective consciousness. The artwork here documents a fragile moment, asserting the presence of the participants whose experiences and existence may oth-erwise go undocumented. The photograph is thus a freeze frame, but one that also transcends the moment of its capture. In Azoulay's words:

> The event of photography is never over. It can only be suspended, caught in the anticipation of the next encounter that will allow for its actualisation: an encounter that might allow a certain spectator to remark on the excess or lack inscribed in the photograph so as to re-articulate every detail including those that some believe to be fixed in place by the glossy emulsion of the photograph. (Azoulay 2015: 25)

Photographic images, as acknowledged by many scholars (such as Susan Sontag 1977, 2003; Roland Barthes 2000; John Berger 1967), are objects in their own right and as such merit deep investigation, since they are texts that contain multiple, nuanced layers of meaning. A photograph that carries potential for political interpretation re-states these meanings with each new, separate viewing. The act of spectatorship enlivens the object, in addition to its own display of itself. For communication to occur, however, of course there must be an interlocutor or recipient. I argue that this reading may also be applied not just to photographs but also to artefacts such as those constructed by Margolles from found objects and debris, with narratives being woven using multiple objects and across different media.

Margolles' work is concerned with memory, visibility and the wresting of absent bodies into presence through re-materialisation of bodily traces and remains, or via the creation of objects and images that document and testify. She confronts the spectator with the Kristevan notion of the abject in its most extreme form – death and the dead body – and also in a broader sense in that the abject is also waste, the discarded, the Other that threatens a stable sense of identity and therefore must be eliminated (see Kristeva 1982).

The notion of the abject offers a conceptual foundation for looking at the performance of corpses and partial bodies as a deconstruction of the premise that bodily, or even existential, boundaries are impermeable. It is therefore of some use when considering works that deal in and with the material of the body, though it is not unproblematic. Imogen Tyler (2009) points out Kristeva's adherence to a concept of the maternal as abject and a rootedness in the abject as the condition of a writer, being an outside observer, rather than focusing on how the concept is a helpful way to understand processes of social exclusion. Young helps by developing Kristevan abjection beyond the psychoanalytical, positing that social groups labelled Other are positioned as abject, waste, hence excluded and oppressed on grounds of race, gender identity, age, ability and sexuality via 'symptoms of avoidance, objectification, disgust, dislike, or discomfort' (1990: 202). Our very society is thereby structured around discrimination against that which inspires feelings of insecurity in members of the so-called 'centre', namely the bodies of individuals and communities that are felt to threaten the identity of the mainstream. Young states that

> [m]embers of oppressed groups constantly experience such behaviours of avoidance, aversion, expressions of nervousness, condescension, and stereotyping [. . .] Such behaviours throw them back onto their group identity, making them feel noticed, marked, or *conversely invisible*, not taken seriously, or worse, demeaned. (1990: 205, italics mine)

Consciousness raising can, then, according to Young, 'be considered a kind of social therapy' (1990: 213) that can be used to confront fears of identity loss and propose a reconceptualisation of group subjectivity that does not rely for its own sense of identity on being defined against an Other.

Rebecca Solnit explores the connection between the ruin, visibility and memory in relation to the construction, demolition and reconstruction of the architecture of cities. She says:

> Ruins stand as reminders. Memory is always incomplete, always imperfect, always falling into ruin; but the ruins themselves, like other traces, are treasures; our links

to what came before, our guide to situating ourselves in a landscape of time. To erase the ruins is to erase the visible public triggers of memory; a city without ruins and traces of age is like a mind without memories. (Solnit 2011: 151)

This idea is intensely relevant to Margolles' work with derelict and neglected spaces, particularly concerning the sites of demolished night-clubs that have provided material for found-object installations. Also exhibited are photographs depicting these locations, showing sections of broken wall and fragments of the dancefloor *in situ*. The redevelopment of the historic centre of Ciudad Juárez will create what Solnit calls an 'amnesiac landscape' (Solnit 2011: 151) devoid of evidence of what was swept away. Margolles' series of photographs *Esta finca no será demolida* [*This Property Will Not Be Demolished*] 2009–13 depicts nightclubs in the centre of Ciudad Juárez before demolition; some then featured in the *Pistas de baile* series after demolition had occurred. The two series together form visual bookends, documenting the process of enforced change and the aftermath of destruction. The artist insists in this title that these spaces will have an afterlife and will not be forgotten; images survive them.

Margolles, like the aforementioned Colombian artist Salcedo, works with trauma experienced by others and, like Salcedo, Margolles 'approach[es] this task ... with a particular cultural affinity' (Bennett 2005: 53). She engages with others' individual and collective trauma not through the objectifying lens of an outsider but as someone with a deep understanding forged by spending considerable lengths of time in the communities she works with; as Bennett states of Salcedo, 'a relationship forged with the primary subjects of violence that enables the artist to enact the state of grief as a form of embodied perception' (Bennett 2005: 54). Nowhere is this more apparent than in the artist's work in Ciudad Juárez.

The dancefloors depicted in the *Pistas de baile* series are no longer enclosed spaces bounded by walls. They are trace evidence written on the ground plane. Jesse O'Neill says of the ground plane, that 'ground is fundamental in orienting spatial experience, providing a divided community that ties together countryside, city streets and interior as we step from one surface to another. Ground links spaces when walls divide them' (2015: 158). Dividing walls are absent, and the previously neat edges of the dancefloors have been disrupted. The process of demolition itself, and the act of the participants' occupation of the marked space, challenge and unsettle the boundary between public and private, interior and exterior. The building's destruction also transgresses the divide between earth – the ground outside – and floor – the ground inside – both of which function symbolically as 'abstract synechdochic devices, created to represent the qualities of more complex, real human spaces' (O'Neill 2015: 168).

Nightclubs are indoor spaces with a public function. They carry strong connotations about belonging, culture, subculture and identity. The presence of transgender sex workers in the now derelict spaces documented in the *Pistas de baile* images, individuals whom Zeppetelli describes as 'doubly marginalized' (Zeppetelli, St-Gelais, Uzel and Morales Mendoza 2017: 85), becomes an act of defiance, of witnessing and memorialisation. Floor tiles are overlain onto the ground beneath. Churchill and Smith explore the symbolism of earth:

> The concept of earth has been laden with themes of social identity, belonging, exclusion and collective memory, all of which refer back to the mythical image of a first ground on which societies were formed. Earth is ground that retains the markings of time, where the bodies of ancestors are buried, and therefore a common element that binds a people to a tradition. It is often treated as collective memory given material form. (O'Neill 2015: 168)

The photographic fragment, the capturing of this moment, then serves multiple functions as memorial and testament, asserting the presence and the agency of the individuals who are photographed on the *Pistas de baile*. The water the artist has used to mark the spaces will quickly evaporate, leaving minute traces of its passing, the tiniest metonymic reminders of the act that intervened and passed away.

The *Pistas de baile* were displayed at an exhibition of Margolles' work that took place at the Musée d'Art Contemporain de Montréal (MAC) in early 2017. The exhibition, entitled '*Mundos*', takes its name from a found-object piece, the neon sign from one of the demolished nightclubs. The boldly illuminated text has a dual function, spelling out the name of the now-demolished club and also the artwork, and its displacement and display re-contextualises it as metonymic memorial. Margolles performs the ruin, making presence from the traces of the absent building, ruined spaces temporarily occupied by individual bodies. The present of the space seals its passing and becomes the boundary between the past and the future, between the life and afterlife of the object in different spaces.

The catalogue from *Mundos* features 'Testimonies', text excerpts from interviews with the sex workers who posed for the *Pistas de baile* photographs. One of them, 'La Gata', speaks in a textual afterlife about her experiences, and friends' testimonies talk about her, her abuse, health problems and death, and also about the city, the changes enforced upon it and the effect it has had on their lives. La Gata says, in her testimony taken from 2015 (the interviews with her friends were conducted in January 2017):

> ... there were many bars and many people coming from El Paso. There was a lot of bustle. Now that they've been demolishing, people have left, and there were also murders, so now the gringos are afraid of coming to Juárez because if you bring money they'll rob you or kill you. Not everyone, but because of some, we all have to pay. (*Mundos* catalogue, translated by Oscar Gardea, 2017: 80)

La Gata is witness to the destruction of the architecture and the spaces that provided her with a living, and she has seen the changes wrought by the demolitions.

In the immediate moment when documentary images such as the *Pistas de baile* series are captured, the spaces they depict are irrevocably altered although they still show traces of their previous life, evidencing the function disrupted by the dismantling of the architectural structure. However, the assertive presence of the sex workers who reclaim and occupy the places where they worked challenges the idea that these ruins are empty, barren or useless once the architectural structures have been dismantled. One could surmise that the ruin itself represents death - the ceasing of the space to function as it did previous to the building's collapse or destruction.

Viney explains the function of built spaces in the following way:

> A building makes explicit a particular, enclosed relationship between use, place and environment, which might unravel if and when a building goes to ruin. [...] buildings differ from other objects in that, when they go to waste, they *retain their place but alter how the enclosure of space and time might be experienced*. (Viney 2014: 132, italics mine)

Thus a demolished nightclub with no walls and only a partial dancefloor as evidence of the previous function of the now ruined space becomes a site for performance. The fragments of floor are sufficiently intact as to support the weight of a body, and to provide a foundation for an act of defiant self-display. As can be seen in the images, the participants' body language is universally confident, with all the photographs showing subjects standing upright, looking directly into the camera and meeting the viewer's gaze via the mediating lens. They stand in resistance to the deliberate wasting that sees spaces inhabited by non-mainstream cultures policed, invaded and ultimately effaced. In this way, Margolles re-places the peripheral, the marginalised, in spaces whose original function has been irrevocably altered.

Like *Mundos* (2016), *Espejos* (2016) is a work that was created from found objects removed from their original settings and relocated to a site of exhibition. *Espejos* is a mirror also taken from a demolished club. Both *Mundos* and *Espejos* metonymically represent the buildings they originally occupied, in which they had specific functions that are now directly referenced by their function in the exhibition space. The architectural death of the now fragmented building has yielded artefacts that, beyond their function as memorials to the defunct nightclubs, are reconfigured and repurposed in a life-after-death of objects.

Layered Meanings, Experiences and Border Crossings

Much of Margolles' work deals in metonyms, so that a body part or some residual substance may stand in for a corpse, a group of people, society as a whole, or even for death itself. Merleau-Ponty poses a question that is highly pertinent to the dynamics of memory in Margolles' works, and the potential for interpretation of these works as memorials or secular 'relics':

> Whether it be a question of vestiges of the body of another person, we need to know how an object in space can become the eloquent relic of an existence [. . .] The constitution of the other person does not fully elucidate that of society, which is not an existence involving two or even three people, but co-existence involving an indefinite number of consciousness. ([1962] 2008: 406)

While this concern is well founded, it is problematic to label 'society' as a whole in the way Merleau-Ponty does above. To do so further perpetuates the marginalisation of the excluded individuals and groups to whom Margolles' work aims to draw attention. As we have seen, the artist has throughout her career focused on many marginalised and disenfranchised groups, such as cis and trans women and girls who are victims of abuse and murder; people murdered in connection with the narcotics trade; people whose bodies end up in unmarked graves; migrants who lose their lives in their journey. She focuses on the stories of people who are made invisible when they slip through the cracks in society's veneer and are conveniently lost – unless a process of investigation is undertaken. For such individuals, how else can visibility be recovered but by a process of archaeological forensic investigation that uncovers, and in some cases creates, a series of 'eloquent relics'?

Exhibited found objects carry multiple potential meanings. They may refer back to their original function – neon lighting that spells out the name of a bar or nightclub, for instance – or depart from it to create a new, repurposed function specific to their relocation and exhibition. This can be said of traces and residues in carrier materials such as water or earth that are shaped or vaporised as much as it can be said of tangible objects. Works that rely heavily on encoded meanings may consequently garner widely varying responses; explanatory text mitigates this to some extent with minimal works but spectators may choose to simply walk past without reading and therefore miss some of the compound interrelated messages. This is not to privilege different levels of engagement in relation to one another, of course; it almost goes without saying that individuals may move through and engage with exhibition spaces, whether in a gallery or in the public realm, in multiple and diverse ways.

A further problem with metonymic symbolism is its danger of being reductive, even essentialising, since it relies on the distillation of wider meanings into a single artefact or fragment. This is further compounded by some problems with representation of trauma, particularly that undergone by others. Jill Bennett (2005) examines the operation of affect in trauma imagery and its potential to trigger trauma responses either in those who have witnessed it first hand or in spectators who later view such images. She paraphrases Lefebvre who dismissed the potential for such imagery to educate its viewers and identifies 'a gap between affect and understanding' (2005: 64) that does not foment deep understanding or encourage reflection on the causes and effects of the trauma being referenced. Clearly, the potential for strong emotional reaction is higher in individuals with direct experience of or connection to individuals who have experienced the trauma being depicted or referenced, and much has been written on the potential for spectators to simply turn away from an oversaturation with violent and disturbing imagery or on the possibility of emotional burnout caused by feelings of powerlessness in the face of evidence of trauma.

Aesthetically, many of Margolles' works, particularly those produced post the shift into her greater presence in the public realm, employ a spare minimalist style as visual language. Far from being safe or sterile, however, objects perform as 'contact relic [by means of which] the viewer is to experience a transformation through contact' (Gygax 2018: 222). It is of importance that these relics contain materials that derive directly from, or have come into contact with, the bodies of victims of brutalising violence, so that contact is immediate and impactful, even though objects may be aesthetically aligned with Minimalist qualities. The often innocuous formal characteristics of the objects themselves, therefore, invite the viewer into physical contact with the materiality of death and the reality of how victimised individuals are positioned, consumed and destroyed by violence enacted along lines of race, class and gender.

It is vital to acknowledge that Margolles is a transnational artist not only in terms of the reception of her work but also in its production. Since early in her artistic career, Margolles has travelled outside of Mexico to produce works in disparate locations, often involving local communities. For the 1999 collective work *Andén*, for example, the artist travelled to

Figure 8.3   *Frazada (La Sombra)* [Blanket (The Shade)], 2017.

the city of Cali, Colombia, where she dug up a section of ground in Las Banderas park (Grevenbrock 2015: unnumbered page). Items belonging to individuals who had been killed were placed in the ground by their families, and then the hole was covered over, erasing any indication that the earth had been disturbed. Only the people directly involved in the production of this work would know of its existence were it not for its documentation in photographs and reporting via text, meaning that they have a privileged intimate connection with the materiality of the intervention itself as well as with the objects belonging to their deceased loved ones. Viewers may be positioned as witnesses by photographs, but they are displaced in temporal and geographical terms. Therefore, they cannot achieve the level of connection experienced by those who participated in the action alongside the artist-facilitator. The site functions doubly as loving memorial and symbolic tomb whose excavation and re-filling constitute a singular and specific life-and-death cycle of ritual and artefact.

Frazada (La sombra) (2016) (Figure 8.3), a touring installation created in La Paz, Bolivia and exhibited in cities across the world, is another Margolles work that specifically references gendered violence. The piece is a metal structure upon which a blanket is supported. The blanket has come from a morgue in La Paz, and it was used to cover the body of a murdered woman. It is reported that 'whoever uses the space generated by the shadow to cool off in the scorching heat cannot fail to notice the strong odour of blood that emanates in the air' (Guerisoli 2018: 198). The permeability of fabric makes it an ideal carrier material for bodily traces. Blood functions on many symbolic levels, connoting life, death, violence and fertility. In this installation, the substance is a relic from one woman's body. Its strong smell makes it an enduring testament to the violence she suffered; the sensory experience, and by extension the injustice, cannot be ignored. Guerisoli is clear that Margolles' work confronts the serious and pervasive nature of gendered violence in Bolivia, which according to the National Office of Statistics, affects as many as 87% of women (2018: 198).

Conclusion

As we can see from the observations made above, Margolles appeals to us using the language of loss, of grief, of mourning - experiences as universal as love and death. Her works trick the viewer with their understated minimalism, and then unveil their messages, revealing the artist's call to feeling and action. People reduced to statistics, victims of systemic violence, gain visibility through the challenge to consciousness.

Margolles' work is fundamentally concerned with transition; liminality; the traces left behind after death. She recuperates the absent and the invisible into the present and into embodied space. Participants and spectators become witnesses, tied into a reciprocal relationship via contact with the artwork as relic. Intervention by the artist herself and by participants into public space and exhibition space produces works that wound and hurt as a response to individual and collective trauma and also function as a call to response. Since the experience of an artwork is in itself embodied, entailing an interaction of the senses with the object, spectators are invited, sometimes challenged, to become active participants rather than passive recipients. Space itself becomes a medium, a place that is occupied by individuals and communities responding to their own lived experience. Objects, images and text interrelate, weaving a tapestry of multiple meanings.

Throughout her career, Teresa Margolles' focus has been on trauma and its aftermath. She has worked mostly in Mexico but also travelled far afield to examine the impact of traumatic events. Her position as a Mexican artist of international standing means that, while she is inevitably taken to be a national representative, as she has herself stated, 'whether I like it or not' (quoted in Pimentel 2009: 84), [she] is able to relocate the materials of trauma and death, and re-tell stories in many settings. The act of transporting works that deal with local and national traumas creates new structures and networks of communication of the realities of violence, injustice and loss.

Note

1. Unless otherwise stated, all translations are my own.

Bibliography

Adorno, Theodor [1970] (1986), *Aesthetic Theory*, London and New York: Routledge.

Azoulay, Ariella (2015), *Civil Imagination: A Political Ontology of Photography*, translated by Louise Bethlehem, London and New York: Verso.

Bacal, Edward (2015), 'The Concrete and the Abstract: On Doris Salcedo, Teresa Margolles and Santiago Sierra's Tenuous Bodies', *Parallax*, 21:3, pp. 259–70.

Barthes, Roland (1977), *Image, Music, Text*, London: Flamingo.

Bennett, Jill (2005), *Empathic Vision: Affect, Trauma, and Contemporary Art*, Stanford: Stanford University Press.

Bowden, Charles (2010), *Murder City: Ciudad Juárez and the Global Economy's New Killing Fields*, New York: Bold Type Books.

Churchill, Lynn, and Dianne Smith (eds) (2015), *Occupation: Ruin, Revolution, Repudiation*, Farnham and Burlington, VT: Ashgate Publishing.

Gallo, Rubén (2004), *New Tendencies in Mexican Art: The 1990s*, New York: Palgrave Macmillan.

Görner, Klaus, and Udo Kittelman (2004), *Muerte Sin Fin*, exhibition catalogue, Frankfurt: Hatje Kantz.

Grevenbrock, Christina (2015), '"Each Bubble is a body": Teresa Margolles – Hidden Terror', *Seismopolite: Journal of Art and Politics*, 8 October. Available at <http://seismopolite.com/each-bubble-is-a-body-teresa-margolles> (last accessed 19 February 2020).

Guerisoli, Francesca (2018), 'Cemento – Cement', *Ya basta hijos de puta*, exhibition catalogue, Milan: Silvana Editoriale, p. 195.

Gygax, Raphael (2018), 'Assenza/Absence', Teresa Margolles, *Ya basta hijos de puta*, exhibition catalogue, Milan: Silvana Editoriale, pp. 221–30.

Jonquères, Antoine Henry (2018), 'Luoghi/Places', in Teresa Margolles (ed.), *Ya basta hijos de puta*, exhibition catalogue, Milan: Silvana Editoriale, pp. 249–54.

Kristeva, Julia (1982), *Powers of Horror: An Essay on Abjection*, New York: Columbia University Press.

La Jornada (2019), 'Feminicidio: realidad intolerable', *La Jornada*, 29 December. Available at <https://www.jornada.com.mx/2019/12/29/opinion/002a1edi?partner=rss> (last accessed 19 February 2020).

La Verdad Juárez (2019), 'Galería: Glitter Rosa, la marcha feminista en Ciudad Juárez', *La Verdad Juárez*, 16 August. Available at https://laverdadjuarez.com/index.php/2019/08/16/galeria-la-marcha-feminista-del-glitter-rosa-en-ciudad-juarez/> (last accessed 19 February 2019).

Lefebvre, Henri (1996), edited and translated by Eleonore Kofman and Elizabeth Lebas, *Writings on Cities*, Malden, MA and Oxford: Blackwell Publishing.

Merleau-Ponty, Maurice [1962] (2008), *Phenomenology of Perception*, London and New York: Routledge Classics.

O'Neill, Jesse (2015), 'With Feet Firmly Planted on Unstable Ground', in Lynn Churchill and Dianne Smith (eds), *Occupation: Ruin, Revolution, Repudiation*, Farnham and Burlington, VT: Ashgate Publishing, pp. 157–70.

Pimentel, Taiyana (2009), 'Conversation between Taiyana Pimentel, Teresa Margolles and Cuauhtémoc Medina', *¿De qué otra cosa podríamos hablar?/What Else Could We Talk About?*, exhibition catalogue, Venice Biennale, Mexican Pavilion, Barcelona: RM Verlag, pp. 83–99.

Simmel, Georg [1911] (2011), 'The Ruin', in Brian Dillon (ed.), *Documents of Contemporary Art: Ruins*, London: Whitechapel Gallery, pp. 23–4.

Solnit, Rebecca (2011), 'The Ruins of Memory', in Brian Dillon (ed.), *Documents of Contemporary Art: Ruins*, London: Whitechapel Gallery, pp. 150–2.

Tyler, Imogen (2009), 'Against Abjection', *Feminist Theory*, 10:1, pp. 77–98.

Vicario, Gilbert (2018), 'Memoria/Memory', in Teresa Margolles (ed.), *Ya basta hijos de puta*, exhibition catalogue, Milan: Silvana Editoriale, pp. 121–35.

Viney, William (2014), *Waste: A Philosophy of Things*, London and New York: Bloomsbury.

Watt, Peter, and Roberto Zepeda (2012), *Drug War Mexico: Politics, Neoliberalism and Violence in the New Narcoeconomy*, London: Zed Books.

Young, Iris Marion (1990), 'Abjection and Oppression: Dynamics of Unconscious Racism, Sexism, and Homophobia', in Arleen B. Dallery and Charles E. Scott (eds), *Crises in Continental Philosophy*, Albany, NY: State University of New York Press, pp. 201–13.

Zeppetelli, John, Thérèse St-Gelais, Jean-Philippe Uzel, and Lulu Morales Mendoza (2017), *Teresa Margolles: Mundos*. Montreal: Musée d'art contemporain de Montréal.

Index